AGAINST THE HERESIES

Papal Encyclicals Condemning Modern Errors Infecting the Church and Society

MARCEL LEFEBVRE

Angelus Press

PO Box 217 | Saint Marys, KS 66536

Translated from the French: *C'est moi, l'accusé, qui devrais vous juger!: Commentaires des actes du magistère condamnant les erreurs modernes*, with permission from the publisher (editions Fideliter, 1994) by Angelus Press.

©1997 by Angelus Press
All rights reserved. No part of this book may be reproduced or transmitted in any form or by any means, electronic or mechanical, including photocopying, recording, or by any information storage and retrieval systems without permission in writing from the publisher except by a reviewer who may quote brief passages in a review.

ANGELUS PRESS
PO Box 217
Saint Marys, Kansas 66536
Phone (816) 753-3150
Fax (816) 753-3557
Order Line 1-800-966-7337
www.angeluspress.org

Library of Congress Control Number: 98118521

ISBN 978-0-935952-28-5
FIRST PRINTING—February 1997
EIGHTH PRINTING—January 2021

Printed in the United States of America

Contents

Preface xiii
Outline of the Course on the Acts of the Magisterium xv
Introduction xix

I. *E Supremi Apostolatus* of Pope St. Pius X 1
The Abandonment of God 2
To Restore All Things in Christ 2
Secularism 3
The Coming of the Antichrist 4
The Cult of Man 5
God Will Have the Victory 5
Salvation by Jesus Christ 6
Christ Is God 8
To Jesus Christ Through the Church 9
The Order Willed by God 9
The Formation of Priests 10
Increase the Number of Seminaries 11
Form Holy Priests 13
Solicitude for Young Priests 13
A Patient Charity 15
Refrain From Hasty Conclusions 16
The Priest Is a Physician of Souls 17
Catholic Action 18
Piety First 19

PART I:
PONTIFICAL DOCUMENTS
ON FREEMASONRY

II. *Quo Graviora* of Pope Leo XII on Freemasonry ... 23
Clement XII: Excommunication of Freemasons 24
Benedict XIV: Fight Against Indifferentism 27
Pius VII: Against the Sacrilege 31

Leo XII: The Infamous Project of the Secret Societies 36
The Duties of Chiefs of State 37

III. *Qui Pluribus* of Pope Pius IX
On Rationalism and the Other Modern
Errors Propagated by the Freemasons 39

The Rationalists' Error.. 40
Philosophy the Handmaid of Theology...................................... 42
The Individual Reason Cannot Demonstrate Everything 42
Even Natural Mysteries Exist 43
The Credibility of Revelation... 44
Other Attacks Against the Church.. 46
Religious Indifferentism... 48
Attacks Against Priestly Celibacy.. 48
The Destructive Doctrine of Communism 49
Pontifical Directives: Defend the Faith 50
Clergy Should Be an Example..52
Yesterday's Magisterium and Today's.. 54
Modernist Influence in the New Mass 56
The Freemasons' Goal: Destruction of the Church 56
The Holiness and Doctrine of the Priests
    the Church's Strength.. 58
Role of Catholic Chiefs of State 59

IV. *Humanum Genus* of Pope Leo XIII
On the Sect of the Freemasons 63

Leo XIII Makes Known the Wickedness of Freemasonry 63
The City of Satan..65
Prior Condemnations... 66
The Advance of Freemasonry... 67
Unity of All Secret Societies.. 69
The Fundamental Pact of Masonry... 70
The Fundamental Principles of Freemasonry 71
The First Principle: Naturalism... 72
Rationalism...74
The Errors of Naturalism and Rationalism 75
Denial of the Supernatural and the Natural Order 76

The Church and Masonry: An Impossible Dialogue 76
Freemasonry Has Not Changed 79
Refusal of a Unique Objective Truth 79
Laicity of the State and the Struggle Against the Church 81
Second Principle: Indifferentism 82
Third Principle: Denial of the Existence of God
    and the Immortality of the Soul 83
Disastrous Consequences of Masonic Principles 84
    Public Immorality 84
    Negation of Original Sin and the Consumer Society 84
    Communist Enslavement 86
    Destruction of the Family by the Destruction of Marriage 87
Christian Marriage: Guarantee of the Dignity of the Woman . 89
Monopolize the Education of Youth 92
The Rights of Man 94
Democratic Ideology Destroys Authority 94
Masonry Opens the Way to Communism 96
Perversity of Freemasonry 97
The Work of Satan 97
Juvenile Delinquency Engendered by Freemasonry 98
The Revolution and the Thirst for Change 100
The *Aggiornamento*: Adaptation to the Liberal Spirit 101
The Combat Against Freemasonry 102
Tear Away the Mask from Freemasonry 103
No Catholic Can Join the Freemasons 104
Rationalism Destroys the Liturgy 104
The Third Order of St. Francis 105
Restore the Guilds 106
Dialectic and Class Warfare 108
The Church's Social Doctrine: *Rerum Novarum* 109
Christian Social Order 110
Protect the Youth from the Sects 111
Prayer for the Combatants in the Fight Against the Sects 112

V. *Custodi* of Pope Leo XIII to the Italian People
    On Freemasonry 115

PART II: PONTIFICAL DOCUMENTS ON LIBERALISM

VI. Liberalism and Catholicism 121
The Liberal Catholic Betrays His Religion 122
Vatican II: the Triumph of Liberalism 123
Paul VI: a Liberal Pope 126
Continual Combat 127
"Liberty of Conscience," an Ambiguous Expression 128
"God, depart!" 129

VII. *Libertas Praestantissimum* of Pope Leo XIII On Human Liberty and Liberalism 131
An Erroneous Mind 131
FIRST PART: What Is Liberty? 132
Psychological and Moral Liberty 133
Liberty the Mark of Intelligence 133
Moral Liberty 134
The Capacity to Do Evil a Defect of Our Liberty 135
What Limits? 136
Liberty: Our Faculty to Choose the Means
 While Respecting the True Order of Ends 137
Law: A Precious Help to Our Liberty 138
Right Reason Is Ordered to the End 139
Eternal Law, Natural Law, Human Law 140
The Necessity of Human Law 141
Bad Laws 142
True Liberty Postulates Law 144
The New Law of the Gospel 144
SECOND PART: Liberalism 146
Naturalists and Rationalists, Abettors of Liberalism 146
Duty Precedes Rights 147
Democratic Ideology and Moral Positivism 148
Society's Self-Destruction 150
Mitigated Liberalism: First Category,
 Refusal of the Supernatural Order 151

Second Category: The Partisans of
 the Separation of Church and State 152
Vatican II, Instigator of the Ruin of Good Concordats 154
THIRD PART: The Modern Liberties 156
First Liberty: Freedom of Worship 156
Sanctity, Mark of the Divinity of the Church 157
The Duty of the State in Regard to Religion 158
"Rights" for All Religions 159
Second Liberty: Freedom of Speech and of the Press 162
Third Liberty: Freedom to Teach 164
The Benefits of Christian Philosophy 166
Fourth Liberty: Liberty of Conscience 169
A Culpable and Fatal Ambiguity 169
True Tolerance 170
To Tolerate Does Not Mean to Recognize a Right 171
FOURTH PART: Degrees of Liberalism 172
The Deadly Sin of Liberalism 173
First Degree: Absolute Liberalism 174
Second Degree: The Church Despoiled or Reduced in Status 174
Third Degree: Liberal Catholics 176
Without the Grace of Jesus Christ, No Society Is Normal 177
Communist Society 178
True Liberty and Coups d'Etat 179
The Forms of Government 180

VIII. *Mirari Vos* of Pope Gregory XVI Condemning Liberalism, Indifferentism, and Freedom of Conscience 183

Immutability of Dogmatic Formulas 184
The Liberal Mentality: Perpetual Incoherence 186
We Fight Liberalism: We Are Anti-Liberals 187
Indifferentism: Death of the Missionary Spirit 188
"Freedom" of Conscience: Freedom of Error 189

IX. *Quanta Cura* of Pope Pius IX Condemning Naturalism, Liberalism, Indifferentism, Communism and Socialism 191

The Liberals' Reaction to the *Syllabus* 191
Condemnation of Naturalism in Politics 192
The False Religions: The Devil's Invention 193
Islam Imprisons Millions of Souls in Error 193
The State's Duty: Repress Religious Error 194
A Right to Freedom of Error 195
Religious Liberty or Toleration? Bea vs. Ottaviani 196
Decisive Influence of Fr. John Courtney Murray, S.J. 197
Council "Experts" Under Condemnation of the Holy Office . 197
Condemnation of Freedom of All Religions 198
The Occupied Church 200
Liberation Theology 201
Destruction of Religious Orders and Christian Education 202
The Infallibility of *Quanta Cura* 203

X. *The Syllabus of Errors* of Pope Pius IX 205

Rationalism 205
Religious Indifferentism 206
Outside of the Church No Salvation 209
The Situation of the Protestants: Ecumenism 210
What Must Be Said 211
Biblical Societies 213
The Rights of the Church 215
The Catholic Church, the One True Religion 215
Analysis of the Council's *Declaration on Religious Liberty* 216
A "Right to the Free Search for Truth" 216
A Right Contrary to the Gospel 217
The Council Professes Religious Relativism 218
Is Our Lord Jesus Christ God? 219
The Union Between Church and State 221
The Error of Separation 222
Natural and Christian Moral Law 224
Errors on Christian Marriage 224
The Pope, Chief of State 226

Liberty Favors Error 227
Liberalism Has Sapped the American Catholic Church 229
The Conciliar *Aggiornamento* Condemned
    Ahead of Its Time 231

XI. *Our Apostolic Mandate* of Pope St. Pius X to the French Bishops on the Sillon 233

The Heyday of the Sillon 234
Appearance of Disturbing Tendencies 235
First Error: Independence From Authority 237
Second Error: Ill-conceived Love of the Poor 238
Liberation Theology... 239
The Suppression and Levelling of the Classes........................241
Third Error: An Erroneous Notion of Human Dignity......... 244
Sillonist Democracy..245
Sillon's Ideal Society: Liberty, Equality, Fraternity 246
False Liberation Leads to Violence 247
Refutation of the Sillonist System 248
Authority Comes From God 249
Liberty and Authority 251
Justice and Equality 252
Fraternity and Pluralism..253
No Real Brotherhood Outside of Christian Charity 254
One God, One Faith...255
False Definition of Human Dignity 258
The Sillon's Action 262
No More Master 263
The Dignity of the Priesthood Debased 263
Opposition to Authority... 264
Seek the Causes.. 266
Secularism and Desecration: A Total Disaster 267
The Lead Came from the Top.. 268
The Church's Past Discredited 269
The Breath of the Revolution 269
St. Pius X's Judgment of the Sillon 271
Catholicism Not Linked to Any Form of Government.......... 272
The Sillon Stood Back While the Church Was Despoiled..... 273
Paul VI: Liberal and Symbol of Contradiction 274

False Ecumenism 274
The Union of Religions 276
Without the True Religion, No Real Civilization 279
Impossible to Be Both Jew and Catholic 280
It Is the Jews Who Have Persecuted the Catholics 281
Respect for Error Prevents Conversion 282
They Put Their Flags in Their Pocket 284
Verbal Confusion and Social Chimera 285
Towards a One-World Religion 286
Baneful Doctrines 288
The Mystery of the Blessed Trinity 290
Instruct, Convert, and Save Souls 290
Texts Not Inspired by the Holy Ghost 292
The Authority of the Vatican II Decrees 292
Holy Ghost Not Obliged to Intervene 293

The Encyclical *Divini Redemptoris* of Pope Pius XI on Communism 295

Christian Civilization 295
The Fight Began With Original Sin 297
Their Goal: Annihilate Christian Civilization 297
A Monstrous Doctrine 299
The Popes' Clairvoyance 301
Abandonment Worse Than Persecution 302
Aggravation of the Peril 303
The Imposture Decried 304
Counterfeit Redemption of the Poor 304
The Capitalist Economy: Fruit of the Revolution 305
Dialectical Materialism, the "Class Struggle" 307
Depersonalization 308
Destruction of Marriage and Family Life 310
Constant Surveillance 311
A Machiavellian Persecution 312
Unceasing Fear 312
Banish God From the Earth 313
A Counterfeit of the Truth 313
Fraud of Propaganda 314
The Spike: Astounding Silence of So-Called "Free" Press 315

Preface

After the founding of the Priestly Society of Saint Pius X, Archbishop Lefebvre drew up a special course for the first year seminarians: Acts of the Magisterium. This course covers the major papal encyclicals and other documents which deal with the Christian social order and the reign of Our Lord Jesus Christ over society. The purpose of the course was to prepare the young candidates to the priesthood for their work in the present situation of the Church and post-Christian society, in which they would be called upon to exercise their apostolate and sanctification.

From 1979-1982, it was Archbishop Lefebvre himself who taught these courses at the Seminary of Ecône, showing thereby the capital importance he attached to our combat against modern errors, especially Liberalism, Modernism, Communism, and their promoters, particularly the Freemasons. He also showed thereby his filial and undying attachment to the teachings of the popes, to the Church's magisterium and to eternal Rome.

His life's great sorrow was to see the Church, with Vatican II—which he referred to many times as the Third World War—infested with all these errors, and its key posts occupied by enemies. He saw the Conciliar and post-Conciliar popes turn their backs on the teachings and warnings of their predecessors. It was also with great sorrow that he saw the priesthood in ruins, the religious life fall to pieces, and Catholic states laicized in the name of the Council's teaching on religious liberty.

However, he did not give up on the situation; on the contrary, his course on the Acts of the Magisterium was a striking elaboration of his declaration of November 21, 1974, which begins thus:

> We cleave, with all our heart and with all our soul, to Catholic Rome, the guardian of the Catholic Faith and of the traditions necessary for the maintenance of that Faith, and to eternal Rome, mistress of wisdom and truth. On the other hand we refuse and have always refused to follow the Rome of the neo-Protestant trend clearly manifested throughout Vatican II and, later, in all the reforms born of it.

The present work is based upon the course given in 1980-81 and carefully transcribed by Mr. and Mrs. André Cagnon, while it draws from the course of 1979-80 for the commentary on *Quanta Cura* and the *Syllabus*. Bishop Tissier de Mallerais edited and arranged the text slightly, adding a few clarifications, and retaining the spoken style of the course for the sake of order and clarity. We can only thank and congratulate them all on their work, which places such a useful and precious book in the hands of Catholics in these closing years of the twentieth century. The reader will find herein the teaching of the living God Himself, pronounced by the mouth of the popes, regarding the modern errors, their promoters and their adherents. Herein he will find light and courage; from this reading he will derive an abiding love for the Holy Roman Catholic Church, Mistress of truth.

May this work, by the intercession of the most Blessed Virgin Mary, Mediatrix of all graces, bear abundant fruit for the Mystical Body of her divine Son.

Menzingen, Wednesday in Holy Week, 30 March 1994

Franz Schmidberger
Superior General
of the Priestly Society of Saint Pius X

Outline of the Course on the Acts of the Magisterium

From the way he had arranged his files in his office, which he personally had labelled, the intention of Archbishop Lefebvre was clear. He had meant them to benefit his priests. All the documents were in order. "When I am gone," he said, "they will find all the documents they need here." That is how Bishop Tissier de Mallerais found the outline which the Archbishop had drafted when he chose to give the seminarians in their year of spirituality a series of classes in which he would comment on the Acts of the Magisterium, of the popes who have condemned the modern errors.

On the whole he remained faithful to his plan, though he could not always adhere rigorously to the outline which he had sketched, and several times he would come back to a point raised in a previous class in order to reinforce his argumentation or refresh the memory of his students. The following is the outline established by Archbishop Lefebvre.

+School Year (1979-1980)

Why devote this course to the "Magisterium of the Church," and especially to the Magisterium of the Sovereign Pontiffs of the last three centuries?

Because all the Popes in succession during these three centuries until Pope Pius XII inclusively have never ceased to proclaim the truth and to condemn the "modern errors" which are poisoning souls and societies.

Present here the words of Pope Pius IX at the beginning of his encyclical letter *Quanta Cura*, the *Syllabus*, the catalogue of modern errors.

The importance of this course: Modern errors so infect the atmosphere we breathe that even the best of the Church's faithful are contaminated. The mind-set resulting from the secularization of society, religious Indifferentism, and Liberalism in every domain is such that we have a hard time receiving the Truth in its integrity, truth that comes to us by sound philosophy and the Catholic faith.

The voice of the popes is heard just when we need it, in order to remind us of the principles that must direct our life and our activity if we are to merit eternal life; and with keen insight, this same voice denounces the obstacles placed in our path by the enemy [i.e. Satan] and enemies [i.e., his instruments] of Our Lord Jesus Christ and His reign.

The purpose of this course is not so much a systematic study of the errors, but a guided tour of the encyclicals themselves, especially those in which the popes made an in-depth study of the truths denied by these errors, or gave a detailed analysis of the errors themselves. One cannot but admire the zeal and faith of these vigilant guardians of the deposit of the faith, and one is all the more stupefied upon remarking how this relentless combat was suddenly abandoned for the sake of compromise with all the promoters of these errors and with their successors, by means of a false ecumenism which is a betrayal of truth.

The program of this course is thus sketched in its general outline. But for a better understanding of the thinking and teaching of the popes, we shall begin by grouping their writings under several headings:

(1) The magisterium dealing with the Secret Societies. This is an impressive study which discloses the causes, the social mechanism where these errors are refined and diffused throughout the world. The list of these documents:

1. The letter *Quo Graviora* of Pope Leo XII of March 13, 1826, which includes the documents of his predecessors:
   i. *In Eminenti* of Clement XII (April 26, 1738);
   ii. *Providas* of Benedict XIV (March 16, 1751);
   iii. *Ecclesiam* of Pius VII (September 13, 1821).

2. *Qui Pluribus* of Pius IX (November 9, 1846); *Quibus Quantisque* (on the occupation of Rome); *Nostis et Nobiscum*; *Syllabus*, ch. IV.

3. *Humanum Genus* (April 20, 1884) of Leo XIII.

4. Canon Law §2335 (Biblical societies, *Inter Praecipuas*, Gregory XVI).

(2) The important documents condemning Liberalism, with special attention given to those of Leo XIII:

1. *Libertas Praestantissimum* of Leo XIII (June 20, 1888).
2. *Mirari Vos* of Gregory XVI (August 15, 1832).
3. *Quanta Cura* of Pius IX (December 8, 1864).
4. *Immortale Dei* of Leo XIII (November 1, 1885).
5. *Inscrutabili* (April 21, 1878).
6. *Quod Apostolici* (December 18, 1878).
7. *Letter on the Sillon* by St. Pius X (August 25, 1910).

(3) Documents condemning Modernism.

(4) Documents condemning Socialism and Communism.

INTRODUCTION

A COMPLETE PAPAL PROGRAM
"TO RESTORE ALL THINGS IN CHRIST"

Why study the Acts of the Church's Magisterium? Quite simply, in order to grasp the situation of the Church today. One notices, in fact, that for nearly three centuries the popes have always condemned the same errors, those which they themselves called "the modern errors."

Liberalism is at the root of all these errors (Protestantism, Sillonism, Progressivism, and even Socialism and Communism) which poison souls and minds, and have led us to where we are today. Well, the popes have long since taken care to pinpoint and denounce error. For their role is to proclaim the truth, as Pope Pius IX said in the first paragraph of the encyclical *Quanta Cura* of December 8, 1864:

> It is well known unto all men, and especially to You, Venerable Brothers, with what great care and pastoral vigilance Our Predecessors, the Roman Pontiffs, have discharged the Office entrusted by Christ Our Lord to them, in the Person of the Most Blessed Peter, Prince of the Apostles, have unremittingly discharged the duty of feeding the lambs and the sheep, and have diligently nourished the Lord's entire flock with the words of faith, imbued it with salutary doctrine, and guarded it from poisoned pastures. And those Our Predecessors, who were the assertors and Champions of the august Catholic Religion, of truth and justice, being as they were chiefly solicitous for the salvation of souls, held nothing to be of so great importance as the duty of exposing and condemning, in their most wise Letters and Constitutions, all heresies and errors which are hostile to moral honesty and to the eternal salvation of mankind, and which have frequently stirred up terrible commotions and have damaged both the Christian and civil commonwealths in a disastrous manner.

A distinct knowledge of what the popes have taught and condemned is thus indispensable for a correct evaluation of the extremely grave events which are the order of the day.

Society Without God

We are surrounded by an environment that is no longer Catholic. Those who were fortunate enough to be born in a Christian family should thank the good Lord. They have known therein, I would say, a little oasis of what the Church desires and requires of Christian parents. But everywhere else, in schools, colleges and universities, the youth come in contact with people who do not believe, and who in fact have no true notion of the Catholic faith. Society today is imbued with the modern errors to such a degree that they appear normal; it is nearly impossible to get rid of certain preconceived notions. Take, for example, religious indifferentism, which the popes have condemned. Well, now this idea has gained acceptance even in Catholic circles, the notion that all religions are equal, that they all have their place, and hence that man is free to choose and to practice the religion he prefers. After all, you can't force religion on people.

Well, this is a grave error: men are not free in this regard. Why? Because the good Lord Himself founded a religion. Are men allowed to say to Him then, Your religion doesn't suit me; I prefer another, Mohammed's, Buddha's, Luther's? How can one admit such an attitude? Our Lord Jesus Christ, Who is God, founds the Catholic Church. He endows it with the Holy Sacrifice of the Mass, the sacraments, a hierarchy and a priesthood; and should we be free to answer: No, thank you, we will look into another religion?

Now Indifferentism has been adopted by State constitutions. Since Vatican II, States that were still Catholic, thus in which the Catholic religion was the only one officially recognized, have been urged by the Holy See to change their constitutions. That is where the spirit of religious liberalism leads. And this is the climate in which we live: a climate where error prevails.

Church and State

Here is another example. When I entered the French Seminary at Rome (in 1923), had I been asked about the question of the separation of Church and State, I would have answered: Yes, there should be separation, Church and State have different goals; everything in its place. Well, it took the Fathers of the French Seminary to introduce me to the encyclicals, especially those of Leo XIII and St. Pius X, to deliver me from this error. No, the Church should not be separated from the State. At least in principle, for in reality one is often obliged to tolerate a situation which one cannot change. But in principle, Church and State should be united and work together for the salvation of souls. The State was created by God, it is of divine origin, and thus cannot remain indifferent on the question of religion.

As I said, not long ago there were a good number of States—Italy, (Southern) Ireland, Spain, the countries of South America, several cantons of Switzerland (Valais, Ticino, Fribourg)—that affirmed their officially Catholic status in the first article of their constitutions. But that has disappeared. The modern world will not stand for the influence that a Catholic State might exercise to stunt the growth of the Protestant, Moslem or Buddhist religions. Religions, after all, have to be free.

This is absurd. Other religions have States with constitutions proclaiming the State religion, and they have no intention of changing their constitutions. England has a Protestant constitution, as do Sweden, Norway, Denmark, Geneva and Zurich. And the Moslem States are Islamic without apology or concession. There the religion is an integral part of society. And what about the Communist States? No one belongs to the government who does not belong to the party.

And should we Catholics, then, hold that Church and State must be separated? What an error; and what consequences for society, the family, and every walk of life. We must steep ourselves anew in the Catholic faith; that is why we study the encyclicals. How do the popes stand on the major issues? How did they view and judge the world in their time?

We can see how they condemned the same errors and shortcomings that we know today. We can thus rely upon these official declarations to combat the errors of our time, and tell how they destroy the plan of God in society.

Our Course of Study

We shall begin with an encyclical of St. Pius X, because we place our teaching, like our Society, under the protection of him who is the greatest pope of our time, the only one canonized since St. Pius V! If the Church declared this pope from the beginning of the century as a light for his time, then we appeal to this light, and we implore St. Pius X to give us the light we need. We shall begin, then, with the first encyclical of this holy pontiff, which contains the major themes of his pontificate.

Then we shall see how the popes put their finger on the sources of these modern errors: the social mechanisms where they have been devised, the secret societies, Freemasonry. There are a number of encyclicals on this topic, which nowadays are swept under the carpet. No one wants to hear about them. Yet these documents are informative; they explain how these errors were able to be circulated throughout the world, and how they succeeded in changing society. For the Freemasons have indeed successfully overturned society, not only by means of violent revolution, but also by a complete revolution in the realm of ideas; by diffusing false ideas, they have radically transformed society, and, to a certain extent, the Church.

In a series of documents, the first of which, by Clement XII, dates from 1738, the Popes Pius VII, Benedict XIV, Leo XII, Pius IX, and Leo XIII made a serious and pertinent study of the sects which are at the origin of the current evils.

Then we shall look at the encyclicals condemning Liberalism and, consequently, Socialism, Communism, and Modernism: encyclicals by Gregory XVI, Pius IX, Leo XIII, and St. Pius X. These texts are of capital importance, for I do not refuse what the Holy See now asks of us, to interpret Vatican II in light of the Church's constant teaching. This very teaching or Magisterium is found in the documents of these popes. If, then, there are things in the Council which disagree with or which contradict what previous popes have said, how can we accept them? There is no room for contradictions; the popes teach, and the matter is settled. Pope

Pius IX even wrote an entire syllabus, that is, a catalogue of truths to which we must assent. St. Pius X did the same in the decree *Lamentabili*. Then how could we accept truths taught by these seven or eight popes, and at the same time accept a teaching given by the Council that contradicts what these popes have affirmed most explicitly?

For two centuries the popes have neither taught errors, nor permitted them to be taught. They might do so momentarily, as Pope Paul VI or Pope John Paul II have done today, to our great dismay. They themselves might personally be convinced of a false teaching. But in that case we are obliged to resist by relying on the constant teaching of the Church throughout the centuries.

Chapter 1

The Encyclical Letter *E Supremi Apostolatus* of Pope St. Pius X

(October 4, 1903)

St. Pius X's first encyclical, dated October 4, 1903, is entitled *E Supremi Apostolatus*. The Pope had been crowned August 4th; hence it is just two months after his accession to the throne that he published this relatively short and clearly developed encyclical. Just after the prologue, he exposes the program he intends to follow during the course of his pontificate, while at the same time sketching his vision of the state of the world. He then encourages the bishops to give their support, insisting especially on the formation of seminarians, the care of the clergy, and Catholic action.

The Pope begins with some reflections on his nomination. In point of fact, he had never thought nor even imagined that he would be elected by the conclave; indeed, he had promised his parishioners of Venice that he would return...Thus, he begins:

> In addressing you for the first time from the Chair of the supreme apostolate to which we have, by the inscrutable disposition of God, been elevated, it is not necessary to remind you with what tears and warm instance We exerted Ourselves to ward off this formidable burden of the Pontificate.

He borrows the words of St. Anselm on the occasion of his elevation to the episcopacy:

> For to show with what dispositions of mind and will We subjected Ourselves to the most serious charge of feeding the flock of Christ, We can well adduce those same proofs of grief which he invokes in his own behalf. "My tears are witnesses," he wrote, "and the sounds and moanings issuing from the anguish of my heart, such as I never remember before to have come from me for any sorrow, before that day on which there seemed to fall upon

me that great misfortune of the archbishop of Canterbury. And those who fixed their gaze on my face that day could not fail to see it...."

In truth reasons both numerous and most weighty were not lacking to justify this resistance of Ours....Then again, to omit other motives, We were terrified beyond all else by the disastrous state of human society to-day. For who can fail to see that society is at the present time, more than in any past age, suffering from a terrible and deep-rooted malady which, developing every day and eating into its inmost being, is dragging it to destruction? You understand, Venerable Brethren, what this disease is—apostasy from God.

The Abandonment of God

Thus, for St. Pius X, the great malady of his time is the abandonment of God, apostasy. The abandonment of God! How much more could we speak of this today! If St. Pius X were living today, I think he would be even more terrified than he was in his own time. Back then, there were still seminaries, many priests, many religious and many souls animated by a lively faith. The churches were still full. Let's continue the reading:

> We say therefore that, in virtue of the ministry of the Pontificate, which was to be entrusted to Us, We must hasten to find a remedy for this great evil.

To Restore All Things in Christ

What remedy does he propose?

> We considered as addressed to Us that Divine command: "Lo, I have set thee this day over the nations and over kingdoms, to root up, and to pull down, and to waste, and to destroy, and to build, and to plant" (Jer. 1:10). But, cognizant of Our weakness, We recoiled in terror from a task as urgent as it is arduous. Since, however, it has been pleasing to the Divine Will to raise Our Lowliness to such sublimity of power, we take courage in Him who strengthens Us; and setting Ourselves to work, relying on the power of God, we proclaim....

Here follows an official declaration, short and to the point:

> We proclaim that We have no other program in the Supreme Pontificate but that "of restoring all things in Christ" (Ephes. 1:10), so that "Christ may be all in all" (Col. 3:2).

Such is the program of St. Pius X.

This motto is truly admirable, for if we read St. Paul in his letter to the Ephesians or the Colossians, and if we read the verses that follow and complete the affirmations of St. Pius X, we perceive that this was also the main purpose of St. Paul's apostolate. St. Paul says to the Ephesians and Colossians that he has been chosen as an apostle to announce a great mystery, a mystery hidden since the beginning of the world, hidden even, to a certain degree, from the angels, an extraordinary mystery. What is Pope Pius X going to announce? His mystery is just this: *Instaurare omnia in Christo.* "*Recapitulare omnia in Christo*," I would say. To make of Christ both the center of human history and the solution to the problems of mankind: not only *instaurare* but *recapitulare* (from the Greek word *kephalos*, head). Our Lord Jesus Christ is the head, and everything proceeds from the head. This was the great mystery announced by St. Paul to the Gentiles. St. Pius X takes it up as the program of his pontificate.

There are some, the Pope adds, who will deny that this is our goal, claiming we have political ambitions:

> Should anyone ask Us for a symbol as the expression of Our will, We will give this and no other: "To renew all things in Christ."

That is clear enough. We find clarity of ideas, limpidity of expression—contrary to what we hear too often in today's pontifical documents where ambiguities and popular phrases abound. Here everything is simple, and there is no doubt as to what the Holy Father thinks.

Secularism

He then casts a glance at the world:

> In undertaking this glorious task, We are greatly quickened by the certainty that We shall have all of you, Venerable Brethren, as generous co-operators.

He counts on the support of the bishops to come to his aid:

> For in truth, "The nations have raged and the peoples imagined vain things" (Ps. 2:1) against their Creator, so frequent is the cry of the enemies of God: "Depart from us" (Job. 21:14). And as might be expected we find extinguished among the majority of men all respect for the Eternal God, and no regard paid in the manifestations of public and private life to the supreme Will."

Described here is the introduction of Secularism, which perhaps nowadays would be called secularization. Religion plays no part in public life: man is by himself, he organizes the world, society and everything else as if God simply did not exist. This is complete and utter Secularism.

The Pope continues:

> Nay, every effort and every artifice is used to destroy utterly the memory and the knowledge of God.

What would he have said had he lived at the time of Communism with its schools of atheism.

The Coming of the Antichrist

Then, curiously enough, comes an allusion to the Antichrist:

> When all this is considered there is good reason to fear lest this great perversity may be as it were a foretaste, and perhaps the beginning of those evils which are reserved for the last days; and that there may be already in the world the "Son of Perdition" of whom the Apostle speaks (II Thess. 2:3).

Something undoubtedly inspired Pope Pius X to say this at the very beginning of his pontificate, as though it seemed to him that the Antichrist were already present in the society of his time. The holy Pope continues:

> ...[O]n the other hand, and this according to the same apostle is the distinguishing mark of Antichrist, man has with infinite temerity put himself in the place of God, raising himself above all that is called God.

We know that the coming of the Antichrist will correspond to a moment when men will reject God in every way. Now, this open struggle began long ago; to tell the truth, since Satan, since original sin. But during the course of the Church's history, one lived in an era when God was known, loved and respected in the majority of nations.

The Cult of Man

With the Renaissance and Protestantism arose certain thinkers who desired to transform society and make it secular, hence atheistic. They could not achieve their goal, however, as long as there were Catholic kings and princes. Thus they made a revolution by killing kings and massacring princes; and having overturned the ancient order, they succeeded, little by little, in establishing a truly secularized society, parcel by parcel, and more or less according to the country. Today legislatures pay no attention to the law of God or to the decalogue, but only to the rights of man.

Well, St. Pius X foresaw all of this:

> ...although [man] cannot utterly extinguish in himself all knowledge of God, he has contemned God's majesty and, as it were, made of the universe a temple wherein he himself is to be adored.

All this is prophetic. Speaking of his own time, the Pope already directs his thoughts to the future: he senses the oncoming of terrible times, where the persecution of Our Lord will be overt. Did he have a premonition of the coming of atheistic Communism? In any case, he saw the Antichrist at work.

God Will Have the Victory

Let's continue our reading.

> Verily no one of sound mind can doubt the issue of this contest between man and the Most High. Man, abusing his liberty, can violate the right and the majesty of the Creator of the Universe; but the victory will ever be with God.

It's clear, then; God shall win. But when?

>...[N]ay, defeat is at hand at the moment when man, under the delusion of his triumph, rises up with most audacity. Of this we are assured in the holy books by God Himself. Unmindful, as it were, of His strength and greatness, He "overlooks the sins of men" (Wisd. 11:24), but swiftly, after these apparent retreats, "awaked like a mighty man that hath been surfeited with wine" (Ps. 77:65), "He shall break the heads of his enemies" (Ps. 67:22)...

The Pope quotes the words of Scripture:

>...that all may know "that God is the king of all the earth" (Ps. 66:8), "That the Gentiles may know themselves to be men."

What St. Pius X says, we can say all the more: God "closes his eyes"; we feel a little abandoned by God. Men commit the worst crimes, things that one would not have dared think of at the time of St. Pius X. Think of the laws permitting abortion, inviting the massacre of hundreds of millions of innocent lives in the so-called civilized countries. Immorality is everywhere: one cannot open a newspaper without reading of rapes, crimes, robberies....And so we ask ourselves, What is the good Lord waiting for before he shakes up the world and makes men tremble a bit?

God is patient; He has His own time; we cannot know when He will decide to manifest it. This could happen suddenly; He comes "like a thief," a little like when He comes at death.

On God's triumph, continues St. Pius X:

>All this, Venerable Brethren, We believe and expect with unshakable faith. But this does not prevent us also, according to the measure given to each, from exerting ourselves to hasten the work of God—and not merely by praying assiduously: "Arise, O Lord, let not man be strengthened" (Ps. 9:19), but, more important still, by affirming both by word and deed and in the light of day, God's supreme dominion over man and all things, so that His right to command and His authority may be fully realized and respected.

Salvation by Jesus Christ

That is the plan: work for the reign of Our Lord Jesus Christ. It's clear. For St. Pius X, it is not a question of the rights of man, or progress, or changing structures; no, uniquely Our Lord. It is by Him that salvation will come. As he says later, let us do our duty, and if we seek peace, we cannot find it outside of God:

> But to want peace without God is an absurdity, seeing that where God is absent thence too justice flies, and when justice is taken away it is vain to cherish the hope of peace. "Peace is the work of justice, *Pax opus justitiae*" (Is. 22:17).

Render to God the things that are God's, render to one's neighbor his due: such is the virtue of justice. Peace reigns by justice.

However, says St. Pius X:

> There are many, We are well aware, who, in their yearning for peace, that is for the tranquillity of order, band themselves into societies and parties, which they style parties of order. Hope and labor lost.

And yet, isn't the Church's program a call to order? For St. Pius X, that does not suffice:

> For there is but one party of order capable of restoring peace in the midst of all this turmoil, and that is the party of God. It is this party, therefore, that we must advance, and to it attract as many as possible, if we are really urged by the love of peace.

This is what we no longer understand today. The current Pope in his discourse at Paris at the UNESCO (June 2, 1980) said that the great means to re-establish peace in the world is to restore "consciousness," to make people aware of the danger to which the world is exposed if efforts are not made to establish peace. "Becoming aware," as they say nowadays, cannot suffice if no remedy is given. But the only remedy is God's law; it is the Decalogue, which is the basis of all civilization, human and Christian.

St. Pius affirms without hesitation:

> But, Venerable Brethren, we shall never, however much we exert ourselves, succeed in calling men back to the majesty and empire of God, except by means of Jesus Christ. *Nunquam nisi per Jesum Christum eveniet.*

Once again, it is very clear. The Apostle warns us: No one can lay another foundation than that which was laid, which is Christ

Jesus. It is He alone whom the Father sanctified and sent into the world, the splendor of the Father and the image of His substance, true God and true Man, without whom no one can know God. For "neither doth any one know the Father, but the Son and he to whom it shall please the Son to reveal Him" (Mt. 11:27).

Christ Is God

For St. Pius X the conclusion that follows is that "to restore all things in Christ and to lead men back to submission to God is one and the same aim." Christ is God: that seems simple, and yet it is this that is always denied as much by the adversaries of Our Lord as by Catholics who no longer have a living faith, for these fail to consider Him as God in their way of life and manner of acting. The mystery of God Incarnate is manifestly a great mystery; we more easily see the man in Jesus Christ, while God is hidden behind His humanity. Yet there are not two persons in Our Lord Jesus Christ, there is only one: the Person of the Word. *Et Verbum caro factum est.* The Word, who is God, took flesh. Then if He is truly God, we must honor Him as God, obey Him as God, and seek the coming of His kingdom.

"This done," the Pope explains:

> We shall have brought [mankind] back to God. When We say to God We do not mean to that inert being heedless of all things human which the dream of materialists has imagined, but to the true and living God, one in nature, triple in person, Creator of the world, most wise Ordainer of all things, Lawgiver most just, who punishes the wicked and has reward in store for virtue.

The question of how immediately arises.

To Jesus Christ Through the Church

Now the way to reach Christ is not hard to find: it is the Church. Rightly does Chrysostom inculcate: "The Church is thy hope, the Church is thy salvation, the Church is thy refuge." (*Hom. de capto Eutropio*, n. 6.)

It was for this that Christ founded it, gaining it at the price of His blood, and made it the depository of His doctrine and His laws, bestowing upon it at the same time an inexhaustible treasury of graces for the sanctification and salvation of men.

And so in this manner we shall sanctify ourselves and honor Our Lord, and His reign shall come through the expansion of the Catholic Church. There is no other way, and it is for this that we are striving. We want to keep the Church as she has always been to give Our Lord Jesus Christ to souls, as He has always wished to give Himself: by the Church, by the faith and grace of the Church.

Let's continue the reading:

> You see, then, Venerable Brethren, the duty that has been imposed alike upon Us and upon you of bringing back to the discipline of the Church human society, now estranged from the wisdom of Christ; the Church will then subject it to Christ, and Christ to God.

The Order Willed by God

> But if our desire to obtain this is to be fulfilled, we must use every means and exert all our energy to bring about the utter disappearance of the enormous and detestable wickedness, so characteristic of our time—the substitution of man for God.

How can we help but think of the novelties of Vatican Council II? What is most striking in them is the place of man in relation to God. It is practically the religion of man. In the new Mass, for example, it is man that stands out, it is a democratic Mass; whereas the Mass of tradition, the one we call the Mass of all times, is hierarchical: God, Christ, the Church in the person of bishop and priest, then the faithful. Even among the faithful a hierarchy is recognized: a distinction used to be made between the princes or magistrates—those who exercise authority, and thus share the authority of Our Lord (because all authority comes from God)—and the rest of the faithful.

These are not mere medieval ideas, this is simply a part of the hierarchy that we shall find in heaven, where God will be first, then the hierarchies of the angels and saints. This is normal, for God has willed that we share in His glory in differing degrees.

And this allows us to practice charity. The very fact that some men have fewer gifts and some men more gives rise to exchanges between men here below, as it does between the saints and the angels in heaven.

According to the modern errors, on the contrary, all men are equal. They form a uniform mass, and it is number that gives authority! Man substitutes himself for God; there is no more God.

St. Pius X recalls the order in society willed by God:

> ...it remains to restore to their ancient place of honor the most holy laws and counsels of the gospel; to proclaim aloud the truths taught by the Church, and her teachings on the sanctity of marriage, on the education and discipline of youth, on the possession and use of property, the duties that men owe to those who rule the State; and lastly to restore equilibrium between the different classes of society according to Christian precept and custom. This is what We, in submitting Ourselves to the manifestations of the Divine will, purpose to aim at during Our Pontificate, and We will use all our industry to attain it.

Such is the program of the holy Pope Pius X: To renew all things in Christ, to put God back in society by the Church, and to restore order in society by means of the Christian institutions which the Church has always protected and promoted.

The Formation of Priests

The Pope then addresses the Bishops. What is their special role? What must they do to bring about the reign of Our Lord Jesus Christ? What suitable means are at hand to attain such a great end? It seems superfluous to name them, they are so obvious:

> Let your first care be to form Christ in those who are destined from the duty of their vocation to form Him in others. We speak of the priests, Venerable Brethren. For all who bear the seal of the priesthood must know that they have the same mission to the people in the midst of whom they live as that which Paul proclaimed that he received in these tender words: "My little children, of whom I am in labor again until Christ be formed in you" (Gal. 4:19).

It is absolutely necessary, then, to think of the seminaries.

...[The priests] are called another Christ, not merely by the communication of power but by reason of the imitation of His works, and they should therefore bear stamped upon themselves the image of Christ.

St. Pius X exhorts the bishops: What will be your first concern? The formation of priests! And this is quite normal: for what is a Church without priests, true priests, holy priests? Now, it is we who are much nearer this catastrophe than they were at the time of St. Pius X. Were he to return, he would emphasize it even more. For there are priests without the spirit of the priesthood, who neither preach the gospel nor teach the true catechism, or else who marry! There are few seminarians, and these are badly trained. What can come of such a situation?

Increase the Number of Seminaries

I repeat: The first concern of the bishops should be the formation of true priests. We could not have chosen a better patron for the Society than St. Pius X. Because the situation is worse today than at the time of the holy Pontiff, as a bishop and having no official function, I thought that I could do nothing better for the Church and the restoration of the reign of Our Lord Jesus Christ in the Church and in society than to form priests, and thus to open seminaries, and to prepare professors to teach there.

Seminaries must be founded. This is the first goal of the Priestly Society of St. Pius X. There should be one in Canada, in Mexico, one in Columbia and in Australia, and in South Africa. There should also be one in Ireland, and England...everywhere. In the measure that it is necessary to renew the Church and to restore the reign of Our Lord Jesus Christ, priests are needed, and not just any kind of priest.

Sometimes one hears the remark: Things are getting better; the number of seminarians is increasing. For example, at the seminary of Paderborn, thirty-nine seminarians entered last year; and in the seminary of Augsburg, twenty-five. In a new seminary in Argentina, a bishop decided to restore tradition somewhat, and many young men are attracted by the use of Latin, and a certain discipline.

Alas, one must closely examine the kind of philosophy they teach, the liturgy they use, and even the general discipline. They are not teaching these young seminarians Scholastic philosophy, which is nonetheless the philosophy of the Church. They teach the history of philosophy, presenting all the philosophies in a few words, but they do not reach the true first principles of philosophy. The same is true for theology: they study Apologetics and Holy Scripture. And so these priests are not formed; they are even deformed.

Recently a professor of Paderborn came to visit our seminary of Zaitzkofen. He told us there are seminarians there, true enough, and when they arrive they are well disposed and desire to learn the truth. But after a year or two, they notice that they are completely deformed; no one teaches them what they came to learn. They become discouraged, or lose the notion of truth, or they look elsewhere!

Another example: Not long ago the seminary of Regensburg (Ratisbonne) was considered to be the best traditional seminary of Germany, and Mgr. Graber was also considered as a traditionalist, having authored a little "reactionary" book against certain positions of the Council. I paid him a visit; and what did he tell me? He has seminarians, he said, and ordained eighteen that year, and he still receives vocations. Are you happy, then, I asked? Not really, he said; many of the seminarians do not go to Mass in the morning, and some of them wear their hair down to their shoulders.

If there were seminaries that were on the right track we would rejoice and say, *Deo gratias*. But this is not the case; and the longer the delay, the fewer professors there will be who know Thomistic philosophy and true theology. That is why a good number of the seminarians of the Society of St. Pius X will be called upon in turn to become professors in our seminaries. This will become necessary.

Form Holy Priests

St. Pius X earnestly invites us to do so:

This being so, Venerable Brethren, of what nature and magnitude is the care that must be taken by you in forming the clergy to holiness! All other tasks must yield to this one. Wherefore the chief part of your diligence will be directed to governing and ordering your seminaries aright so that they may flourish equally in the soundness of their teaching and in the spotlessness of their morals. Regard your seminary as the delight of your hearts, and neglect on its behalf none of those provisions which the Council of Trent has with admirable forethought prescribed. And when the time comes for promoting the youthful candidates to holy orders, ah! do not forget what Paul wrote to Timothy: "Impose not hands lightly upon any man" (I Tim. 5:22), bearing carefully in mind that as a general rule the faithful will be such as are those whom you call to the priesthood. Do not then pay heed to private interests of any kind, but have at heart only God and the Church and the eternal welfare of souls so that, as the Apostle admonishes, "you may not be partakers of the sins of others" (*Ibid.*).

Solicitude for Young Priests

Young priests who have just left the seminary must not be neglected either:

> Then again be not lacking in solicitude for young priests who have just left the seminary. From the bottom of Our heart, We urge you to bring them often close to your breast, which should burn with celestial fire—kindle them, inflame them, so that they may aspire solely after God and the salvation of souls. Rest assured, Venerable Brethren, that We on Our side will use the greatest diligence to prevent the members of the clergy from being drawn to the snares of a certain new and fallacious science, which savoureth not of Christ, but with masked and cunning arguments strives to open the door to the errors of Rationalism and
>
> Semi-Rationalism; against which the Apostle warned Timothy to be on his guard, when he wrote: "Keep that which is committed to thy trust, avoiding the profane novelties of words, and oppositions of knowledge falsely so called which some promising have erred concerning the faith" (I Tim. 4:20 ff.)

Take care of the young priests!

"It is a great grief and a continual sorrow to our heart" (Rom. 9:2) to find Jeremiah's lamentation applicable to our times: "The little ones asked for bread, and there was none to break it to them" (Lam. 4:4). For there are not lacking among the clergy those who adapt themselves according to their bent to works of more apparent than real solidity—but not so numerous perhaps are those who, after the example of Christ, take to themselves the words of the Prophet: "The Spirit of the Lord hath anointed me, hath sent me to evangelize the poor, to heal the contrite of heart, to announce freedom to the captive, and sight to the blind" (Lk. 4:18-19).

I imagine the Pope was thinking of his own diocese when he said, many priests spend their time on many other things than their ministry, teaching the catechism and administering the sacraments.

St. Pius X always stressed the main duty of the priest: teaching catechism. Priests nowadays say that that is not their business, it is the parents' job. Of course parents must teach the rudiments of the catechism to their children; but it is still the priest who possesses the knowledge for giving religious instruction. He has it, not to pronounce learned philosophical discourses for a small elite, but to be able to communicate religious knowledge to children and to simple people. For there is a real danger of letting oneself be absorbed by the speculative sciences and of failing to adapt oneself to people. The priest has to know how to adapt and proportion the science he has received to those to whom he is sent.

This is what St. Pius X says again:

...[T]he principal way to restore the empire of God in their souls is religious instruction.

Then he adds:

How many there are who mimic Christ and abhor the Church and the Gospel more through ignorance than through badness of mind, of whom it may well be said: "They blaspheme whatever things they know not" (Jude 2:10)....The result is for a great many the loss of the faith. For it is not true that the progress of knowledge extinguishes the faith; rather is it ignorance, and the more ignorance prevails the greater is the havoc wrought by incredulity. And this is why Christ commanded the Apostles: "Going forth teach all nations" (Mt. 28:19).

A Patient Charity

St. Pius X then asks the bishops to assure that the priests be charitable.

> But in order that the desired fruit may be derived from this apostolate and this zeal for teaching, and that Christ may be formed in all, be it remembered, Venerable Brethren, that no means is more efficacious than charity.

The advice given here is really important. Think of the problems that many traditionalists have experienced in their parishes. Priests who lack charity have a tendency to judge men as they should be and not as they are; they close their eyes to the realities. If a young priest comes into contact with souls, and has categories in mind, thinking *a priori* what Christians should be like, he will not receive the sinner who comes to him (and we are all sinners!) as a physician—a—physician of souls—but as a judge. Then he will condemn, rebuke, and scold the penitent, with the result, of course, that people will flee. Imagine that in a hospital a doctor were to say to the patient, You are too sick, I can't treat you, you have only to die. Or else a doctor who would have recourse to drastic measures right away: your leg must be amputated. Such a doctor might do analyses, but he would have no feel for diagnosis, the sense that so many of our country doctors used to have to such a high degree, and who could guess the nature of the disease right away. Such doctors were loved.

The priests, then, must be physicians of souls, says St. Pius X, and he explains:

> ..."For the Lord is not in the earthquake" (III Kings 19:11)—it is vain to hope to attract souls to God by a bitter zeal. On the contrary, harm is done more often than good by taunting men harshly with their faults, and reproving their vices with asperity. True the Apostle exhorted Timothy: "Accuse, beseech, rebuke," but he took care to add: "with all patience" (II Tim. 4:2).
>
> Jesus has certainly left us examples of this. "Come to me," we find Him saying, "come to me all ye that labor and are burdened and I will refresh you" (Mt. 11:28). And by those that labor and are burdened he meant only those who are slaves of sin and error. What gentleness was that shown by the Divine Master! What

tenderness, what compassion towards all kinds of misery! Isaias has marvelously described His heart in the words: "I will set my spirit upon him; he shall not contend, nor cry out; the bruised reed he will not break, he will not extinguish the smoking flax" (Is. 42:1 ff.). This charity, "patient and kind" (I Cor. 13:4), will extend itself also to those who are hostile to us and persecute us. "We are reviled," thus did St. Paul protest, "and we bless; we are persecuted and we suffer it; we are blasphemed and we entreat" (I Cor. 4:12 ff.). They perhaps seem to be worse than they really are. Their associations with others, prejudice, the counsel, advice and example of others, and finally an ill-advised shame have dragged them to the side of the impious; but their wills are not so depraved as they themselves would seek to make people believe.

Refrain From Hasty Conclusions

Truly, harshness is a bad counselor. Right away one draws exaggerated conclusions from a single sentence; the words of others are always taken in the most extreme way. For example, some people reason thus: The pope has said this; he is therefore a heretic; he is therefore not pope. Behold an argument that is too simple. It does not suffice, after all, to take a sentence out of context and then rightly conclude: he is a heretic.

To be a heretic it is necessary to be pertinacious in adhering to the error; it is not enough to have uttered an heretical phrase. For example, on the subject of the Blessed Trinity—a very difficult subject—we might make a mistake or blunder in speech and say something that is not very orthodox. If someone points it out to us we retract; but if they accuse us of heresy, or excommunicate us…how frightful.

Some go so far as to draw the most improbable conclusions: Someone said such a sentence, thus he is a liberal. And if he is a liberal, then he must be a mason, and so he is excommunicated. With such argumentation, everyone would be a freemason!

So it is very dangerous to let oneself be drawn into hasty conclusions. Sometimes it is said about the pope: He signed the Decree on Religious Liberty; but this decree is heretical, therefore the pope is a heretic, therefore the pope isn't pope. Firstly, one must study in a very precise way to see if the decree is heretical.

Then, one must ask whether the pope, when he signed it, was quite aware of what he signed. It is known that he himself obliged certain expressions to be added which say, "The Decree on Religious Liberty is in conformity with Tradition." Of course, this isn't true, but in his own mind the pope saw it that way. Hence one cannot conclude too rapidly, the consequences would be too grave.

Some say, "There is no pope." Then the cardinals he has named are not cardinals, and when these elect the next pope, there will be no pope because the cardinals were not cardinals. Where does this lead? Who then will designate the new pope? Providence? Yes, but Providence makes use of men. One falls into a black hole. This is where hasty conclusions lead.

Is it any wonder that the faithful look elsewhere? They go to Palmar de Troya, where Clemente made himself pope, and sits with a court of cardinals. They go to the Latin Church of Toulouse, or elsewhere. They have been driven into seeking an authority; they end up by joining the sects; they break away completely from the Church.

Thus, one must be very careful and very prudent before affirming something. Those who have spoken thus have lacked the spirit of charity, and consequently, Realism. They are idealists, speculative reasoners.

The Priest Is a Physician of Souls

It is the same thing with sinners. When one must examine someone's sin, one must, of course, consider the sin in itself, the action committed that is a grave sin. But it is possible that, subjectively, the penitent is not guilty: perhaps he didn't know that he was committing a grave sin, or he had been pushed, or conditioned, or at the time he was not conscious of what he was doing: so many circumstances to weigh; to examine things outside of their circumstances is not realistic. Now, once again, the priest is the physician of souls, he must question the penitent or the person who has come seeking advice. How did he do that? How did he get himself into such a situation? Explain so as to try later to give a remedy. This is very important. A priest must begin in the seminary to seek the virtue of prudence. He must not let himself become harsh, or enclose himself within arguments by which he leads astray himself and others.

Catholic Action

Next St. Pius X considers the question of means.

> It is true, Venerable Brethren, that in this arduous task of the restoration of the human race in Christ neither you nor your clergy should exclude all assistance.

The Pope requests the bishops to watch over Catholic Action, the society of the faithful who help the priest to spread the teaching that comes from the example of the Christian life:

> For it is not priests alone, but all the faithful without exception, who must concern themselves with the interests of God and souls—not, of course, according to their own views, but always under the direction and orders of the bishops....Our predecessors have long since approved and blessed those Catholics who have banded together in societies of various kinds, but always religious in their aim. We, too, have no hesitation in awarding Our praise to this great idea, and we earnestly desire to see it propagated and flourish in town and country. But We wish that all such associations aim first and chiefly at the constant maintenance of Christian life, among those who belong to them.

To grasp St. Pius X's ideas on Catholic Action, it is necessary to refer to the allocution he pronounced on September 25, 1904. He asks that three principles govern Catholic Action: piety, study, action. In France they are familiar with groups like the Catholic Students youth group (JEC), Young Catholic Workers (JOC), Junior Catholic Farmers (JAC), which were formed under the initiative of a Belgian priest, Cardijn, who later became cardinal; he took as his motto: see, judge, act.

This is quite different from what Pius X proposed: prayer, study, action. Prayer, one may say, envelops study according to the principles of the Catholic religion, and then comes the action that is commanded by prayer and study. Whereas in the program "see, judge, act," seeing comes first, which is an action. It is to conduct oneself like all those who accomplish any undertaking: one begins by seeing, then one judges; finally one acts. But how do they see things? How do they judge them? How is their action guided.

When I was Archbishop of Dakar I remember having visited JOC groups. I would point out to them the danger of this motto. First of all, one sees that something goes wrong at work; then one judges: why did this go wrong? It is because of the authority, the boss; then one acts: one must fight the boss. The same thing happens in the parish: something goes wrong, it is the pastor's fault, and so one must fight the pastor. Thus one falls into the principle of revolution. These young people think that nothing is ever their fault; the authority is always to blame!

This explains how these initially well-intentioned Catholic Action movements ended up by becoming revolutionary associations. What is more revolutionary that the ACO (the Workers' Catholic Action)? Everything is society's fault, hence one revolts against society; one seeks to change all the institutions: it becomes generalized revolution.

Piety First

It is very important to return to the true principles of Catholic action. First of all prayer: beg the good God for His grace. Then study the teaching of the Church in order to act in conformity with the principles of truly Catholic action. Such is the normal order.

St. Pius X continues:

....Such luminous examples given by the great army of soldiers of Christ will be of much greater avail in moving and drawing men than words and sublime dissertations; and it will easily come about that when human respect has been driven out, and prejudices and doubting laid aside, large numbers will be won to Christ, becoming in their turn promoters of His knowledge and love which are the road to true and solid happiness.

The result:

...[T]here will certainly be no more need for us to labor further to see all things restored in Christ. Nor is it for the attainment of eternal welfare alone that this will be of service—it will also contribute largely to temporal welfare and the advantage of human society. For when these conditions have been secured, the upper and wealthy classes will learn to be just and charitable to the lowly, and these will be able to bear with tranquillity and patience the trials of a very hard lot; the citizens will obey not lust but law, reverence and love will be deemed a duty towards those that govern, "whose power comes only from God" (Rom. 13:1). And then? Then, at last, it will be clear to all that the Church, such as it was instituted by Christ, must enjoy full and entire liberty....

St. Pius X, before concluding, expresses a wish:

May God, "who is rich in mercy" (Ephes. 2:4), benignly speed this restoration of the human race in Jesus Christ for "it is not of him that willeth, or of him that runneth, but of God that showeth mercy" (Rom. 9:16). And let us, Venerable Brethren, "in the spirit of humility," with continuous and urgent prayer ask this of Him through the merits of Jesus Christ.

Then he turns towards the Blessed Virgin:

Let us turn, too, to the most powerful intercession of the Divine Mother....with further exhortation that as intercessors with God appeal be also made to the most pure Spouse of Mary, the Patron of the Catholic Church, and the holy Princes of the Apostles, Peter and Paul.

Finally, the Pope gives his apostolic blessing. This beautiful encyclical of Pope St. Pius X practically summarizes all the encyclicals of his predecessors. He puts the accent on what is most important: *Omnia restaurare in Christo*. Today, as in his time, that is the goal of the priesthood.

Part One

PONTIFICAL DOCUMENTS ON FREEMASONRY

Chapter II

THE ENCYCLICAL *QUO GRAVIORA* OF POPE LEO XII ON FREEMASONRY
(MARCH 13, 1826)

The encyclical *Quo Graviora* by Leo XII, dated March 13, 1826, which deals with Freemasonry, is special in that it cites the integral text of letters published by his predecessors, namely, Clement XII (1738), Benedict XIV (1751) and Pius VII (1821). It is interesting to note that as early as 1738, thus a century earlier, the popes were decrying the secret societies, as they continued to do after Leo XII.

Pope Leo XII wanted to bring them once again to the attention of the bishops and the faithful, because, unfortunately, they had not paid enough attention to the previous warnings, and the secret societies were continuing to develop alarmingly.

The encyclical begins:

> The greater are the disasters that threaten the flock of Jesus Christ our God and Savior, the greater must be the solicitude of the Roman Pontiffs, to whom in the person of Peter were confided the power and the responsibility for this flock, to avert them.

He reminds them that the pope, whose duty it is to lead the flock, must indicate where the dangers that threaten the flock lie.

> The Roman Pontiffs, Our Predecessors, having understood the great task that they had to fulfill, like good shepherds always kept watch carefully, and by means of exhortations, instructions and decrees, and even by risking their lives for the sake of their sheep, they tried to utterly destroy the sects that were threatening the Church with total ruin.

Notice that the Pope does not hesitate to say "the sects threaten," and desire the complete destruction of the Church. He continues:

The record of this papal solicitude is not only to be found in ancient ecclesiastic archives; brilliant proofs are met with in the examples of what has been done in our own and in our fathers' day by the Roman Pontiffs to counter the secret associations of the enemies of Jesus Christ.

Then he introduces the letter of Clement XII:

Clement XII, Our Predecessor, having seen that the sect, whether called Freemasons or what other name soever, was gaining new strength daily, and having learned with certitude by numerous proofs that this sect was not only suspected of being an enemy of the Church, but was so openly, he condemned it in an excellent constitution which begins by the words "*In eminenti*," published April 28, 1738.

Clement XII: Excommunication of Freemasons

Here is the text of the letter of Clement XII:

Raised by divine Providence to the highest degree of the apostolate, seconded incessantly by divine grace, We intend to bring our attention to bear with all the zeal of our solicitude upon that which can help conserve the integrity of orthodox religion and, by barring entrance to errors and vices, banish from the Catholic world in these difficult times all dangers of disturbances.

The popes of old knew how to be clear and simple! They said that they were pastors and wanted to protect the flock. Against what? Against errors and vices. Consequently, they denounce errors and proclaim the truth of the Church. Nothing could be clearer. One felt safe with such shepherds, who were not afraid to say, Watch out! avoid this, avoid that; there lies danger, walk according to the truth of the Church.

Such language is unknown now, especially since Pope John XXIII. Before him, Pius XII wrote a strong and magnificent encyclical against the errors of modern times, *Humani Generis* (1950). Since then, it would seem that there are no more modern errors. It is as if because there are elements of truth even in the errors, along with the grain of apparent truth, the error that covers it is swallowed, and the flock is poisoned.

Clement XII's letter continues:

> It has become known to Us, even in truth by public rumor, that great and extensive progress is being made by, and the strength daily increasing of, some Societies, Meetings, Gatherings, Conventicles, or Lodges, commonly known as Freemasons or some other nomenclature according to difference of language, in which men of all religions and sects whatsoever, content with a certain affectation of natural virtue, are associated mutually in a close and exclusive bond in accordance with laws and statutes framed for themselves; and are bound as well by a stringent oath sworn upon the Sacred Bible, as by the imposition of heavy penalties to conceal under inviolable silence, what they secretly do in their meetings.

The definition is magnificent. Note the elements: firstly, men "of all religions," who affect "an appearance of natural virtue," that is, they pretend to be philanthropists, passing themselves off as the friends of the people, of progress, and society. This has not changed! They still have a secret pact which binds them under severe penalties (even death, as was to be learned later on) to an unbreakable silence. It is impossible to learn exactly what is plotted in these societies—absolute secrecy is maintained. The popes have emphasized this fact: things accomplished in such a manner can only be evil; if good things were being done, there would be no reason for it not to be done in broad daylight.

Clement XII evokes the grievances the Church has against these societies: firstly, the suspicions that are raised in the minds of the faithful.

> But since it is the nature of wickedness to betray itself, and to cry aloud so as to reveal itself, hence the aforesaid Societies or Conventicles have excited so strong suspicion in the minds of the faithful that to enroll oneself in these Lodges is quite the same, in the judgment of prudent and virtuous men, as to incur the brand of depravity and perverseness.

Thus, the Pope relies somewhat upon public opinion. The prudent and honorable faithful deem that something wicked goes on in these societies.

> And this repute has spread to such a degree that in very many countries the societies just mentioned have been proscribed, and

with foresight banished long since as though hostile to the safety of kingdoms.

At that time, actually, the States were Catholic. The princes decided to forbid these secret societies. The Pope, one sees, bases his judgment on what he has learned from persons who are in contact with these societies. And so he proclaims:

> We, accordingly, turning over in Our mind the very serious injuries which are in the highest degree inflicted by such Societies or Conventicles, not merely on the tranquillity of the temporal state, but also on the spiritual welfare of souls, and perceiving that they are inconsistent alike with civil and canonical sanctions, being taught by the divine Word that it is Our duty, by day and night, like a faithful servant, and a prudent ruler of his master's household, to watch that no persons of this kind like thieves break into the house, and like foxes strive to ravage the vineyard, that is to say, thereby pervert the hearts of the simple, in order to close the wide road which might be opened thereby for perpetrating iniquity with impunity and for other just and reasonable causes known to Ourselves, have determined and decreed that these same Societies, Meetings, Gatherings, Lodges or Conventicles of Freemasons, or by whatever other name called, herein acting on the advice of some Venerable Brethren of Ours, Cardinals of the Holy Roman Church, and also of Our own motion, and from Our certain knowledge and mature deliberation, and in the plenitude of Apostolic Power, should be condemned and prohibited, as by this present Constitution We do condemn and prohibit them.
>
> Wherefore We direct the faithful in Christ, all and singly, of whatever status, grade, dignity and pre-eminence, whether laymen or clerics as well secular as regular, strictly and in virtue of holy obedience, that no one, under any pretext or farfetched rationale dare or presume to enter the above-mentioned Societies of Freemasons, or otherwise named; or to propagate, foster or receive them whether in their houses or elsewhere, and to conceal them, or be present at them, or to afford them the opportunity or facilities for being convened anywhere, or otherwise to render them advice, help or favor, openly or in secret, directly or indirectly, of themselves or through the agency of others in whatever

way...; but in every particular to abstain utterly as they are in duty bound from the same Societies (...) under pain of excommunication.

Such is the first document: Clement XII was worried by the secret actions taking place in these societies; therefore he excommunicated those who went.

And yet this letter—one can also say this bull—of 1738 did not suffice. Rumors spread after the death of Clement XII according to which the condemnation decreed during his lifetime was no longer valid as long as it was not confirmed by his successor. This is what makes Leo XII say: "This bull did not seem sufficient for our Predecessor of happy memory, Benedict XIV."

Benedict XIV: Fight Against Indifferentism

It was undoubtedly absurd to claim that the bulls of deceased popes became null if they were not expressly approved by their successors. Still, to deny to the contestors any pretext for claiming permission to adhere to Freemasonry, Benedict XIV published a new bull beginning by the word *Providas* and dated March 18, 1751. This is the second document cited by Leo XII.

Benedict XIV firstly explains why he deems it advisable to confirm the act of his predecessor:

> Clement XII of happy memory, Our predecessor, in the year 1738, the eighth year of his pontificate, condemned and proscribed in perpetuity certain societies popularly called Freemasons...forbidding all the faithful of Jesus Christ and each in particular to adhere under pain of excommunication incurred *ipso facto*...and which can only be absolved by the Sovereign Pontiff....As some who have been found who did not fear to aver and publish that the said pain of excommunication levied by Our predecessor no longer holds (...) and as some pious, God-fearing men have suggested to Us that to counter the subterfuges of these calumniators (...) it would be very useful to add the weight of Our own confirmation to the constitution of Our predecessor....

It can be seen here that the Pope clearly confirms what Clement XII said. Then he gives several supplementary reasons worth studying because he states them quite clearly. There are six of them. The first forcefully repeats what Clement XII had already observed: "that in this type of society men of all religions and sects are gathered"; and Benedict XIV adds: "which evidently can cause the gravest damage to the purity of the Catholic religion."

It needs to be remembered that these popes always fought against Indifferentism, the error that consists in affirming that all religions are good, that every man can have his own, and that the Catholic religion must not be set above the others. This is contrary to Catholic truth; a Catholic can not accept it. That is why the popes have always fought against these so-called "interdenominational" meetings, unions or congresses; they give the impression that all religions are identical, and that none is preferable to another. This is absolutely contrary to our faith!

In times of calamity, of course a spontaneous accord results, when some event, like a catastrophe, an earthquake, a tidal wave or cyclone hits, or when everyone is afflicted as in wartime; then it is possible to collaborate with another religious group to go to the rescue and bring aid. That would be a precise activity that does not engage the faith, it would be a normal act of mercy.

But to create permanent institutions is dangerous because the principles are not the same.

We had difficulties of this kind, I well remember, in Cameroon, for example. The government offered to help public schools. As a result, some people thought that it was clever to suggest that since not only Catholics, but also Protestants were involved in private schools, the two groups should unite in order to present their requirements more forcefully to the government. Well, those who, despite the advice of the bishops, acted in this manner were deserted by the Protestants, because finally the Protestants felt it expedient to agree to everything the government asked for in exchange, whether concerning the curriculum, or the location of the schools. There were things agreed to that were unacceptable to the Catholics, and in the end the Catholic schools were nearly ruined. The result was a rupture between the two groups, and a situation worse than before.

The problem is the same in the trade unions. All those involved possess a genuine notion of justice; that of the non-Catholics is more or less good, but when discussions arise the non-Catholics are inclined to push the workers to revolt. A moment always comes when the guiding principles are no longer the same. St. Pius X had to intervene in a division that arose between German bishops over the question of establishing inter-denominational trade unions. He advised them against it in a letter in which he said, roughly, that Catholics have principles that they apply in practice, but that the others do not. The latter's working principles change, because they do not have any clear convictions. It is impossible to collaborate with them.

Returning to the reasons Pope Benedict XIV gives against Freemasonry, the second is:

...the strict pact and impenetrable secret by which everything that is done in their lodges is hidden, to which one can apply this maxim (...): Good things welcome publicity, criminal deeds are hidden.

The third reason follows from the second:

It is the oath that they swear to maintain this inviolable secrecy, as if it were allowable to rely upon the pretext of a promise or oath in order not to be obliged, should one be interrogated by the legitimate authority, to avow everything one might be asked in order to learn if anything is done in these lodges that is contrary to the State and the laws of religion and government.

So, the reasons are the secrecy, the oath sworn, and the refusal to avow anything when interrogated by the legitimate authority. This is illicit. No one can swear to refuse to answer someone who has a legitimate right to question him, someone who must know things that affect the security of the State and even the existence of religion.

Benedict XIV provides a fourth reason:

These societies are no less inimical to civil law than to Canon Law.

Both civil and Canon law forbid secret gatherings, secret meetings, and secret associations unknown to anyone, because all societies gathered without the public authority are forbidden by civil law and are also prohibited by Canon Law.

The fifth reason is that in several countries, these societies have been proscribed and banished by the laws of the secular princes.

Of course, one could retort that the princes act this way because these societies bother them, and that does not necessarily mean that they are bad. But the Pope relies upon the judgment of secular Catholic princes who deem that they cannot tolerate these associations which hide and act in secret. And the sixth reason:

> These societies have a bad reputation among honest and prudent men (...); to enroll in them is quite the same as to incur the brand of depravity and perverseness.

Here the Pope relies upon the opinion of honest and virtuous men. Then he, like his predecessor, urges prelates and bishops, the local ordinaries and ecclesiastical superiors, as well as princes and heads of State, to fight against these secret societies.

Such then is the second document cited by Leo XII, who adds a reflection: He reproaches the governments and heads of State for having not heeded the popes' warnings. For that reason the secret societies continue to spread and to disseminate evil. We cite:

> Would to God that those who possessed the power would have known how to appreciate these decrees as much as the salvation of religion and the State required.

> Would to God that they had been convinced that they should see in the Roman Pontiffs, the successors of Peter, not only pastors and the head of the Catholic Church, but also the firmest stay of the governments and the most vigilant watchmen to discover the perils of society!

> Would to God that they had exercised their power to fight and to destroy the sects whose perfidy had been made known to them by the apostolic See. Then they would have succeeded. But whether because the members had the cunning to hide their plots, or whether by negligence or culpable imprudence the matter had been presented as something of little importance and meriting neglect, the Freemasons have instigated more dangerous and audacious meetings.

One must place at the head of the roster the *Carbonari*, who seem to embrace all of them, and which is the most important in Italy and in several other countries. Divided into different branches and known under diverse names, it has dared to undertake to combat the Catholic religion and to fight against the legitimate authority.

The Pope does not hesitate to designate this new sect which openly attacks the Catholic religion and the legitimate authority of the State.

Pius VII: Against the Sacrilege

Leo XII then presents a third document:

Our Predecessor Pius VII of happy memory, published a bull on September 13, 1821, beginning by the words: *Ecclesiam a Jesu Christo*.

It concerns the condemnation of the sect of the *Carbonari* under gravest penalties. The Revolution had taken place and had subsided materially, but by 1821 it was evident that far from diminishing, the activity of the sects had increased in order to spread the revolution throughout Europe.

The Church which Jesus Christ our Savior founded on the firm rock and against which, according to the promise of the Savior, the gates of hell shall not prevail, has been so often attacked and by enemies so terrible that, without this divine and lovable promise, she would surely have succumbed, overcome either by the might or the subterfuges of her persecutors.

It must be remembered that Pius VII still saw the effects of the Revolution, which had caused the execution of the King of France, the massacres of priests and religious, the destruction of churches, and ruins and persecutions everywhere.

What happened long ago is still being renewed, especially during the deplorable epoch in which we live, an epoch that seems to resemble the last times announced so often by the Apostles, when "there should come mockers, walking according to their own desires in ungodlinesses" (Jude, 18). It is not unknown to anyone what a prodigious number of guilty men have banded together in these very difficult times against the Lord and against His Christ, having done everything to deceive the faithful by the subtleties of a false and vain philosophy, to wrest them from the bosom of the Church in the mad hope of overturning this same Church.

In order to attain this goal more easily, most of them have formed occult societies, clandestine sects, hoping by this means to more freely associate a greater number of men to their conspiracy and their perverse plan.

It is already long ago that the Holy See, having discovered the existence of these sects, rose up against them with strength and courage, and exposed to the light of day the dark designs that they had formed against religion and civil society. For a long time she has been drawing attention to this matter by encouraging the vigilance necessary to prevent the sects from putting into execution their culpable projects. But it is necessary to bemoan the fact that the zeal of the Holy See has not been able to obtain the expected effects.

The popes themselves recognized that their efforts had been in vain. St. Pius X often said that despite their efforts to fight against Liberalism, Modernism and Progressivism, because they were not heeded, the gravest evils would befall mankind. Men want to let themselves go: freedom of all religions, freedom of association, freedom of thought, of the press, of speech. Well, evil will spread more and more, and society will become unbearable, like life under a Communist regime.

Pius VII also laments to see that:

> These perverse men have not ceased from their undertaking, from which have finally resulted all the woes which we have foreseen.

So it is clear: the evils of the Revolution have been caused by the sects. The Pope adds:

> What is more, these prideful men have dared to form new secret societies, among which it is necessary here to point out a newly formed society which has extended throughout Italy and in other countries, and which, though divided into several branches

and bearing different names according to the circumstances, is nevertheless really one by the community of opinion and outlook and by its constitution; it is most often designated by the name of *Carbonari*. They affect a singular respect and an admirable zeal for the Catholic religion and doctrine and for the person of Our Lord Jesus Christ, whom they sometimes have the criminal audacity to call their Grand Master and the head of their society.

But these discourses, which seem smoother than oil, are nothing but the darts which these perfidious men use to wound more surely those who are not on their guard. They come to you like sheep, but at heart they are voracious wolves.

And here once again the grievances against these associations are evoked:

> They swear that never and under no circumstance will they reveal the least detail concerning the society to men who would not be admitted, nor will they ever discuss with members of the lower ranks things pertaining to the higher ranks.

Not only is there secrecy from the outside, but even within Freemasonry, there are degrees, and an oath is imposed upon each member of the superior ranks not to reveal anything to those of the lower ranks! All this must inspire the greatest distrust.

> Moreover, the clandestine and illegitimate meetings which they hold in imitation of several heretics, and this aggregation of people of all religions and all the sects, rather shows (...) that it is impossible to trust their words.

Little by little, the popes gathered information, especially from former members who had converted. Pius VII knows books where certain details are revealed:

> Their books in which are published what takes place at their meetings, especially for the upper ranks, their catechisms, their statutes, and other authentic documents worthy of faith, the testimonies of those who had left the society and revealed to the magistrates their artifices and errors: all prove that the principal goal of the *Carbonari* is to spread indifferentism in matter of religion, the most dangerous of all the systems, which teaches that every one has the absolute freedom to make a religion following

his own inclinations and ideas, to profane, and defile the Passion of the Savior by several of their guilty ceremonies.

Not everything that has been told can be pure invention. There is talk, for example, of black masses; these are horrible sacrileges. The Freemasons need consecrated hosts for them. They look for them where they are sure that the hosts have been consecrated, and if need be they will break into a tabernacle. Their will is explicitly to commit a sacrilege, and this sacrilege is truly abominable.

These accounts are not made up. Black masses are even held at Rome in different locations. In Geneva, according to a public enquiry reported in the press, there are more than fifty secret societies with two thousand adherents. The same can be said of Basel and Zurich. You must not be under any illusions: Switzerland is heavily influenced by Freemasonry, even in the Catholic cantons like the Valais, and certain of the Protestant cantons are veritable hotbeds of the Freemasons. The federal government is infiltrated by them: that is why Switzerland was one of the first countries to close its eyes to abortion, and to attract women from neighboring countries to have abortions. All this is quite real, and reveals a determined will to defile the Passion of Our Lord, and, as Pius VII says:

> ...to despise the sacraments of the Church, for which, by a hideous sacrilege, they seem to have substituted some of their own invention.

I had a chance to see some brochures published by the Masons. They were very well done, very well printed. There were some on the Blessed Virgin, blasphemous from beginning to end, going so far as to compare her to all the obscene pagan goddesses of antiquity. Their initiation ceremony resembles baptism, because they have caricatured everything from the Catholic Church, which is indeed the sign of Satan. They have worship, sanctuaries. They even have an altar, but stripped, without a single cloth, and behind a seat for the president. The new arrangement of the sanctuary in churches since Vatican II surprisingly resembles this; these altars where there is not even a crucifix, the priests who call themselves presidents, turned towards the people and making speeches: there is a real, albeit external, resemblance! The Freemasons, Pius VII says:

> ...despise the sacraments of the Church in order to overthrow the apostolic See, against which, animated by a special hatred because of the primacy of this Chair, they weave the deepest and most detestable plots.

This was in 1821. Fifty years later, the Holy See was to be despoiled of its States, the result of the secret societies' conspiracies.

The moral precepts given by the society of the *Carbonari* are no less culpable, as these same documents show, although it boasts of requiring its votaries to practice charity and the other virtues, and to abstain from all vice. Thus it openly favors the pleasures of the senses; it teaches that it is permitted to kill those who reveal the secret which We have spoken about previously.

The Pope goes so far as to publicize it. There are murders which are never explained. Think of the sudden death of a French minister[1]; at first suicide was suggested, then the newspapers insinuated that it could very well have been an assassination, that Freemasonry was involved. And this was not the first time! Ordinary people, Masons without great influence, disappear one fine day because they revealed a secret or acted in a way they should not have, quite simply. Think of all the assassination attempts that take place today. Those who are in charge of State security either do not know or do not want to say it, but there is most likely a hand that commands or communicates guidance of these deeds from a distance. And this may very well originate in the secret societies.

Let us return to the condemnations recalled and reiterated by Pius VII:

> Such are the dogmas and the precepts of this society as well as others like it. Whence the assassination attempts committed recently in Italy by the *Carbonari*, attempts that have so afflicted honest and pious men. We then, who are constituted the guardian of the house of Israel which is the Holy Church, We who by our pastoral charge must assure that the flock of the Lord which

---

[1] Robert Boulin, deceased October 30, 1979.

has been confided to us avoid all harm, We think that it is impossible for us to abstain from repressing the sacrilegious efforts of this society.

Finally, the Pope states the sentence: excommunication.

Leo XII: The Infamous Project of the Secret Societies

Drawing his conclusions from these three documents, Pope Leo XII then says in turn what he thinks of these societies, and names another:

> Little time had elapsed after the publication of this bull by Pius VII when We were called (...) to succeed him on the Holy See. Immediately We began to study the state and number and the power of these secret associations, and We easily recognized that their audacity had grown by the new sects that had attached themselves to it. The one designated by the name Academic (*Universitaire*) especially held our attention. It has been established in several universities, and the young people, instead of being instructed, are perverted by masters initiated in mysteries that could well be called mysteries of iniquity, and trained for every crime. Whence it comes that such a long time after the flame of revolt had been kindled for the first time in Europe by the secret societies, and had been carried abroad by their agents, after the brilliant victories won by the most powerful princes and which had made Us hope to see the suppression of these societies, nonetheless their culpable exertions have still not ceased. For even in the same countries where the former tempests seemed to have been stilled, are not new disturbances to be feared, new seditions that these societies plot incessantly? Does one not fear the impious daggers with which they strike down in secret those whom they have sentenced to death?

The Pope returns to the observations of his predecessor:

> The frightful calamities that desolate the Church everywhere must be attributed to these associations....Audaciously they attack its dogmas, its most sacred precepts, and attempt to disparage its authority....

> It must not be imagined that by calumny we falsely attribute to these secret associations all these evils and others that we do

not name. The works that their members have dared to publish on religion and on the commonwealth, their contempt for authority, their hatred of sovereignty, their attacks against the divinity of Jesus Christ and the very existence of God, the materialism that they profess, their codes and statutes which demonstrate their projects and their goals, prove what We have related of their efforts to overthrow legitimate princes, to shake the foundations of the Church; and, which is equally certain, these different associations, albeit bearing different designations, are allied in their infamous projects.

There is, then, a real organization. Hence the reminder:

We think that it is Our duty once again to condemn these secret associations.

The Duties of Chiefs of State

Thus falls the fourth condemnation in less than a century! Before concluding, Leo XII addresses the Catholic princes:

Catholic Princes, our very dear sons in Jesus Christ, for whom We have a special affection, We earnestly ask you to come to Our aid. We shall remind you of these words of Leo the Great, Our predecessor whose name we bear although unworthy to be compared to him, addressed to the emperor Leo: "You must incessantly remind yourself that the royal power has not been confided to you just for governing the world, but even more, and mainly, for lending a strong arm to the Church, by repressing the wicked with courage, by upholding good laws, and by re-establishing order wherever it has been disturbed."

This is a principle that many in our day do not grasp: power has not been given to princes merely for the exercise of temporal power, but also for the defense of the Church. The princes must aid the propagation of the good that the Church diffuses throughout society by courageously opposing the wicked.

Nowadays a hue and cry is raised for freedom. When a head of State, for example, limits the freedom of the Protestant religion, howls resound in the progressive world. Yet the fact that the liberty preached by Protestantism quickly becomes a doctrine of revolution must be borne in mind; morality itself is dissolved, contrary to Catholic morals. And if all the liberties were granted to the Moslems, it would mean that polygamy would have to be allowed by the States. Islam does not merely consist in the public prostrations the Moslems make in the streets at the hours of prayer; it is also means the threat of slavery, that is, the *Dhimmi* for all those who are not like them.

Can this be allowed in Catholic States? Can these States be obliged to not defend themselves?

Chapter III

THE ENCYCLICAL *QUI PLURIBUS* OF POPE PIUS IX ON RATIONALISM AND THE OTHER MODERN ERRORS PROPAGATED BY THE FREEMASONS
(NOVEMBER 9, 1846)

Pius IX, in his encyclical *Qui Pluribus*, furnishes even more details than his predecessors on the development of the Freemasons' offensive. It is noteworthy that this is the first encyclical of his pontificate, and it is rather long, which shows the importance the Pope attached to addressing this subject.

Like St. Pius X in his first encyclical, Pius IX begins by expressing his astonishment and the apprehensions provoked by the burden of the office that has just been confided to him:

> ...We were placed, despite Our unworthiness, on this high See of the prince of the apostles as the representative of the blessed Peter, and received from the eternal Prince of Pastors Himself the most serious divinely given office of feeding and ruling not only the lambs, that is, the whole Christian people, but also the sheep, that is, the bishops....

The Pope expresses right away his haste to address the bishops and the faithful:

> Therefore, since We have now assumed the supreme pontificate in Our Lateran[1] Basilica, We are sending this letter to you without delay, in accordance with the established practice of Our predecessors.

The Pope begins by reporting on the state of the Church at the moment when he assumed the office of Sovereign Pontiff:

---

[1] St. John Lateran.

> Each of you has noticed, Venerable Brothers, that a very bitter and fearsome war against the whole Catholic commonwealth is being stirred up by men bound together in a lawless alliance. These men do not preserve sound doctrine, but turn their hearing from the truth. They eagerly attempt to produce from their darkness all sorts of prodigious beliefs....We shudder indeed and suffer bitter pain when We reflect on all their outlandish errors and their many harmful methods, plots and contrivances.

It has been said about Pope Pius IX that during the first years of his reign he had shown himself to be liberal and that afterwards, with the experience gained in the exercise of his pontificate, he had become, contrariwise, very firm and had revealed himself as an admirable fighter, especially, of course, at the moment when he published his encyclical *Quanta Cura* and the famous *Syllabus*, which inspired the horror of all the progressives and liberals of the epoch. Well, this is not true. A legend of the sort has been noised about, but it is false. Pope Pius IX was never a liberal. From his first encyclical he reveals himself to be a man of faith, combative and traditional:

> For you know, Venerable Brothers, that these bitter enemies of the Christian name, are carried wretchedly along by some blind momentum of their mad impiety; they go so far in their rash imagining as to teach without blushing, openly and publicly, daring and unheard-of-doctrines, thereby uttering blasphemies against God. They teach that the most holy mysteries of our religion are fictions of human invention and that the teaching of the Catholic Church is opposed to the good and the prerogatives of human society. They are not even afraid to deny Christ Himself and God.

The Pope also notes that these sects, condemned for over a century by his predecessors, are still very active, and he in turn denounces the evil they continue to perpetrate by their perverse doctrines.

The Rationalists' Error

> These enemies never stop invoking the power and excellence of human reason; they raise it up against the most holy faith of

Christ, and they blather with great foolhardiness that this faith is opposed to human reason. Without doubt, nothing more insane than such a doctrine, nothing more impious or more opposed to reason itself could be devised.

Of course, this is the radical vice of these enemies of the Church: They proclaim that human reason is independent, and postulate that everything that is above human reason, all that is not intelligible by human reason, such as the mysteries of faith, of course, are inadmissible. Human reason is preponderant, they say, and reason must dominate, and thus it cannot be required to subject itself to someone or something that it cannot understand.

Pope Pius IX then affirms the superiority of faith over reason, and shows why the two cannot be contradictory:

> For although faith is above reason, no real disagreement or opposition can ever be found between them; this is because both of them come from the same greatest source of unchanging and eternal truth, God.

Faith, then, is above reason; reason by its natural light cannot understand the supernatural mysteries which are the object of faith. And yet faith is not something unreasonable. We do not comprehend, of course, our faith and our mysteries. But the faith we have in these mysteries is a reasonable faith founded upon valid motives, on apologetics, on the credibility of those who have taught us what we know, and particularly upon Our Lord Jesus Christ, who taught us these mysteries.

Why do we believe? Because of the authority of God who reveals, of course! But we also have solid reasons to believe humanly speaking. When the Church commands us to believe, it is a matter of an act that *is not contrary* to reason. Evidently, the Church asks us to accomplish an act that is *above* our reason, and to consent to mysteries that we cannot comprehend here below: the mystery of the Holy Trinity, the mystery of the Incarnation, the mystery of the Redemption.

If the Church requires us to believe in the mysteries, it is not in an unreasonable way, but, on the contrary, founded upon motives of credibility such as the miracles Our Lord worked manifesting that He is God. Once He has proved that He is God, then we must believe His words because they come to us from God, and we have no right to resist.

Faith, far from contradicting our knowledge, is an infinitely higher and greater complement to it, because this knowledge comes to us from God, and not merely from our human reason.

Philosophy the Handmaid of Theology

St. Thomas Aquinas said it: Philosophy is the handmaid of theology, because theological knowledge is elevated far above philosophical knowledge. Philosophical knowledge must serve theology in order, precisely, to show us that theology is not opposed to reason, even if we cannot understand it, because it is above reason. But the fundamental first principle of all modern philosophies absolutely rejects as impossible all received truths. Their argument postulates that it must be reason alone that grasps, by its own natural light, all truths.

The Individual Reason Cannot Demonstrate Everything

This conception is false, not only for what concerns theology and the truths of faith, but also for purely natural truths, philosophy and all the sciences. After all, how many things are we obliged to accept without being able to prove them?

One will object that reason could prove them. Agreed. For example, in philosophy we are taught some principles that are not evident, and this is true for all of the sciences. It is impossible for everyone to go and repeat the line of reasoning that men have followed and developed over the course of centuries, ever since science took its first steps. For since men have existed, the body of science has accumulated, and it is not possible to know everything, and to rediscover everything by oneself.

Can it even be conceived that any man as he is born should say, "As for me, I refuse to receive any lessons, I want no professors, I want no master, I want to learn everything by myself?" Of course not. Who is the man who can know everything, and learn all the sciences by himself? We are all most certainly obliged to have masters, to receive lessons, precisely in order to progress more rapidly in knowledge. If it were necessary to repeat all scientific reasoning, and rediscover the origin and the development of law, or how they succeeded in defining this or that principle of philosophy or law of chemistry, no one would succeed.

Even Natural Mysteries Exist

Those who protest that they will not believe anything they are told, who must know it or prove it themselves, are fools, for if one acted in this way, one would not know anything. Mysteries also exist in nature. And one inevitably comes to the conclusion that there is a God, Creator of all things, that it is God who has created us.

For example, by philosophy one demonstrates that there is a First Being infinitely active, intelligent and powerful who is called God, who must be the author of all we see and of all we are. When we seek to deepen our understanding of the notion of creation, we conclude that it is a great mystery. How can God, who is the author of all being, make beings who are not Himself and who are not outside of Himself either, for nothing can be outside of God? It is a great mystery.[2]

Consider the mystery of human liberty and the omnipotence of God. Even our free acts are in a certain way held in being by God, such that we cannot accomplish a free act without God's concurrence. Some are inclined to say that it is God who does almost all, and that, so to speak, we are not free. Others, on the contrary, affirm that, as man is free, he does everything and God has no part in our free acts. This is not possible, because one would then falsely pretend that in any given act, God is not present. But there is not a being that exists nor an act that is accomplished without God giving the means; without which, we would be God. If we could accomplish a single act by ourselves without God's support, then we would be the authors of that being, and hence we could make all beings. This is false, for we are incapable. This is what those who refuse to accept that there are natural mysteries refuse to admit.

---

[2] "I could not therefore exist at all, O my God, unless Thou wert in me. Or should I not rather say, that I could not exist unless I were in thee from whom are all things, by whom are all things, in whom are all things" (St. Augustine, *Confessions*, Book I, Chapter 2).

We see, then, that by apologetics, reason demonstrates the rational foundations of the faith, and that in return, faith enlightens us on even the simply natural mysteries. Far from being in opposition, says Pope Pius IX, faith and reason:

> ...give such reciprocal help to each other that true reason shows, maintains and protects the truth of the faith, while faith frees reason from all errors and wondrously enlightens, strengthens and perfects reason with the knowledge of divine matters.

And as other rationalists appeal to the indefinite progress of human reason against the supremacy of the faith, and against the immutability of the truths of faith, the Pope condemns them also:

> It is with no less deceit, Venerable Brothers, that other enemies of divine revelation, with reckless and sacrilegious effrontery, want to import the doctrine of human progress into the Catholic religion. They extol it with the highest praise, as if religion itself were not of God but the work of men, or a philosophical discovery which can be perfected by human means.

The Pope states even more precisely the refutation of what will later be called Semi-Rationalism:

> Our holy religion was not invented by human reason, but was most mercifully revealed by God; therefore, one can quite easily understand that religion itself acquires all its power from the authority of God who made the revelation, and that it can never be arrived at or perfected by human reason.

The Credibility of Revelation

Let us develop, following the Pope, the question of the motives for the credibility of revelation, and thus of our faith:

> In order not to be deceived and go astray in a matter of such great importance, human reason should indeed carefully investigate the fact of divine revelation. Having done this, one would be definitely convinced that God has spoken and therefore would show Him rational obedience, as the Apostle very wisely teaches (Rom. 13:1).

The Church in no way requires us to accomplish an act contrary to reason. The faith is above reason, but the act of faith is "*rationi consentaneus*," that is, in accord with reason.

There is an analogy with what is called human faith: when masters dispense their teaching, quite rightly one thinks that one can believe them. There are enough reasons to demonstrate that the teaching put forth by the master shows all the marks of credibility. One can trust him because one really believes that he knows the subject matter he teaches, and that the books whence he draws his knowledge are legitimate and valid sources. What he says, then, we believe.

Human faith exists. Then, just as we give our assent to the natural sciences by putting our faith in the authority of the masters who teach them, there is no reason why we should not act in the same manner when it is God who speaks. And this we should do, even if it is only because of the miracles that He worked and the fulfillment of all the prophecies made through the centuries and which Our Lord accomplished point by point, word for word. How is it possible not to believe that the One who has spoken to us thus is God? And, consequently, how is it possible not to assent to what He teaches?

A supplementary reason offers itself. He showed Himself to be the master of nature, by commanding the waves, the wind, and life itself: He resurrected dead men. And even more extraordinarily, He resurrected himself. As He thus proved that He is God, we should quite reasonably believe His words.

And to those who retort, that they haven't seen, and that they haven't heard, well, the Church offers all the proofs of her own credibility, as the Church is the successor of Our Lord, carrying the word of Our Lord from generation to generation. These and other proofs the Church carries within her, and above all the proof that is the most irrefutable: her holiness.

God is holy. It is impossible to imagine that God would not be holy. God must produce fruits of sanctity. Now, it is clear that the Church herself is holy, if only by those saints that she has counted, those who, formed by her, are her sons, and by all the good works that she has extended throughout the whole world. The Church offers a sufficient number of proofs for us to be sure that it is the good Lord who speaks to us by her mediation. From this comes the necessity of the Church's holiness. And this must be so down to the littlest details. For example, for the faithful, the priest in his parish represents the Church. If the priest fails in his duty of holiness, this creates a great problem for the faithful. Evidently, they well know that their pastor is not the Church's only priest. They are sufficiently instructed to know that they belong to a diocese, and that it is the diocese that constitutes the Christian family. Thus, they have access to other proofs.

But still, for them, the priest represents the Church. He is truly the man of the Church. Thus, if the priest does not manifest a certain holiness, they are scandalized, and that threatens to make some of them lose their faith. Many have lost the faith because of priests who conducted themselves badly or who quit the priesthood. When this happens again once or twice, they lose the faith. That is normal. People need reasons for belief, they need to have proofs.

The Pope continues his letter by denouncing these men who perversely reject the faith, who most unreasonably refuse it and who disseminate errors, pretending that Our Lord is not God, that the Church was not divinely founded, and that she teaches fables and fiction. All this happened after the Christian era during which no one would have dared, or even dreamed, of affirming such lies. An enormous scandal took place in Christendom when intelligent men and self-styled philosophers began to spread, in newspapers, reviews, and all the media, their ideas against the Church and the Catholic faith.

Other Attacks Against the Church

The Pope continues his address to the bishops, and reaffirms the condemnations made by his predecessors:

> This consideration too clarifies the great error of those others as well who boldly venture to explain and interpret the words of God by their own judgment, misusing their reason and holding the opinion that these words are like a human work. God Himself has set up a living authority to establish and teach the true and legitimate meaning of His heavenly revelation. This authority judges *infallibly* all disputes which concern matters of faith

and morals, lest the faithful be swirled around by every wind of doctrine which springs from the evilness of men in encompassing error.

God established Peter so that by his infallible judgments, when he speaks as head of the Church, he confirms and specifies the definition of the faith.

How grave it is when the successors of Peter no longer use clear and precise language, as most of the popes have done when expressing the truth, and when they use new modern, ambiguous terms that confuse because they are not precise. After the Second Vatican Council one no longer knows what to trust. This casts a great perplexity in the minds of the faithful, and this is very serious:

> We, therefore, placed inscrutably by God upon this Chair of truth, eagerly call forth in the Lord your outstanding piety, Venerable Brothers. We urge you to strive carefully and zealously to continually warn and exhort the faithful entrusted to your care to hold to these first principles....You already know well, Venerable Brothers, the other portentous errors and deceits by which the sons of this world try most bitterly to attack the Catholic religion and the divine authority of the Church and its laws. They would even trample underfoot the rights both of the sacred and of the civil power. For this is the goal of the lawless activities against this Roman See in which Christ placed the impregnable foundation of His Church. This is the goal of those secret sects who have come forth from the darkness to destroy and desolate both the sacred and the civil commonwealth. These have been condemned with repeated anathema in the Apostolic letters of the Roman Pontiffs who preceded Us.

Like his predecessors, the Pope shows that, in the same spirit of Rationalism, other assaults have been made against the Church and her doctrine in order to destroy her. In particular he denounces the Biblical societies which distribute free falsified versions of sacred Scripture.

Religious Indifferentism

He brings up another reason to condemn the Masonic sects, the "horrible system of indifference in the matter of religion" that they propagate, which is utterly repugnant to the natural light of reason:

> By means of this theory, those crafty men remove all distinction between virtue and vice, truth and error, honorable and vile action. They pretend that men can gain eternal salvation by the practice of any religion...

Now here is a clearly expressed statement that could well be meditated upon by the successors of Peter who have strayed from sound doctrine:

> ...as if there could ever be any sharing between justice and iniquity, any collaboration between light and darkness, or any agreement between Christ and Belial.

Attacks Against Priestly Celibacy

Coming to the fourth objective of these sects, Pius IX writes:

> The sacred celibacy of clerics has also been the victim of conspiracy.

The attack against clerical celibacy did not start yesterday; the Pope wrote this in 1846! So it isn't new to see in our day multiple pressures being brought to bear—although today it is even by bishops—in favor of the marriage of priests and the ordination of married men, in order thereby to suppress the celibacy of the clergy:

> Indeed, some churchmen have wretchedly forgotten their own rank and let themselves be converted by the charms and snares of pleasure.

There are members of the clergy who collaborate with the Freemasons to try and destroy priestly celibacy:

> This is the aim too of the prevalent but wrong method of teaching, especially in the philosophical disciplines, a method which deceives and corrupts incautious youth in a wretched manner....

The Destructive Doctrine of Communism

In addition to the attacks against the celibacy of priests, the Pope denounces the formidable dangers of Communism:

> To this goal also tends the unspeakable doctrine of *Communism*, as it is called, a doctrine most opposed to the very natural law.

Already, over a hundred years ago, the Pope stigmatizes the sects that originated the false and abominable doctrine of Communism. He describes a century ahead of time what will come to pass with Communism.

With astonishing perspicacity the popes published solemn warnings, but no one listened. The chiefs of State remained deaf, and none heeded their harsh rebukes. Even the bishops lacked the courage. And so this perverse doctrine spread so widely that events have come to pass even as Pius IX foresaw:

> For if this doctrine were accepted, the complete destruction of everyone's laws, government, property, and even of human society itself would follow.

It could not be better expressed. What is left of the rights of men in the countries where Communist governments have been established? There is no more property, it has been replaced by Collectivism. As for human society, it has been replaced by slavery.

Finally, the Pope describes the means taken by the sects in order to attain their goals, and especially the mass media, the press and publishing:

> To this end, finally—to omit other dangers which are too well known to you—tends the widespread disgusting infection from books and pamphlets which teach the lessons of sinning. These works, well-written and filled with deceit and cunning, are scattered at immense cost through every region for the destruction of the Christian people....As a result of this filthy medley of errors which creeps in from every side, and as the result of the unbridled license to think, speak and write, We see the following: morals deteriorated, Christ's most holy religion despised, the majesty of divine worship rejected, the power of this Apostolic See plundered, the authority of the Church attacked and reduced

to base slavery, the rights of bishops trampled on, the sanctity of marriage infringed....

What would he say if he were alive today! In his time "the unbridled license" he decries, even then undoubtedly unacceptable, was a far cry from what we know today. For example, at this time, one would have been unable to imagine the number of families destroyed by the laws instituting divorce, in violation of the holiness and indissolubility of marriage. After the introduction of the divorce legislation in Italy, thousands of divorces were filed. In France, there are between eighty to one hundred thousand divorces per year. This marks the complete destruction of the family.

Children do not know where to turn, to the mother or to the father; they are completely abandoned. Left to themselves, children become the prey of delinquency, and crimes, thefts and children in prison follow. Here is what divorce gave rise to, the fruits of our lovely liberal society:

> ....and many other losses for both the Christian and the civil commonwealth. Venerable Brothers, We are compelled to weep and share in your lament that this is the case.

Pontifical Directives: Defend the Faith

Faced with the sinister tableau of the work accomplished by the secret societies, the Pope asks what is to be done. And so he addresses the bishops:

> You must also care for and defend the Catholic faith with episcopal strength and see that the flock entrusted to you stands to the end firm and unmoved in the faith.

This is what Pope St. Pius X will request with regard to religious instruction. Confronted by religious ignorance and attacks against the faith, one must defend the Catholic faith:

> So, in accordance with your pastoral care, work assiduously to protect and preserve this faith. Never cease to instruct all men in it, to encourage the wavering, to convince dissenters, to strengthen the weak in faith by never tolerating and letting pass anything which could in the slightest degree defile the purity of this faith.

The Encyclical *Qui Pluribus* of Pope Pius IX On Rationalism

It is good for us to be reminded of what we must do. Each one in his place must defend the Catholic faith. It is attacked from all sides, and today to an unmatched degree. It is even attacked by the clergy, and even by bishops, when they publish catechisms that are not in conformity with the faith. The Dutch Catechism and those derived from it no longer teach the Catholic faith. It is terrifying to observe that the bishops whose mission is to defend the faith are the very ones who are corrupting it.

St. Pius X said that the Liturgy together with the Mass are the rampart of our faith. But presently the rampart has been demolished. Why should one be surprised, then, that faith disappears and the people no longer believe and are ignorant of the rudiments of the faith. It is the logical outcome; it is fatal.

Let us return to the good popes who were truly vigilant defenders of the faith, and who fought to preserve and propagate it. We have heard the language of Pius IX, Leo XIII, of St. Pius X, and we shall hear that of Popes Pius XI and Pius XII. These popes never ceased to exhort the bishops to defend and conserve the purity of the faith.

One is obliged to observe that despite so many reminders ("despite our vigilance"), the errors continued and still continue to spread ("the evil has continued"). We can say today that, despite all the efforts employed by the last popes until Pius XII (for unfortunately one cannot include Paul VI among them), no one has listened. The voice of the Popes has not been heeded, and we find ourselves in total darkness.

Pius IX, after asking the bishops to protect the faith, demands that they denounce the sects and their artifices:

> It is an act of great piety to expose the concealments of the impious and to defeat there the devil himself, whose slaves they are.

As Pope Leo XIII will say, one must tear away the mask that conceals masonry in order to reveal it for what it is. One must expose its errors, secrets, and its conventicles of crime:

> Therefore We entreat you to use every means of revealing to your faithful people the many kinds of plot, pretense, error,

deceit and contrivance which our enemies use. This will turn them carefully away from infectious books.

The bishops, then, are conjured to denounce the errors and to impede the circulation among the faithful of "infectious books," whence the need for the Index. Yet the suppression of the Index was the first thing the modernists demanded the Council to do. There were some who said, "It suffices to place a book on the Index to ensure that everyone will read it. It is a little like when a movie is called pornographic and so is forbidden. Everyone goes to see it."

Firstly, this is not true. Then, one does not cease to denounce evil under the pretext that if one does so there will be some who will deliberately seek it out, and thereby let everyone be poisoned. When a book was placed on the Index there were nonetheless a great number of people who would not read it. In the seminaries, these books were prohibited; and in the universities, Catholic schools and bookstores one could not find books that had been placed on the Index. So in fact this was an important means. But the modernists insisted that this had to be suppressed, as it was contrary to freedom of expression, freedom of research, and so on. And now the poison is spread throughout. People read anything. There are no more limits. One is free to imbibe poison, it doesn't matter.

The Pope gives one other piece of advice, which I summarize: strive with all your might to see that the faithful love charity, and make peace reign amongst themselves; see that there are no quarrels within the Church, that they have the same love for Our Lord Jesus Christ, the love of the truth, and the love of His words.

Clergy Should Be an Example

Pius IX speaks then of priests, and, as the popes have always done, reminds the bishops that the first condition for assuring that the faithful receive effective and exemplary instruction is the good formation of priests:

> However, priests are the best examples of piety and God's worship, and people tend generally to be of the same quality as their priests.

The people will be like their priests. There is an adage in the Church that confirms this judgment: "A holy priest will have a fervent parish; a fervent priest, a mediocre one; a mediocre priest, a bad one; and a bad priest will have nothing left." Always one level less!

....[as] people tend generally to be of the same quality as their priests, [t]herefore devote the greatest care and zeal to making the clergy resplendent for the earnestness of their morals, the integrity, holiness and wisdom of their lives.

To have a good clergy, one must necessarily think of their formation, that is to say, of establishing good seminaries. This goes without saying for it is plain common sense:

You know that suitable ministers can only come from clergy who are very well trained, and that the proper training greatly influences the whole future life of clerics. Therefore, continually strive to ensure that young clerics are properly molded even from their earliest years.

Here the Pope is referring to the minor seminaries. This is an institution that existed more or less everywhere, although not in the same manner. For example, in Italy, most of the vocations in the major seminaries, as many as 95%, would come from the minor seminaries.

There were academies, minor seminaries, where the parish priests identified the children they deemed more or less apt to be directed towards the priesthood. Of course, at the age of ten or twelve it is quite difficult to discern the seed of a vocation in a boy. But nevertheless the parish priests would send them to the minor seminary, where the practical preparation for the major seminary was undertaken. A certain number of the boys would quit, but not that many, ultimately. And the minor seminaries were in fact the seedbed of the vocations to the major seminaries. Very few seminarians would come from the academies or universities. In France, about 50% of the postulants to the priesthood came from the minor seminaries.

The popes have always encouraged the bishops to create or maintain minor seminaries. It was especially among the Latin peoples that the minor seminaries were propagated, in South America, Spain, Portugal.

But one can also say in all truth that some academies were tantamount to minor seminaries, because these establishments were true Catholic schools, entirely dependent upon the diocese, and with many of the professors priests. This encouraged the students to reflect and consider whether to follow their example.

When I was a student at the Sacred Heart Academy of Lille, each year half of the senior philosophy class, about fifteen students, would go into the Congregation of the Holy Ghost Fathers, or into the seminaries. This school was the equivalent of a minor seminary. I should say that at that epoch there were thirty-five priests for professors, and that for just five hundred students. Evidently, that was considerable; but this number enabled the priests to see the students individually, to follow their progress, to speak with them, hear their confessions, and guide them. That is why the school produced so many vocations.

Now the academies have become co-ed! This is the case of the example just given; even the chapel has been suppressed. From time to time a great ceremony is held in the gymnasium. There are just four or five priests, all the other professors are laymen. The result: no more vocations.

We hope to reproduce the good Catholic academies of old with our schools, like St. Mary's in Kansas, and others. We should like these establishments to be good Catholic schools, and not restricted to those who feel they may have a vocation. But it is certain that most of our vocations will come from these schools.

Already encouraging results have come from our St. Michael's, near Chateauroux, as well as from Morning Star School, and the schools of the Dominican Teaching Sisters of Fanjeaux and Saint-Pré. These schools will certainly bring forth vocations. This is what the popes have asked for. Without opening minor seminaries, we have secondary schools that can serve this function.

Yesterday's Magisterium and Today's

We are accused, in the letters we receive from Rome and from those who attack us, of not accepting the magisterium of the Church. Yet I do not believe there is any other seminary in the world besides Ecône where the documents of the popes are studied in order to know the Church's magisterium and to give it entire assent. Precisely, it is because we are attached to this magisterium and because we feel great respect towards the pontifical acts which constitute the magisterium of the Church, that we are accused and persecuted. And this we incur because we cannot conceive that it is possible to adhere to what is now in contradiction with what the popes have always upheld. That is the crux of the problem ever since Vatican Council II. Can one adhere to Modernism, Liberalism, Laicism, and Religious Indifferentism whereas all the popes have unceasingly denounced their perverse effects and condemned them?

On the contrary, rather it is by obedience to all that the popes have taught that we refuse a magisterium opposed to that of the Church of all times. Who can answer this? Not only do we oppose this recent magisterium that has been influenced by Modernism and Liberalism, but also an entirely new conception of the Church.

Let us take a very simple example, and read the declaration *Dignitatis Humanae* on "religious liberty." Let us too accomplish the little task that a layman, Professor Salet, under his pseudonym of Michael Martin, undertook for the review *Le Courrier de Rome*. He made a comparison by juxtaposing the acts of the magisterium of Popes Gregory XVI and Pius IX and the *Declaration on Religious Liberty*, in order to manifest the formal and flagrant contradiction between these documents.

What is to be done? If one adheres to today's magisterium, to this declaration on religious liberty, one opposes yesterday's magisterium, that of Gregory XVI and Pius IX. Which will one choose? Necessarily, we are obliged to choose the more traditional, because this is what establishes the rule in the Church: that which was taught before, and not what is taught today. What is taught today can only be appreciated in relation to what is in conformity with the entire antecedent magisterium of the Church.

Now the past is rejected and some say, now the past must be considered no longer, you must submit to the magisterium of today. If the latter were in conformity with the traditional magisterium we would agree, but it is contrary to it. And so adherence isn't possible.

Let us recall the solemn warning of St. Paul, who foresaw the danger: "But though we, or an angel from heaven, preach a gospel to you besides that which we have preached to you, let him be anathema" (Gal. 1:8). Even at the time of St. Paul, then, the question arose about a choice to be made between what he himself had taught at the beginning of his apostolate, which was in conformity with what Our Lord had revealed to him, and what those professed about whom St. Paul said "let [them] be anathema." Let those whose teaching is not in conformity with the ancient teaching be anathema: this is the rule.

And so we too say: What we are being asked to assent to is not what was originally taught, thus we cannot accept it; the same applies for the case of the Mass.

Modernist Influence in the New Mass

If one studies well the New Mass, one finds that it is imbued with modernist ideas. It was drafted under the influence of the modernist spirit execrated and condemned by Pope St. Pius X in his encyclical *Pascendi Dominici Gregis*, in which he demonstrated the error and banefulness of Modernism, which he calls the synthesis of all heresies.

Whom are we to believe? St. Pius X or the modernist influence that has penetrated the Church and which is currently at work there. There is a choice to be made. And we have made it. We cannot submit to such an orientation. It is impossible to accept this teaching that is in contradiction with tradition and which, under the empire of the very Modernism condemned by the magisterium, has presided over the entire reform of the Church since Vatican Council II, whose bad fruits and disastrous consequences it is painful to behold.

The Freemasons' Goal: Destruction of the Church

Hence it is important for all Catholics to really study the magisterium of the Church in a practical way. Why have the popes published so many documents and placed so much emphasis on the warnings against Freemasonry? It is precisely because they saw in masonry the infectious source of all these errors. The Freemasons are the originators of the ideas that are killing us: Rationalism, Naturalism, which destroys the supernatural and hence all that Our Lord Jesus Christ came to bring us. If one destroys the supernatural and grace, one destroys revelation, the Church, the sacraments, the Mass; in short, everything. Nothing can remain.

The popes, in their vigilance, have understood that it was necessary to denounce the Freemasons and, as they themselves said, "tear away the mask," unmask these sects. Unmask them, because they hide behind a front of philanthropy, progress, Humanitarianism and universal brotherhood, etc. These are only false and illusory beacons. By their encyclicals, the popes have clearly demonstrated the true nature of masonry, by tearing away the mask behind which it concealed itself.

Towards the end of his encyclical *Qui Pluribus*, of November 9, 1846, and which we have been studying, Pope Pius IX calls upon the bishops to fight vigorously and courageously against these sects, and he reminded them of the first duty of their office:

You must...care for and defend the Catholic faith with episcopal strength.

How are they to go about it?

...Expose the concealments of the impious;

...Never stop preaching the Gospel;

...Instruct the faithful to follow after love and search for peace;

...Devote the greatest care and zeal to making the clergy resplendent....

And he gave advice for the selection of future priests, "Take the utmost care, as the Apostle commands, not to impose hands on anyone in haste...."

This is the concern of the popes. Recall that from the first encyclical of his pontificate, St. Pius X deemed that the great remedy for the current ills was the formation of priests.

The Holiness and Doctrine of the Priests the Church's Strength

This is understandable. What constitutes the Church's strength? Who are those responsible for teaching the faith of the Church and showing by their conduct and the example of their life what the Church is and teaches? It is the priests. The Church will be holy, and the faithful will be holy in proportion to the holiness of the priests. Hence the capital importance attached by the popes to priestly formation and the choice of seminary professors. St. Pius X will order that any professor with the least hint of an attachment to Modernism be expelled from the seminary, as well as those who would not be sincerely attached to the doctrine of the Church as she would have it be taught.

Is this what is sought in today's seminaries? Is there a real concern to choose good professors? It is reported that there are more entering the seminaries in Germany, Argentina and Italy. These seminarians undoubtedly come with good dispositions, because they enter the seminaries that still have a traditional bent. But what will happen if the professors who instruct them do not teach the truth of the Church, or the philosophy of St. Thomas, which the Church has made her own philosophy. For it is no longer, in a certain way, the philosophy of St. Thomas; the Church has adopted it, and has judged that it is the true philosophy, the one that teaches the truth about being, the nature of things, reality, truth. Thus it is this philosophy that must be taught, the Church has so judged.[3]

If the professors do not teach this philosophy, or if, on the contrary, they contradict it, the young people are badly formed. And then, either they stay and are deformed, or else they leave because they see that they are not taught the truth. They lose their vocation. This is currently what is happening. Hence the importance that the formation of priests takes on, and which the Pope emphasizes:

---

[3] Cf. Leo XIII, Encyclical *Aeterni Patris*, of August 4, 1879; Pius XI, Encyclical *Studiorum Ducem*, of June 29, 1923, on the philosophy and theology of St. Thomas Aquinas.

Furthermore, you realize that spiritual exercises contribute greatly to the preservation of the dignity and holiness of ecclesiastical orders. Therefore do not neglect to promote this work of salvation and to advise and exhort all clergy to often retreat to a suitable place for making these exercises.

To help the priests complete their ascent towards holiness, the Pope encourages the practice of the *Spiritual Exercises* of St. Ignatius, and asks the bishops to commit their priests to making them:

> Laying aside external cares and being free to meditate zealously on eternal divine matters, they will be able to wipe away stains caused by the dust of the world and renew their ecclesiastical spirit. And stripping off the old man and his deeds, they will put on the new man who was created in justice and holiness.

Then Pius IX encourages the bishops themselves to be models and to fulfill their duties:

> At no time do you spare either cares or plans or toils in religiously fulfilling your pastoral duties and defending all Our beloved sheep who, redeemed by Christ, have been entrusted to your care from the rage, assault and snares of ravening wolves. You keep them away from poisonous pasture land and drive them on to safe ground, and in all possible ways you lead them by deed, word and example to the harbor of eternal salvation. Therefore, to assure the greater glory of God and the Church, Venerable Brothers, join together with all eagerness, care and wakefulness to repulse error and to root out vice. When this is accomplished, faith, religion, piety and virtue will increase daily.

Role of Catholic Chiefs of State

The Pope then confides to the princes his desire to preserve the principles of piety and religion. At his time, there were still Catholic princes, despite the onslaught of Freemasonry and the nearly desperate situation of the Church. The Pope addresses the princes. Unfortunately, one must admit, all these princes one by one let themselves be influenced by masonry. And that brought on an ever increasing degradation of Catholic politics and Christian society:

We hope that Our political leaders will keep in mind, in accordance with their piety and religion, that "the kingly power has been conferred on them not only for ruling the world but especially for the protection of the Church."[4] Sometimes We "act both for the sake of their rule and safety that they may possess their provinces by peaceful right."[5]

During the pontificate of Pius IX, there was still collaboration between the princes and the Church, the latter upholding the princes in their authority, and the princes accomplishing their duty, which was to uphold the Church and further its extension.

This is a notion that has become completely foreign to almost everyone, even Catholics. Such an idea is inadmissible in current thinking. The States are supposed to have nothing to do with the Church. It is not their business to defend the Church, or support a particular religion. They should be indifferent to all religions, give free reign to all religions, make no distinction between true and false religion. The old idea should go; and the freedom of cults should be recognized.

The freedom of religions, as is meant today by the expression religious liberty, that is, the free external exercise of religions, leads to the freedom of error, and error always triumphs over truth. Not that truth will not ultimately triumph over error, but here below, with all the means that error disposes of, it can contribute to the loss of many souls. Error has at its disposal all the money of the world, and the means of communication. Because, after all, men are always drawn more by false liberty than by discipline. Order is always more difficult, because less inviting. Unbridled license is the consequence of this liberty. We sadly observe it everywhere; nothing withstands.

The Pope confides them to the most Blessed Virgin, urging them to:

> ...call as intercessor Her who is always with Him, the most holy Virgin Mary, Immaculate Mother of God. She is the most sweet mother of us all; she is our mediatrix, advocate, firmest hope, and greatest source of confidence.

---

[4] St. Leo, epistle 156 (123) to Emperor Leo.
[5] St. Leo, epistle 43 (34) to Emperor Theodosius.

According to the custom, Pius IX concludes the encyclical *Qui Pluribus* by giving his apostolic blessing.

Chapter IV

THE ENCYCLICAL *HUMANUM GENUS* OF POPE LEO XIII ON THE SECT OF THE FREEMASONS
(APRIL 20, 1884)

Leo XIII Makes Known the Wickedness of Freemasonry

The most important and complete encyclical on Freemasonry, the one with the most exhaustive description of its nature and the perversity of its goals, is due to Pope Leo XIII. It is, of course, his encyclical letter *Humanum Genus*.

Leo XIII has been reproached for his weakness on certain points, and in practice he was unable to perceive the malice of those who governed France, which led to his policy of rallying to the Republic. But over and above this tactical error, which had very pernicious repercussions, the encyclicals written by this Pope are truly magnificent, wonderful theological treatises.

Let us then look carefully at the encyclical *Humanum Genus*. We shall look at it quite closely, because if one studies Masonry following the papal documents, one holds the key to understanding everything that is happening today. Without the study of these pontifical documents, it is impossible to understand the very grave situation in which the Church finds herself today, as do all our so-called civilized societies, which were in fact the beneficiaries for centuries and centuries of Christian civilization and its principles of Christian virtues.

As Pope Leo XIII expresses quite well, the goal of the Freemasons is to destroy all Christian institutions, to bring to an end all that was built up and instituted by the Church over ten or twelve centuries. They intend to annihilate it all from top to bottom. The Church's morals, principles and dogmas: all must be destroyed. How can this destruction in fact be explained, save by the intervention of an extremely efficient organization? For it has succeeded over a period of centuries in bringing about what it foresaw and announced: "We shall take centuries if need be, but we shall prevail."

How can such a project be explained unless it is founded upon an enduring principle? Well, this enduring principle is Satan. The Pope says it quite clearly. One cannot otherwise explain the fury that fuels Freemasonry against the Church and, definitively, against Our Lord Jesus Christ, than by the hatred of Satan. No other explanation is possible. Moreover, when one knows the veritable bonds linking Freemasonry and Satan in its secret ceremonies and in all it does under cover of secretness, one understands the reason for this perseverance, and then this extraordinary subtlety by which everything is conducted. This can only be the sign of the working of an extraordinary intelligence remarkable for its cunning.

Freemasonry has never been as powerful and its influence as widespread as now. The number of Freemasons and the audacity of their action grow at an astonishing rate. They now hold their meetings in broad daylight because they no longer have anything to fear from the governments, which have been infiltrated by their own in great number. They have no reason to hide. No doubt they still meet discretely to discuss strategy, fix their plans and make big decisions. But as for their existence, they no longer conceal it. At present, they no longer overtly attack the Church, which is easily understandable because the Church herself is accomplishing what they had aimed at. One could almost say that the Church has placed herself at the service of the Freemasonry which she formerly condemned.

Leo XIII was clear and categoric, and declared vigorously that "No collaboration whatsoever is possible between Christianity and Masonry." But in our time it has been thought allowable to practice a false ecumenism towards Freemasonry. And the Freemasons are quite content, as the Church ostensibly has adopted their thoughts and desires, and offers no more opposition.

Leo XIII dated the encyclical *Humanum Genus*, On the Sect of the Freemasons, April 20, 1884. It is entitled *De Secta Massonum*. As the title shows the Pope does not intend to treat of the topic in an ephemeral way,.

The City of Satan

Pope Leo XIII uses an image to begin his consideration of the topic, the image used by St. Augustine in *The City of God*, that of the opposition between two cities. The same image is encountered in the *Spiritual Exercises* of St. Ignatius. The human race is divided into two hostile camps:

> The race of man, after its miserable fall from God, the Creator and the Giver of heavenly gifts, "through the envy of the devil," separated into two diverse and opposite parts, of which the one steadfastly contends for truth and virtue, the other for those things which are contrary to virtue and to truth. The one is the kingdom of God on earth, namely, the true Church of Jesus Christ....The other is the kingdom of Satan.

The Pope develops his simple, limpid description:

> This twofold kingdom St. Augustine keenly discerned and described after the manner of two cities, contrary in their laws because striving for contrary objects; and with a subtle brevity he expressed the efficient cause of each....

He quotes St. Augustine:

> Two loves formed two cities: the love of self, reaching even to contempt of God, an earthly city; and the love of God, reaching to contempt of self, a heavenly one.

So they are exactly contrary. For the love of God we hold ourselves in contempt, the Christian despises himself; while, on the contrary, Satan carries the love of self, self-centeredness, to contempt of God and opposition to Him:

> At every period of time each has been in conflict with the other, with a variety and multiplicity of weapons, and of warfare, although not always with equal ardor and assault.

The Pope describes the two cities by drawing upon the text of St. Augustine and the history of the Church:

> At this period, however, the partisans of evil seem to be combining together, and to be struggling with united vehemence, led on or assisted by that strongly organized and widespread association called the Freemasons.

Thus, Leo XIII characterizes the society of the Freemasons by calling it the city of the devil, the city of Satan. He specifies their goals:

> No longer making any secret of their purposes, they are now boldly rising up against God Himself. They are planning the destruction of holy Church publicly and openly, and this with the set purpose of utterly despoiling the nations of Christendom, if it were possible, of the blessings obtained for us through Jesus Christ our Savior.

Faced with these facts, and confronted with such an urgent situation, the Pope concludes that as Sovereign Pontiff it is his duty to raise the hue and cry:

> ...it is Our office to point out the danger, to mark who are the adversaries, and to the best of Our power to make head against their plans and devices...that the kingdom of Jesus Christ entrusted to Our charge may not only stand and remain whole, but may be enlarged by an ever-increasing growth throughout the world.

Prior Condemnations

The Pope rests upon the prior magisterium, and remarks that he is not the first to have sounded the alarm when faced with the attack of such terrible enemies. His predecessors have done likewise. He refers to the documents that have been cited and studied in this class, those of Clement XII, Benedict XIV, and Pius VII. This is very important, because when a pope condemns or approves something by basing himself upon the past, this reinforces his own word. This practice of reviewing what so many popes have already said and repeated on the same subject is what makes the strength of the Church: "And I confirm all that my predecessors have said."

A doctrine that is taught in this manner, a condemnation that is made under these conditions seems to be infallible because it is truly the magisterium of the Church, which is much clearer than when a pope simply sets forth a personal opinion. In this case, Leo XIII does not express a personal opinion; rather, he recalls all that the popes have previously said. He recounts that the popes, having

The Encyclical *Humanum Genus* of Pope Leo XIII

deemed it their duty to denounce the danger, had recourse to the measures of excommunication and canonical penalties against the Freemasons and their sect:

> The members, indignant at this, thinking to elude or to weaken the force of these decrees, partly by contempt of them, and partly by calumny, accused the Sovereign Pontiffs who had passed them either of exceeding the bounds of moderation in their decrees or of decreeing what was not just. This was the manner in which they endeavored to elude the authority and the weight of the Apostolic Constitutions of Clement XII and Benedict XIV, as well as of Pius VII and Pius IX.

Leo XIII bases himself not only on what the popes have done, but also on what the heads of State have done, recounting that many of them had taken measures to prevent these sects from existing within their States, and he enumerates them:

> ...many princes and heads of governments...made it their business either to delate the Masonic society to the Apostolic See, or of their own accord by special enactments to brand it as pernicious, as, for example, in Holland, Austria, Switzerland, Spain, Bavaria, Savoy, and other parts of Italy. But, what is of highest importance, the course of events has demonstrated the prudence of Our predecessors.

The Advance of Freemasonry

The Pope is forced to observe that despite the intervention of his predecessors and the chiefs of State:

> ...the sect of Freemasons grew with a rapidity beyond conception in the course of a century and a half.

Unfortunately, we too are forced to observe that, despite all that the popes did, the Freemasons have made such inroads that there remains not a single head of State who opposes the actions of Freemasonry. There is not a single power left among the countries where Masonry had been banished, to uphold and second the action of the popes.

There was, at the time of the last war, a slight attempt to resist made by Marshall Petain or by Salazar, who took a few measures against Masonry. But these were only sporadic attempts emanating from persons who came to the fore in special circumstances, because of anarchy or war, and who were able to discern the cause of the evil, observing that there were traitors in the ranks of the Freemasons. So they opposed them, but it did not last. After the end of World War II and the disappearance of these courageous personalities, it was over. There is no more resistance. On the contrary, it is now Freemasons who govern all these countries, even the so-called Catholic ones:

> Henceforth there will be grave reason to fear...

The Pope, farsighted, fears for the future, and asserts that the danger is grave:

> ...not, indeed for the Church—for her foundation is much too firm to be overturned by the effort of men....

If he had witnessed what is happening now, what would have been his reactions? Of course, he would have affirmed that the Church cannot be overturned, as he said, but no one before the Second Vatican Council could have imagined that the Church would be infiltrated by her enemies, by the Freemasons, and that Freemasonry would succeed in having its adepts or its dupes counted among the cardinals of the Roman Curia:

> ...but for those States in which prevails the power, either of the sect of which we are speaking or of other sects not dissimilar....

So the Pope declares that he must speak, he cannot remain silent faced with this generalized conspiracy:

> It is now Our intention, following the example of Our predecessors, directly to treat of the Masonic society itself, of its whole teaching, of its aims, and of its manner of thinking and acting, in order to bring more and more into the light its power for evil, and to do what We can to arrest the contagion of this fatal plague.

It is one more attempt of the Pope to attempt to impede the sect from having too great an influence. First, he will speak of its existence, then of its goals and will set forth, in explaining them, the deplorable consequences of these doctrines, and finally he will propose remedies. The outline of the encyclical is, then,

(1) the affirmation of the existence of these sects, (2) the goal towards which they act, (3) the description of their principles, (4) the consequence of these principles; (5) the correct judgment of them; (6) the remedies to apply to them.

Unity of All Secret Societies

There are several organized bodies which, though differing in name, in ceremonial, in form and origin, are nevertheless so bound together by community of purpose and by the similarity of their main opinions, as to make in fact one thing with the sect of the Freemasons, which is a kind of center whence they all go forth, and whither they all return. Now, these no longer show a desire to remain concealed; for they hold their meetings in the daylight and before the public eye, and publish their own newspaper organs; and yet, when thoroughly understood, they are found still to retain the nature and the habits of secret societies. There are many things like mysteries which it is the fixed rule to hide with extreme care, not only from strangers, but from very many members also; such as their secret and final designs, the names of the chief leaders, and certain secret and inner meetings, as well as their decisions, and the ways and means of carrying them out. This is, no doubt, the object of the manifold difference among the members as to right, office, and privilege—of the received distinction of orders and grades, and of that severe discipline which is maintained.

Candidates are generally commanded to promise—nay, with a special oath, to swear—that they will never, to any person, at any time or in any way, make known the members, the passes, or the subjects discussed. Thus, with a fraudulent external appearance, and with a style of simulation which is always the same, the Freemasons, like the Manichees of old, strive, as far as possible, to conceal themselves, and to admit no witnesses but their own members.

The Pope, observing that these societies exist, points out that they try to appear to be other than what they are:

...They assume the character of literary men and scholars associated for purposes of learning. They speak of their zeal for a more cultured refinement, and of their love for the poor; and they declare their one wish to be the amelioration of the condition of the masses, and to share with the largest possible number all the benefits of civic life....

But to simulate and wish to lie hid; to bind men like slaves in the very tightest bonds, and without giving any sufficient reason; to make use of men enslaved to the will of another for any arbitrary act; to arm men's right hands for bloodshed after securing impunity for the crime—all this is an enormity from which nature recoils.

The Pope stresses the secretiveness with which these societies cloak themselves, and denounces the crimes they commit, whose bad fruits make them appear as they are.

The Fundamental Pact of Masonry

Then, in a profoundly perspicacious sentence, which must be kept in mind, the Pope categorically states the goal the Freemasons have set themselves:

Their ultimate purpose forces itself into view—namely, the utter overthrow of that whole religious and political order of the world which the Christian teaching has produced, and the substitution of a new state of things in accordance with their ideas, of which the foundations and laws shall be drawn from mere "Naturalism."

To completely change the foundations of our society: this is what the Masons undertook and, unfortunately, what they have achieved with diabolical skill. This change of mindset, of thinking, of worldview was inculcated by them little by little through the schools and all the levels of instruction which they seized hold of, by a sinister subversion such that people were unaware, and drank in the poison little by little over the years. The result is that their mental framework has been unwittingly changed.

In the same way, the changes and reforms that were effected during and after Vatican Council II, and which were inspired by a Modernism and false ecumenism that take their origin from Masonic doctrine, are infectious reforms. I cease not to repeat: these reforms are vitiated, because they no longer contain the Catholic spirit. They exude another spirit. Those who accustom themselves to live according to these reforms and to use them no longer have the Catholic spirit; they have lost the spirit of penance, of sacrifice, of renunciation. They no longer have the spirit nor the respect for the hierarchy or the authority of anyone. All this is manifest.

One of the most beautiful things that the liturgy of the ages teaches is respect, because the respect of the sacred is respect for God, God present in the liturgy, God present in persons and things. This is what is meant by the sacred. The desacralization and the vulgarity encountered in the modern rites destroy respect. There is no more respect for the Blessed Sacrament, or for persons, or for the hierarchy. The flower of Christian courtesy is respect. Every Christian respects God, God present in persons, in things, God present in the reality of the sacraments. All the magnificent ceremonies that govern the liturgy are endowed with signs of respect for God, by genuflections, inclinations, but also by the gestures of respect shown to the objects that are used in the course of our offices, the sacred vessels, for example, or by the kissing of the stole by the priest before he puts it on, and so on.

We must also respect our neighbor, we must respect one another. There is nothing more unpleasant than the widespread vulgarity by which men mutually treat each other without any signs of respect, and which would make of men a kind of herd without any sense of feeling. Our souls are temples of the Holy Ghost. Thus there is something eminently holy in us, in our persons, in our souls, that others should respect in us as we must respect it in them. Vulgarity in our relations with others must be banished, for we should not conduct ourselves towards those around us as if there were nothing sacred in them.

The Fundamental Principles of Freemasonry

After having clearly exposed the goal of Freemasonry, which is to do everything to bring about the destruction of the Church and the Catholic religion, Leo XIII draws up the list of the fundamental principles that govern it. It does not suffice, he says, to scrutinize their acts; it is also necessary to discern the principles that govern them:

Some of these [affiliated societies], again, are led by circumstances of times and places either to aim at smaller things than the others usually attempt, or than they themselves would wish to attempt. They are not, however, for this reason, to be reckoned as alien to the Masonic federation; for the Masonic federation is to be judged not so much by the things which it has done, or brought to completion, as by the sum of its pronounced opinions.

This is very important, because, more than did his predecessors, Leo XIII seeks to examine more deeply the principles of Masonry. The popes of the beginning of the nineteenth century especially emphasized the secrecy with which the Freemasons cloak themselves, and the crimes they commit, but they did not thoroughly investigate their principles.

The First Principle: Naturalism

Now, the fundamental doctrine of the Naturalists, is that human nature and human reason ought in all things to be mistress and guide.

Naturalism is the first principle for which the Pope condemns Freemasonry. At first glance one might think that, after all, Naturalism believes in human nature and takes it as its rule. That would be an error, for one must not forget that human nature was wounded by original sin.

The faith teaches that ever since the occurrence of original sin in the history of mankind with the sin of Adam and Eve, it not only robbed men of grace, but it also destroyed, disorganized and disordered nature. One must bear this in mind constantly. It is absolutely indispensable for really understanding these problems, which St. Thomas studied in a very explicit way: Human nature was wounded four ways by original sin. And these wounds, says St. Thomas, remain even after grace has been given to us. They remain in our nature. If original sin as sin is taken away by the grace of baptism, nonetheless it leaves vestiges, effects in our nature.

These four wounds are, firstly, the wound of ignorance. It is the virtue of prudence that is wounded by ignorance, and it is no longer what it should be. Someone who is ignorant, and who has a tendency to error, is not prudent. Being badly enlightened, he errs necessarily. The four cardinal virtues are wounded; the virtue of prudence, by error.

The virtue of justice, which is the fundamental, capital virtue of our human life, renders to God, to our neighbor and to ourselves what is due to each. This virtue is wounded by the wound of malice. There is a resident tendency in us to do evil, to not render to God what we owe, nor to our neighbor, nor even to ourselves. Thus, there is a tendency to evil. This is so obvious that there is no need to know the principles to perceive the reality. Unfortunately, one sees it in men: there is a tendency to malice.

The third wound is the weakness that undermines the virtue of fortitude. Man no longer resists temptation. He has been weakened, his strength to resist has been diminished. The virtue of fortitude faced with the difficulties of life is less virile.

And lastly, the fourth wound is the one that attacks the virtue of temperance: concupiscence. Man is tempted to enjoy the goods of this world, that is, money and pleasure, and he needs the virtue of temperance to oppose the attraction of concupiscence. He is in the grips of the desire to enjoy these pleasures. Man is also moved by pride, by the desire for honors, we well know.

So, these four wounds remain. When one speaks of Naturalism, the Freemasons, the Modernists and the liberals have a tendency to say that, on the contrary, nature is good, and consequently all that the Church calls disorders are not disorders for us. All the pleasures that men desire should be granted, for it is nature that demands them. Thus, there is a right, and he must satisfy them. But if we admit, on the contrary, that man is wounded in his very nature, and that he is consequently disordered in his desires...then if he is encouraged to follow his disorders, we see where that leads.

Or, if we denounce the weakness of man, they reply, no, he is not weak. The desires he experiences are not a sign of weakness. He needs and has a right to these pleasures. And then they continue to expound on the rights of man to develop according to his nature. The only bound is that he not disturb the public order. This is the only limit to man's liberty recognized by those who contradict and combat us. The only limit to a man's right to follow his base instincts is that he not disturb the peace, that he avoid run-ins with the police (and even so, it is the police who are often blamed).

Behold where we are led when society is based upon the false principles of Freemasonry. This is what their naturalism amounts to. And when the popes condemn "Naturalism," understand that it is neither nature in itself nor human nature that they designate, but the error that consists in affirming that human nature was not wounded by original sin, and consequently that everything that is disordered in our nature is quite natural, and that one has no right to oppose the instincts that are in man. That is what they mean by the rights of man: one has a right to freedom. The liberals have a tendency to agree with these doctrines of Freemasonry.

Rationalism

The Pope continues:

> Now, the fundamental doctrine of the Naturalists...is that human nature and human reason ought in all things to be mistress and guide....For they deny that anything has been taught by God; they allow no dogma of religion or truth which cannot be understood by the human intelligence, nor any teacher who ought to be believed by reason of his authority.

So, in the society in which we live one no longer wants God nor any master. This is what explains all the transformations that have taken place in the teaching that issues abundantly in all the nations in our day. The teaching is no longer authoritative, as coming from someone who teaches; rather does it consist of dialogues, because no one can bear the thought of any truth being imposed. This is in effect what the Pope is saying:

> For they allow...[no] teacher who ought to be believed by reason of his authority.

One must no longer have faith in any teacher, because the teacher cannot, nor has he the right, to impose any truth as if one were obliged to think or believe it. Oh no, everyone can think as he likes. It is from the clash of ideas, they say, that the light bursts forth. Everyone expresses his thought as he thinks it, and this is how progress in knowledge is made. This is absolutely absurd! This is what is currently contributing to destroy true knowledge, because one refuses to submit to the teaching of a magisterium, that is, all that comes from a tradition and a truth already acquired. Of course, in the physical sciences—chemistry, engineering, etc.—one is obliged to proceed otherwise. In these sciences no one can follow his own whim. There are rules to follow. If one chose not to follow them, he would wind up with a lovely mess that his neighbors would surely exploit to his discomfiture.

Let us take, for example, the two super powers Russia and the United States, both of which have accumulated fantastic arsenals. Suppose one were to say, that there is no ballistic or mechanical science—everyone can think as he likes about these topics; whereas the other would continue to prepare to destroy its rival, who would have no resistance to offer, having abandoned the principles that allowed it to build its armaments, the artillery, the bombs, the surface-to-air and air-to-surface missiles and so on. This would certainly cause an unpleasant predicament. So then, it is quite necessary to follow principles, to teach things as they are. No one thinks of following his opinion in these matters.

So then, can it be that in philosophy and theology everyone can follow his own opinion without that having any important repercussions? No, the consequences are grave. It is in this way that the intellect is killed, for it has no foundation, no truth, nothing. And this is why one perceives that even in the universities there reigns an incredible ignorance, even about the most fundamental principles.

The Errors of Naturalism and Rationalism

Understanding Naturalism is necessary. It is a term that appears again and again in the writings of these popes. They speak constantly of Naturalism, and thus it is essential to understand the significance they attach to it, namely, the error opposed to the Church's doctrine on the disequilibrium of the human soul, wounded as a consequence of original sin, even after this sin has been pardoned. We ourselves feel this very well. We experience the attraction of desires that are not normal, and which we must restrain by the virtues of temperance, fortitude, justice and prudence.

Were we to agree with the Freemasons, who think that it is good for man to satisfy his instincts, esteeming that these are good, where would we be heading? The results appear already: disorder, drugs, corruption, ruin and suicide. Ultimately, this theory leads to suicide, to annihilation, even physically. That is where these ideas have led: the number of young people who kill themselves ceases not to grow.

Denial of the Supernatural and the Natural Order

We need to have a good understanding of the doctrine of nature as the Church teaches and of the Naturalism and Rationalism professed by those who are in error and who contradict the truths of the faith. By refusing all truth and all religious dogma, the Freemasons seek the annihilation of the Church. And what is the Church, but the society founded by Our Lord Jesus Christ who gave it a commission to teach, as Pope XIII reminds us:

> ...it is the special and exclusive duty of the Catholic Church fully to set forth in words truths divinely received, to teach, besides other divine helps to salvation, the authority of its office, and to defend the same with perfect purity....

The helps meant are grace, the sacraments, prayer, the holy sacrifice of the Mass. That is the role of the magisterium and the purpose of the Church. No one has any right to change or modify the dogmas. If they no longer exist, as the Freemasons say, if there is no sound and immutable doctrine, the truth becomes relative. There is no absolute truth concerning nature, man and God.

The Church and Masonry: An Impossible Dialogue

Freemasonry has never renounced any of these objectives; but since Vatican Council II, churchmen have acted as if everything were possible: union with Freemasonry was part and parcel of the "opening" to the world announced by the Council, which was a council of dialogue, of ecumenism.

Recently, the German bishops published a document that is most instructive:

During the years 1974-1980, by a mandate of the Bishops' Conference and the united grand lodges of Germany, official meetings were held between the Church and Freemasonry. The German Bishops' Conference had commissioned the participants of the colloquia firstly, to ascertain the changes that have taken place in Freemasonry, and secondly, to investigate the compatibility of membership in both the Church and Freemasonry.

(You think you must be dreaming when you read the like, it is so incredible.)

...thirdly, in case of an affirmative answer to the preceding point, prepare public opinion to receive the change in position by publicity campaigns....

The German bishops were ready to make publicity in favor of the union between the Church and Freemasonry. They were going quite far in the "opening," as Ploncard d'Assac wrote. Why? The German bishops tell:

Because the Church is open to dialogue with all men of good will, and willing to meet with all groups who are well disposed.

Moreover, Paul VI insisted on this by widening the theoretical foundations, and he indicated the practical orientations to follow, the various circles with whom it would be suitable to open dialogue, since the freedom, correctly understood, of man in his private, religious, and public life, as recognized by the Church in a special way in Vatican Council II, offered a basis for dialogue with Freemasonry.

What the German bishops explained in this text is very serious. For the adopting of religious liberty, in almost the same terms as Freemasonry, would mean permitting the freedom to believe, the freedom of all religions, and thus the freedom of error. Freemasonry is all in favor of this, in as much as by its humanist attitude they consider themselves bound to enlist themselves in favor of human liberty, which is tantamount to their position on the rights of man. Evidently, the rights of man to do all he likes, and to have all he desires.

The German bishops also suggest that since German Freemasonry supports charitable institutions, this would permit certain points of contact between them and the Church, whose vocation is essentially one of charity. "Finally," the German bishops say:

> ...from the fact that in our disoriented time certain people find the satisfaction of unsatisfied needs in the symbols and rites of Freemasonry, just as in the Catholic Church symbols and rites have always had a place, one can presume that here also can be found a point in common and a basis for mutual understanding....

A point in common between the diabolical, satanic rites of Freemasonry and the liturgy of the Church! That such a phrase could appear in an official episcopal document is truly inconceivable.

Fortunately, they correct themselves a little, in a certain manner, as Ploncard d'Assac observes: "Now the text of the Bishops' Conference takes on its weight and worth. Up to this point it seemed to be woven of the gullibility, illusions, and compromises we have just heard. But then suddenly the tone of the text changes, fortunately."

> This opinion on the dual membership in the Church and Freemasonry was favored by a completely false way of interpreting the last Council, which followed upon the press campaign that was just mentioned.

Well, then, where do they stand?

> In order to make a really adequate examination of the problems, it was necessary to study the essence of Freemasonry.

So, the Bishops have studied this official ritual:

> Behold what was learned: the fact that Freemasonry calls into question the very existence of the Church has not changed. It suffices to read the Masonic program *Theses for the Year Two Thousand*, published this year shortly after the conclusion of the colloquium. There they deny in principle the worth of revealed truth (hence they deny dogma), and as a consequence of this Indifferentism, all revealed religion is discarded from the outset.

These are exactly the same words that Leo XIII used: for the Freemasons, there is no revealed religion:

From the first thesis, undoubtedly the most important, no philosophico-religious system exists that can impose an exclusive obligation.

Thus, according to their thesis, there is no religion that can say that it alone is true:

> Hence, whatever the tone employed, even if insults are not bandied, even if the Church knows that today she is obliged to collaborate with other religious denominations, the impression must not be taken that the Church has no reason to consider as outmoded her attitude of wariness towards and refusal of Freemasonry.

Freemasonry Has Not Changed

Thus, as soon as the Catholic Church began to examine the purport of the first three Masonic grades, she was obliged to note the existence of fundamental and insurmountable oppositions: Freemasonry has not changed in essence. Moreover, the Freemasons' worldview is essentially relativist.

The international lexicon of the Freemasons, which is recognized as an objective source, affirms that Freemasonry is truly the only institution which has succeeded in preserving itself free, to a great extent, of dogmas, ideologies, and *praxis*. Freemasonry can be considered as a movement that aims to gather men of relativist persuasion to promote the humanist ideal. Such subjectivism cannot be reconciled with faith in the revealed word of God.

The Freemasons deny the possibility of an objective knowledge of truth. The German bishops continue their findings:

Refusal of a Unique Objective Truth

> During the course of the colloquies, the maxim of the Freemason Lessing was notably cited: "If God held in his right hand all the truth, and in his left hand just the search for truth, even in conceding that I was eternally mistaken, and He said to me, 'Choose,' I would fling myself with humility to His left."

So, if God held the truth in one hand and in the other the search for truth, Lessing would go towards the left hand in order to remain in the search for truth, rather than receive truth. It is unbelievable:

> [And the Freemason continues]: "And I would say to Him, to God, Father, damn me, the pure truth is for you alone;...as for me, I prefer to be always seeking truth. I choose the search for truth."

How frightening it is to reject truth, and to say, Let the good Lord damn me rather than give me the truth!

Let us remark, moreover, that if one studies attentively the texts issued by the Vatican Council II, whether *Gaudium et Spes*, or *Dignitatis Humanae* on religious liberty, one finds the same notion: we are all together, all the religions seek the truth. How could the Church have affirmed such a thing? We are not seeking the truth. We have it. All that was to please the Freemasons and the Protestants, who also share the Masonic theories expressed by Relativism:

> The relativity of all truth constitutes the basis of Freemasonry, the German bishops continue (there is thus no objective truth), which involves a refusal in principle of all the dogmatic positions. Such a concept of truth is not compatible with the Catholic concept of truth, nor with the point of view of natural theology, nor with that of the theology of revelation.
>
> For the Freemasons, the conception of religion is relativist, all the religions are concurrent attempts to express divine truth.

Behold how the Freemasons define the religions even now.

Fortunately, the German bishops mustered some courage, and published this text, which is the first since the Council to express the matter so clearly.

Might one not then be astonished to read in the *Civilta cattolica*, which is published at Rome, an article by a famous Jesuit who during the Council showed himself to be ardently in favor of dialogue with the Freemasons, that scorns the German bishops' findings. He writes: "Oh, that may be true for Germany, but not elsewhere." And this is what is found in the most important

Catholic journal published at Rome and directed by Jesuits. It is frightening! Ever since the Council, then, there has been a will to come to terms with the Freemasons. Yet this is impossible: it would spell the ruin of our theology and our philosophy. Nothing would remain.

It is not without interest to make this digression when studying the declaration of Leo XIII made over one hundred years ago. A century later, in our period the principles of the Freemasons are the same. They have not changed; they cannot stand the Church.

The Church is necessarily, fundamentally opposed to Freemasonry. They affirm that truth is relative, we, that it is objective. They declare that there are no dogmas, and we, that there is a revealed truth and dogmas. Accord is therefore impossible. That is why the Freemasons will continue to do everything, as Leo XIII affirmed, to attempt to destroy the Church, because, necessarily, she is against them. There is an essential incompatibility. Their naturalist principle is in formal opposition to the Church's doctrine. This is what the Pope affirms:

> In those matters which regard religion let it be seen how the sect of the Freemasons acts, especially where it is more free to act without restraint, and then let any one judge whether in fact it does not wish to carry out the policy of the Naturalists. By a long and persevering labor, they endeavor to bring about this result—namely, that the office and authority of the Church may become of no account in the civil State.

Laicity of the State and the Struggle Against the Church

> For this same reason they declare to the people and contend that Church and State ought to be altogether disunited.

As a consequence of their Naturalism, the Freemasons preach the secularization of the State: Church and State must be separated, dogmas and objective truth eliminated. To bring it about, they will influence the instruction dispensed by the State in public schools and in the universities. Thereby they will secularize minds and souls, and infiltrate their relativist ideas, which practically lead to the suppression of God. Leo XIII specifies:

> Nor do they think it enough to disregard the Church—the best of guides—unless they also injure it by their hostility....

The least possible liberty to manage affairs is left to the Church; and this is done by laws not apparently very hostile, but in reality framed and fitted to hinder freedom of action. Moreover, We see exceptional and onerous laws imposed upon the clergy, to the end that they may be continually diminished in number and necessary means.

The clergy will be forced to serve in the military. The strangle hold of the State on the property of the Church will deprive the clergy of the means to create and support schools and works of charity:

> We see also the remnants of the possessions of the Church fettered by the strictest conditions, and subjected to the power and arbitrary will of the administrators of the State.

Second Principle: Indifferentism

The second principle of the Freemasons is Indifferentism, a necessary consequence of Naturalism, but which is still a distinct principle. Indifferentism is a word that occurs frequently in the pontifical documents. It has a precise meaning: Indifferentism postulates and propagates the idea that all the religions are equal, that there is none which is worth more than another:

> As all who offer themselves are received whatever may be their form of religion, they thereby teach the great error of this age—that a regard for religion should be held as an indifferent matter, and that all religions are alike. This manner of reasoning is calculated to bring about the ruin of all forms of religion, and especially of the Catholic religion, which, as it is the only one that is true, cannot without great injustice, be regarded as merely equal to their religions.

This tenor of language is no longer spoken. After Vatican II it disappears. As for Leo XIII, he affirms quite rightly that it is impossible to put error and truth on the same level.

Third Principle: Denial of the Existence of God and the Immortality of the Soul

The Pope comments on this principle:

> They no longer consider as certain and permanent those things which are fully understood by the natural light of reason, such as certainly are—the existence of God, the immaterial nature of the human soul, and its immortality....Neither do they conceal that this question about God is the greatest source and cause of discords among them....

If the Freemasons speak of the Great Architect, it does not mean that they believe in the existence of God. Ultimately, for them, the Great Architect signifies the forces of nature that uphold the existence of the world, but that in no wise means a personal God who created, governs, and maintains the world in existence. On the contrary, it is rather a form of Pantheism, as Leo XIII says:

> When this greatest fundamental truth has been overturned or weakened, it follows that those truths also which are known by the teaching of nature must begin to fall.

The consequence of these denials is the disappearance of the most vital truths:

> When these truths are done away with, which are as the principles of nature and important for knowledge and for practical use, it is easy to see what will become of both public and private morality. We say nothing of those more heavenly virtues, which no one can exercise or even acquire without a special gift and grace of God; of which necessarily no trace can be found in those who reject as unknown the redemption of mankind, the grace of God, the sacraments, and the happiness to be obtained in heaven. We speak now of the duties which have their origin in natural probity. That God is the Creator of the world and its provident Ruler; that the eternal law commands the natural order to be maintained, and forbids that it be disturbed; that the last end of men is a destiny far above human things and beyond this sojourning upon the earth: these are the sources and these the principles of all justice and morality.

If these be taken away, as the Naturalists and Freemasons desire, there will immediately be no knowledge as to what constitutes justice and injustice, or upon what principle morality is founded. And, in truth, the teaching of morality which alone finds favor with the sect of Freemasons, and in which they contend that youth should be instructed, is that which they call "civil," and "independent," and "free," namely, that which does not contain any religious belief.

Nowadays one would say "permissive morality."

Disastrous Consequences of Masonic Principles

After having defined the principles of Freemasonry, Leo XIII comes to the consequences they engender. The results are utterly deplorable.

Public Immorality

For wherever, by removing Christian education, the sect has begun more completely to rule, there goodness and integrity of morals have begun quickly to perish, monstrous and shameful opinions have grown up, and the audacity of evil deeds has risen to a high degree. All this is commonly complained of and deplored; and not a few of those who by no means wish to do so are compelled by abundant evidence to give not infrequently the same testimony.

In reading this passage, one might believe that Leo XIII was writing in our day, speaking of the audacity of evil deeds that the newspapers daily report: kidnappings, crimes, assassinations, in France and Spain and elsewhere, the bombs that go off killing the innocent. It is atrocious. "The audacity of evil deeds" is truly the spectacle we are met with. Then the Pope alludes to the negation of original sin, the cause of all these disorders.

Negation of Original Sin and the Consumer Society

Moreover, human nature was stained by original sin, and is therefore more disposed to vice than to virtue. For a virtuous life it is absolutely necessary to restrain the disorderly movements of the soul, and to make the passions obedient to reason. In this conflict human things must very often be despised, and the greatest labors and hardships must be undergone, in order that reason may always hold its sway. Both the Naturalists and Freemasons, having no faith in those things which we have learned by the revelation of God, deny that our first parents sinned, and consequently think that free will is not at all weakened and inclined to evil. On the contrary, exaggerating rather our natural virtue and excellence and placing therein alone the principle and rule of justice, they cannot even imagine that there is any need at all of a constant struggle and a perfect steadfastness to overcome the violence and rule of our passions.

Wherefore we see that men are publicly tempted by the many allurements of pleasure; that there are journals and pamphlets with neither moderation nor shame; that stage-plays are remarkable for license; that designs for works of art are shamelessly sought in the laws of a so-called *Realism*; that the contrivances of a soft and delicate life are most carefully devised; and that all the blandishments of pleasure are diligently sought out by which virtue may be lulled to sleep.

So, man finds himself subject to the slavery of passion to all that is afforded by the so-called consumer society. How else can the consumer society be described, than by the will to put as many material goods as possible at the disposition of men, and then to urge them to pursue pleasure, money, gain, and goods.

If it were only a question of placing useful and honorable goods at men's disposition, that would be tolerable; but evil and indecent goods are put on a par with the good. Ultimately, everything is done to encourage sin. Let us not be surprised to see society on the way to suicide, heading towards its own annihilation.

Original sin, virtue, the immaterial nature of the soul, the spiritual element that must prevail over the material, all are discounted. Man is but a body made to consume. He must be incited to consume as much as possible so as to earn as much money as possible, and he must be given all the means that lead to sin.

Communist Enslavement

When the Communists come to power, however, the people no longer receive the superfluities of the consumer society, as this all goes to the rulers. Man becomes just a slave, a tool for work for the State, and who must eat just what is necessary to keep body and soul together so as to go on working. All the rest must go to the State, to serve the devil, Freemasonry, Communism; to serve the world revolution and the destruction of the Church.

For men in the consumer society, the slavery of the passions holds sway, which may seem less serious than the slavery to which are reduced the peoples subject to Communism; but in a certain sense, the slavery of the passions is more detrimental to the life of the soul and faith and the conservation of religion, than is the slavery of Communism. By depriving men of all the goods that are offered by the consumer society, the Communist slavery puts them in a state of penance, of mortification, and in this condition men are led to think more, and to seek the goods of the spirit.

This explains why religion is perhaps more alive and keen behind the "iron curtain" than in the West. For there is no surer way to sink souls in the enjoyment of pleasures and bring an end to religion than by satisfying all the passions of men. It is undoubtedly easier for the Freemasons to try and wrest men from the hold of religion in this pleasure-seeking society than for the Communists to do as much to the peoples who have been deprived of these goods and forced to work like slaves. For if indeed the people of these lands suffer from the brutalized condition in which they are held, one notices that, deprived of the goods of this world, they turn more readily towards the goods of the soul. Whence the tenacious battle the Communists wage against religion, so that it gain no advantage from the mortified state in which Communism has put men. In all the schools whence God has been banished, the professors of atheism still relentlessly pursue the war against religion.

Destruction of the Family by the Destruction of Marriage

After having studied the principles of Masonry and the deplorable results that ensue when they are applied to the spiritual life, private morals and even politics; and after having denounced the criminality, and the slavery of completely unbridled passions, Leo XIII broaches the subject of the destruction of the family:

> Generally no one is accustomed to obey crafty and clever men so submissively as those whose soul is weakened and broken down by the domination of the passions, there have been in the sect of the Freemasons some who have plainly determined and proposed that, artfully and of set purpose, the multitude should be satiated with a boundless license of vice, as, when this had been done, it would easily come under their power and authority for any acts of daring.

To develop the systematic corruption of the populace is for the Freemasons one of the most effective ways to bring about the destruction of the family:

> What refers to domestic life in the teaching of the Naturalists is almost all contained in the following declarations. That marriage belongs to the genus of commercial contracts, which can rightly be revoked by the will of those who made them.

In principle, every contract can be revoked. There is no reason why a contract cannot be dissolved if those who have concluded it decide to break it. Because it was made by the will of the contracting parties, they can also terminate it.

If this reasoning applies to free acts, depending solely upon the will of the contracting parties, this is so. While marriage is truly a contract, nonetheless it is only free as concerns the choice of persons, but not as to the conditions according to which it is concluded. The conditions of the contract have been inscribed in the very nature of man and woman. It is God Himself who placed the conditions of the contract in nature itself. Men are not obliged to enter the contract. But as soon as they have, they can no longer dissolve it, because the conditions in which it was established manifest that it cannot be broken. This contract is binding until the death of the spouses.

The family is made for procreation, for increasing the human race. Thus the parents cannot break at their good pleasure this contract, as such a separation would leave the children abandoned. This is what we have seen ever since the legalization of divorce. That is why the Church has always taught the indissolubility of marriage: the bond cannot be broken. In extreme cases, the Church tolerates the separation of bodies, but she never admits divorce.

In certain cases, she recognizes the nullity of a marriage, but this can only be for certain reasons. When the Church recognizes the nullity of a marriage, it is because she has discovered that one of the conditions of the contract has not been fulfilled, for example, because there was the presence of fear or threat. The woman was married under the pressure of her parents, under threat of harm and so felt such fear that she dared not say no. Without this constraint, she would have said no. If truly one can discover that before the contract there was imposed moral pressure such that the will was not free, the contract did not take place, for it lacked the liberty of one of the parties. This is one of the reasons that can be invoked.

Let us cite another case. If one or other of the spouses clearly states before the marriage, and in the presence of witnesses who can testify to the fact, that he did not want children, this is another condition that constitutes the nullity of the contract. The contract is made for the spouses to have children. If they cannot have any for particular reasons, that is something else. But the will to not have children renders void the marriage contract.

Outside these rare conditions that occasionally occur, the Church never breaks a marriage. If the marriage is seen to exist and there is no cause of nullity, the Church cannot break the marriage, it is not within her power. The pope himself cannot; he has no right to break a marriage, it is not within his power.[1]

---

[1] There are two notable exceptions: A marriage that has not been consummated can be dissolved by the pope for serious reasons; and the marriage of pagans can be dissolved "in favor of the faith" of the pagan who receives baptism, if the pagan spouse refuses to dwell peacefully with the other.

God instituted marriage and made known the conditions and the end. It is He himself, the Author of nature, who conceived marriage and its purpose. And for the sake of the end of marriage, which is precisely the procreation and education of children, the contract is indissoluble, because children need their parents, the stability of their union, the continuous existence of the family in order to be brought up well.

But the Freemasons have an entirely different idea. For them, marriage is a contract like any other, "which can rightly be revoked by the will of those who made them." It is good to remind oneself that the indissolubility of marriage is specific to the Catholic religion. She alone professes this doctrine which is fundamental, because if there is anything at the basis of human society, it is the family. All the other religions whatsoever accept grounds for divorce, more or less leniently, even the Orthodox and the Protestants. It is truly a mark of the Catholic religion not to admit divorce, as the divine institution of marriage prevents it.

Christian Marriage:
Guarantee of the Dignity of the Woman

By proposing to women the model of the Blessed Virgin Mary, whom God himself chose to be the mother of Our Lord Jesus Christ, the Church proves the esteem in which she holds women. Whereas in all the ancient civilizations, and in all the history of paganism, one finds universally the contempt of women. She is considered as a mere object. She has no civil rights; she can be repudiated and even sold.

The Church gives to the woman freedom and she guarantees it. I was able to observe in Africa that in all the pagan tribes that I encountered, the great problem is always that of the woman. The men spend their time selling their daughters or purchasing wives or reselling them. They term this arranging the dowry.

This is false, for it constitutes a real commerce. Scarcely are they born when the girls become the object of trade, someone puts down money to purchase them. As soon as someone else comes along with more money than what a husband has paid, the parents arrange for the daughter to leave her present husband. They return the "dowry" to the husband who had purchased her first, and keep the rest. If a woman is sold for two hundred dollars and another comes along with four hundred, they return two hundred to the first and keep two hundred. It is a real traffic that is almost impossible to imagine.

The missionaries had to fight to uphold Christian marriages, and even then it was difficult because this habit is so deeply rooted in their mores. And then, the parents were not always Christian, but pagan, and acted towards the daughter who had become a Christian and married in the Church as if she were a pagan. The women who had left their husbands at the behest of their parents had nothing against them; they simply were obeying the injunctions of the parents, who always command. If the father tells his daughter to come home and that he will marry her to another, the daughter can do nothing. She is subjugated by her father. If her father dies, she belongs to her oldest brother. She always belongs to someone; she is not free.

Sometimes we were obliged to go and seek in the villages a wife who had thus left her husband. We would go off like commandos with a few young men in a dug-out in pursuit of the woman, because the catechists advised us, that if the missionary Father did not go and fetch her, all the others would go too. Going to look for women in this way struck me as a rather droll duty.

We made a few examples. But when the parents learned that we were coming to fetch the wife they were intimidating, they made her go and hide in the forest to keep us from finding her. There was always someone in the village, though, who would inform us, and so we always succeeded in finding the woman, for often the woman desired to return to her husband. But in front of her parents she had to show the opposite. Then she would start screaming to prove that she left without her consent. The parents dared not say much in front of the priest. Sometimes we even had to take the woman by force, binding her and putting her in the boat to take her back to the village. As soon as the boat had put out a little distance from the parents, the woman would clap her hands, and show her pleasure at finding herself back with her husband. But before, oh, she put on such incredible scenes: I am going to kill myself... (and then she would jump into the river)... I am going to drown myself. And the young people would go and fetch her back. All this proved quite well that these poor women were not free to dispose of themselves and that they were the object of a veritable traffic.

To protect Christian marriage in such conditions is very difficult! When one considers Islam and the conduct of Moslems, one observes the same contempt of the woman. When I was in Algeria and Morocco I had a chance to visit some harems. It is atrocious; the women are enclosed their entire lives in a very restricted space, three or four together. They too are bought, sold and resold. It is an abominable traffic.

Christian marriage is the guarantee of the respect paid to the woman, respect that still exists, thank God, in our Christian families and in many of the Christian regions. But, to the degree that the Masonic doctrines spread with divorce, we see that the woman is more and more despised, less and less respected. Marriage is one of the marks of Christian civilization; that is why the Church has tried to do all in her power to prevent the legalization of divorce. But currently, in most of the countries where divorce has not yet been admitted, the Freemasons have launched campaigns and exerted pressure to introduce its legalization.

Catholics even, and bishops, have helped to a certain extent to encourage divorce, like Cardinal Tarancon, who recommended the institution of two types of marriage, one for those who desired an indissoluble union, and then a civil marriage for those who might eventually like to divorce. I read this in a renowned Spanish journal; the Cardinal explicitly campaigned for the establishment of two kinds of marriage. Yet it is known that Spain is a country of Catholic tradition, therefore he was not speaking of marriage for people who are non-Catholics, but for Catholics. It is inconceivable to see such a proposition emanate from a cardinal!

All this comes from the fact that it is the Freemasons who are at the origin of these ideas, because it involves a worldwide movement. If this were only occurring in a single country, one might think that it was being instigated by the head of the government. But no, it is in every country, one after the other, that the legislative assemblies are occupied with legislation for laws instituting divorce. And that is the work of Masonry: it wants the heads of government to have power over the marriage bond.

Monopolize the Education of Youth

But that is not enough; Masonry also wants to take control of the education of youth, as Pope Leo XIII affirms:

> With the greatest unanimity the sect of the Freemasons also endeavors to take to itself the education of youth.

After imposing divorce, the education of youth is the next target. This is so clear it is blinding. The advance of the secularization of teaching in all the countries of the world is manifest. The organizations like UNESCO, whose self-proclaimed goal is the spread of education and the end of illiteracy, are in fact directed by Masonry in order to extend anti-clerical, atheistic education throughout the world, under the fallacious pretext of giving all men access to a higher culture.

We observed all of this in the missions. We had the worst troubles with the organs of UNESCO because they had a lot of money to spend, and would establish public schools wherever we had established Catholic schools, even though there were many other places where they could have established schools and which were without any schools at all. Oh, no, they expressly established schools in the same vicinity in order to destroy the influence of the Catholic Church. With the money they had at their disposition, this was easy. They could pay their professors much more than we could afford to.

Fortunately, there were still many Africans with respect for religion who preferred to place their children in our schools, even among the Moslems. We always had a good number of Moslems in our schools, although we did not allow the number to exceed fifteen percent. But among the first to enroll their children in our schools were the Moslems, and this for religious reasons. The parents knew that we taught religion, not to convert them or to make them Catholics, which, unfortunately, was impossible; even if a good little Moslem were the best student in catechism, it was impossible to allow him to make his first holy Communion. Sometimes the child would cry when he saw all the others go forward to receive Communion, while he, the first in the class, was unable to go. He couldn't understand. But there was nothing to be done about the parents. Had they ever learned that we permitted the child to receive holy Communion secretly, they would have burned down the school. It was impossible, then, to convert them, but they still had this feeling for religion such that they wanted to see it taught to their children.

The Pope denounces Masonry's hold on the education of youth:

> With the greatest unanimity the sect of the Freemasons also endeavors to take to itself the education of youth. They think that they can easily mold to their opinions that soft and pliant age, and bend it whither they will; and that nothing can be more fitted than this to enable them to bring up the youth of the State after their own plan. Therefore in the education and instruction of children they allow no share, either of teaching or of discipline, to the ministers of the Church; and in many places they have procured that the education of youth shall be exclusively in the hands of laymen, and that nothing which treats of the most important and most holy duties of men to God shall be introduced into the instructions on morals.

Now, even in countries like Italy, where until just recently the obligation to teach the Catholic religion in the schools had the force of law, it is all over; in Italy, it was ended by the new concordat.[2] The law has not completely entered into effect, and the new secularized legislation still tolerates priests teaching religion in the schools. For the time being, parents are still free to have their children given, either at the school or not, Catholic instruction, and the priests are still remunerated by the State. But the intention of the legislators is to suppress the remuneration of the priests; and because of this, there will no longer be priests dispensing Catholic instruction in the schools.

It will become necessary, then, as is the case in France, for the priests to organize catechism outside the schools. And in this case, the Freemasons, who seek to destroy Catholic education,

---

[2] The new concordat, replacing the one concluded under Pius XI between the Holy See and Italy, was signed February 18, 1984, by Cardinal Casaroli and Italian President Bettino Craxi.

will arrange things such that, all the while appearing to grant a certain liberty to the children to attend catechism, the courses are scheduled during the recreations, when the children need to unwind. It is just then that they allow the children to go to catechism, when it will make the class more difficult. They will have to make a sacrifice in order to receive Catholic education. And then go and have all the parents sign a sheet that they desire the Catholic education of their children!

The Rights of Man

Leo XIII then takes up the thesis according to which all men are equal by right:

> Then come their doctrines of politics, in which the Naturalists lay down that all men have the same right, and are in every respect of equal and like condition.

This is the first article of "the rights of man": all men are equal. Of course, as the Pope says later on, all men by their common nature are equal with respect to God; but in fact, all men are not equal according to their natural talents nor by the role they play in society.

Continuing to analyze the democracy sought by Masonry, the Pope denounces another false principle: man's natural social freedom:

> Each one is naturally free;...no one has the right to command another;...it is an act of violence to require men to obey any authority other than that which is obtained from themselves.

Democratic Ideology Destroys Authority

This false principle is the basis of the modern democratic system: popular sovereignty. Authority resides in all men, in the people. And it is the people who confer the authority that they hold to another. Yet no one has of himself the right to command another. Thomist philosophy says the same thing, but because it is God who commands us. We say that those who exercise authority participate in the authority of God. It isn't because it is so and so, but because they have been endowed with an authority that has been conferred upon them by natural circumstances, or even by an election. But the authority comes from God. This is what the Church teaches, and it matters little by what means they receive the authority. For example, the authority of the father of a family is a natural authority, conferred by nature. Certainly it isn't the children who confer authority on the father. We haven't yet reached such an absurdity!

Think how many events took place by which certain families became royal families. There were personalities who came to the fore, I should say, with the tacit consent of the populace; notably when it was necessary to defend the country against enemies. They needed a leader to command and organize the society, for its own good, and, precisely, to protect the people against foreign enemies. Instinctively the people recognized the authority of someone who had succeeded by his intelligence and talents in protecting the people against their enemies. He was considered as a king. These talents were natural gifts given by God to these men who, having become king or else recognized as princes, founded a dynasty. Because, as the Pope says, it is ridiculous to say that we are all equal. We do not have the same qualities, nor intelligence, nor even the same physical strength. Some are very skillful with their hands, others are all thumbs. Some are very intelligent, others less so. We are all unequal, and the good God wanted it that way. He desired this inequality, these differences, precisely so that we might complement each other, and help each other, and share our gifts with those who have received less. This is what society is.

If some men are bosses, who own an industry and manage it, they need others. If there was no one who worked with his hands, what would they do? A complementary need exists. The workers need a manager who thinks of the organization of the factory, of marketing the products, of seeking new markets. The good God created men thus. He desired society to be organized, ordered, organic, and not, as the Freemasons and liberals would have, an indistinct mass of identical men with identical rights. This conception is completely false. It is against nature.

Leo XIII stigmatizes this entirely erroneous conception, and describes it thus:

>...All things belong to the free people; power is held by the command or permission of the people, so that, when the popular will changes, rulers may lawfully be deposed....

Now we well see the situation of peoples with the multiplication of elections. The candidates have scarcely been elected when they begin to think of the next election and prepare for the next vote. The politicians will flatter the people, give them one thing or the other in order to win their votes for the next balloting. This is absurd, and leads to an absolutely ridiculous society. The one who will be elected is the one who has at his disposal the most resources, the most money; the one who knows best how to seduce the most electors, or who has the most influence. It is not the candidate with the best qualities for being head of State who will succeed, but the strongest or the richest.

Leo XIII additionally points out not only the unnatural character of Masonic democracy, but also its atheistic strain:

> It is held also that the State should be without God; that in the various forms of religion there is no reason why one should have precedence of another; and that they are all to occupy the same place.

Masonry Opens the Way to Communism

The Pope foresees the ultimate consequences of the political principles professed by Freemasonry:

> They prepare the way for not a few bolder men who are hurrying on even to worse things, in their endeavor to obtain equality and community of all goods by the destruction of every distinction of rank and property.

This notion is that of the communists, says the Pope, and by professing it the Freemasons open the way to Communism. It would be an error to think that the Freemasons are not the cause of Communism itself. Perhaps they do not want to see come to pass all the consequences which stem from Communism, but, in fact, their own principles prepare the ground for Communism.

Perversity of Freemasonry

The Pope, having exposed the Freemasons' principles and their consequences, indicates the judgment that must be passed on them:

> What therefore the sect of the Freemasons is, and what course it pursues, appears sufficiently from the summary We have briefly given. Their chief dogmas are so greatly and manifestly at variance with reason, that nothing can be more perverse.

So, there is a total opposition to rational principles. Although the Freemasons call themselves naturalists and rationalists, their principles are absolutely contrary to the natural principles of reason:

> To wish to destroy the religion and the Church which God Himself has established, and whose perpetuity He insures by His protection, and to bring back after a lapse of eighteen centuries the manners and customs of the pagans, is signal folly and audacious impiety....In this insane and wicked endeavor we may almost see the implacable hatred and spirit of revenge with which Satan himself is inflamed against Jesus Christ.

The Work of Satan

The judgment the Pope formulates is clear and formal: this program comes from Satan; the plans of the Freemasons are quite simply Satanic and inspired by the hatred of Our Lord Jesus Christ. One must well see things as Pope Leo XIII describes them, in order to well understand the origin and the motives of this war, a war that is being led with such intelligence and prudence—human prudence—against Christian institutions, and, consequently, against the reign of Our Lord Jesus Christ. They have pursued this war for several centuries throughout the whole world. That is why it can not be that mere men are behind such a plan and such a work. It can only be the devil. It is truly the City of Satan that is being organized against Our Lord Jesus Christ, against the City of God.

Evidently, Satan is cunning and remarkably intelligent. He knows how to play his hand, sometimes by violence, sometimes by hiding beneath a veil of humanitarianism, sometimes by absolutist doctrines like Communism, and then by Liberalism, which is such a fabric of nuances that one loses himself in it. Many let themselves be taken in by ambiguous language destined to attract weak minds, unused to reflection and which let themselves be seduced.

Manifestly, all men are free, all are equal, all are brothers. But in fact, it is not a question of true liberty, veritable equality, real brotherhood. One must apply himself to really understand the motives and objectives of this truly Satanic warfare. The Pope does not mince his words, and categorically accuses Satan of being at the origin of all these Masonic doctrines which dishonor man, the family and society:

> So also the studious endeavor of the Freemasons to destroy the chief foundations of justice and honesty, and to co-operate with those who would wish, as if they were mere animals, to do what they please, tends only to the ignominious and disgraceful ruin of the human race. The evil, too, is increased by the dangers which threaten both domestic and civil society. As We have elsewhere shown, in marriage, according to the belief of almost every nation, there is something sacred and religious; and the law of God has determined that marriages shall not be dissolved. If they are deprived of their sacred character, and made dissoluble, trouble and confusion in the family will be the result, the wife being deprived of her dignity and the children left without protection as to their interests and well-being.

Juvenile Delinquency Engendered by Freemasonry

It is curious to observe the contradictions which result from the conduct of the Freemasons. On the one hand they create secular works for youth and children, and then at the same time they do all they can to fill the prisons with children. They refuse to allow the Church the care of giving Christian education, for they reject its morals and violate chastity. They propagate vice, and pornographic books and movies. They do everything to corrupt youth. And after that, it becomes necessary to construct prisons, psychiatric hospitals and halfway houses for delinquent children.

It is just overwhelming, for before these things were unknown. There were no prisons for children. The halfway houses were often orphanages for children where Sisters or the Brothers of St. John of God took care of them. In France, for example, there are still the Sisters of Pontcalec to whom the police would bring children abandoned by their parents. There were still works such as these where the children were embraced by a family spirit, and welcomed with affection by the sisters or brothers who took them in. Well, these congregations were persecuted, the brothers and sisters driven out. Everything was undertaken to make their works disappear, ostensibly to create secular works. The result: They have had to build prisons for children, which are in fact veritable concentration camps where all the vices prevail. Or else, there are too many juvenile delinquents, and so they let them run loose. They cannot shut them all up. Thus it has come to pass that in every country we see an increase of delinquency, thefts, and drugs.

Even Switzerland has not escaped these disturbances which affect the youth. One can see at Zurich and Lausanne bands of youth who steal cars, break shop front windows to rob them, and who conduct themselves like bandits; and the police simply look on. They don't know what to do about it. They collect data, arrest a few and question them. They put them in prison for a few days and then let them go. And it goes on and on. The responsible authorities no longer know how to govern society, the moral foundations of which have all been destroyed. Everything capable of offering children and youth a stable, regular life has been suppressed. All the barriers have been removed in the name of liberty. It is absolutely horrendous.

The spreading of drug use is an example. It is a frightful plague that has spread even into schools that are still Catholic. No one is able to say what must be done to stop this evil that spreads wider and wider. If things have come to this point, then it is because men no longer will to impose the moral law, the law of God. The ten commandments are no longer the basis of society, the family, and education. Only the "rights of man" remain: the right to liberty. Liberty! The results speak for themselves.

The Revolution and the Thirst for Change

The doctrine of the Freemasons according to which all men are equal inherently undermines all authority in the political organization of civil society. If such a concept were applied to the Church, its entire structure would collapse. The Church is essentially hierarchic, and authority is conferred by the higher authority, the election of the pope during the conclave excepted. The bishops are designated by the Pope, the priests are called by the bishops, and so on. The Church is thus entirely an hierarchic society whose organization is in opposition to the rationalist doctrines of the Freemasons.

The putting into practice of the Freemasons' doctrines, says the Pope, leads to revolution:

> Now, from the disturbing errors which We have described the greatest dangers to States are to be feared. For, the fear of God and reverence for divine laws being taken away, the authority of rulers despised, sedition permitted and approved, and the popular passions urged on to lawlessness, with no restraint save that of punishment, a change and overthrow of all things will necessarily follow. Yea, this change and overthrow is deliberately planned and put forward by many associations of *Communists* and *Socialists*; and to their undertakings the sect of Freemasons is not hostile, but greatly favors their designs, and holds in common with them their chief opinions. And if these men do not at once and everywhere endeavor to carry out their extreme views, it is not to be attributed to their teaching and their will, but to the virtue of that divine religion which cannot be destroyed; and also because the sounder part of men, refusing to be enslaved to secret societies, vigorously resist their insane attempts.

> Would that all men would judge of the tree by its fruits, and would acknowledge the seed and origin of the evils which press upon us, and of the dangers that are impending! We have to deal with a deceitful and crafty enemy, who, gratifying the ears of people and of princes, has ensnared them by smooth speeches and by adulation. Ingratiating themselves with rulers under a pretense of friendship, the Freemasons have endeavored to make them their allies and powerful helpers for the destruction of the Christian name;...In like manner they have by flattery deluded

the people. Proclaiming with a loud voice liberty and public prosperity, and saying that it was owing to the Church and to sovereigns that the multitude were not drawn out of their unjust servitude and poverty, they have imposed upon the people; and, exciting them by a thirst for novelty, they have urged them to assail both the Church and the civil power.

The *Aggiornamento*: Adaptation to the Liberal Spirit

The Popes have often denounced the thirst for change. The desire for change is the evil of modern man, and it throve at the Council. They wanted to change everything under the pretext of *aggiornamento,* under the pretext of adaptation: it is necessary to be attuned to the wavelength of modern man. And as modern man is ever-changing, one must follow suit and adapt indefinitely.

It is true, to a certain extent, that the methods of the apostolate must be adapted; this goes without saying, it is self-evident. Clearly, one does not preach to adults in the same way as to children; one does not address intellectuals in the same way as the common people. One adapts, evidently; this is quite natural and there was no need to hold a Council about this.

But in fact they desired to touch the untouchable: they wanted to change the very formulas by which the faith is expressed, allegedly to make it more accessible to modern man. These are ravings! The rights of man: Which man is it? For there are men, not "man" separated from reality. When they speak about adapting to modern man as he is to be found in Europe, South America, China or elsewhere. What man is meant? It doesn't make sense. Modern man is, quite simply, the man whose mind has been fashioned by Masonic doctrines, by ideas completely contrary to the Church, to the laws of nature, laws conceived by God. To pretend that the ideas and the vocabulary of this "modern man" can be Christianized is entirely unrealistic. It is vain to suppose that, surely the "rights of man can be made evangelistic." It is simply impossible. For the Masons deliberately developed them in opposition to the ten commandments. One never speaks of men's duties, but only their rights, in order to destroy God's law in such a way that it is no longer at the basis of society, and is replaced by liberty.

The rights of man, the goddess Reason, adoration of human reason—this is the revolution. Man is put in God's place. How could they have imagined that they could adapt to such people. It is impossible. They wanted to adapt so much that they ended up by rationalizing the liturgy, which contained such beautiful things, so sacred, mysterious, and divine. They made of it a rationalist concoction. They debased the sacred rite of the Mass to make of it a meal. They had to democratize and abandon hierarchy: the hierarchy is gone; the priest is just the designated president, but who could also be designated by the community. It is truly frightening to consider where we have been led by this will to adapt.

We cannot use the language of others, because it has a precise meaning which well expresses what they wish. One cannot use the language of Protestants or rationalists without becoming, little by little, a rationalist oneself.

The Combat Against Freemasonry

Having exposed the Freemasons' principles, and the consequences of their application, Leo XIII proposes remedies. What is to be done?

> Whatever the future may be, in this grave and widespread evil it is Our duty, Venerable Brethren, to endeavor to find a remedy. And because We know that Our best and firmest hope of a remedy is in the power of that divine religion which the Freemasons hate in proportion to their fear of it, We think it to be of chief importance to call that most saving power to Our aid against the common enemy.

We must, says the Pope, affirm our holy religion.

> Therefore, whatsoever the Roman Pontiffs Our predecessors have decreed for the purpose of opposing the undertakings and endeavors of the Masonic sect, and whatsoever they have enacted to deter or withdraw men from societies of this kind, We ratify and confirm it all by Our Apostolic authority: and trusting greatly to the good-will of Christians, We pray and beseech each one, for the sake of his eternal salvation, to be most conscientiously careful not in the least to depart from what the Apostolic See has commanded in this matter.

Tear Away the Mask from Freemasonry

Then Leo XIII addresses himself to the bishops:

> ...But as it befits the authority of Our office that We Ourselves should point out some suitable way of proceeding, We wish it to be your rule first of all to tear away the mask from Freemasonry, and to let it be seen as it really is....

The Pope tells the bishops that their first duty is to denounce Masonry, tear away the mask it hides behind with its deceitful language, and the various so-called charitable institutions it operates, and the devotion it displays. Behind all this there hides a satanic spirit.

The Freemasons do not like to be unmasked. They do not like to be talked about. I drew down their attacks several times because in a few conferences I spoke about Freemasonry. This provoked immediate reaction in the newspapers. As soon as one touches upon Freemasonry or criticizes it publicly, its adepts respond. They cannot tolerate it. Feeling themselves exposed, which they fear, they are infuriated and they strike.

In a homily I gave at Lille in 1977, I had spoken openly about Freemasonry. I said that it was at the origin of all these revolutions and the war against the Church, and that it is still at work. They did not direct the reaction. (And it is in such circumstances that they reveal themselves.) After the declaration, a journalist who directed a well-done review with a rather traditionalist outlook, such that he had a fairly wide readership in our traditionalist circles, showed his true colors. His father had been a Freemason, which he himself would admit. In the article he wrote, he was very displeased because I had attacked Freemasonry. I should never have done it, it was completely unacceptable. He did more than show the lobe of his ear. His violent reaction made him come out of the shadow and reveal his true affiliation. This surprised a good number of his readership, who could not believe that he would defend Freemasonry. For them it was quite a revelation; and much harm was done among the traditionalists who read his review, where they always found very interesting information and even very traditional articles on religion.

No Catholic Can Join the Freemasons

So, the Pope first asks the bishops to denounce Freemasonry: "Let it be seen as it really is":

> By sermons and Pastoral Letters instruct the people as to the artifices used by societies of this kind in seducing men and enticing them into their ranks, and as to the depravity of their opinions and the wickedness of their acts. As Our predecessors have many times repeated, let no man think that he may for any reasons whatsoever join the Masonic sect, if he values his Catholic name and his eternal salvation as he ought to value them....
>
> Further, by assiduous teaching and exhortation, the multitude must be drawn to learn diligently the precepts of religion.... By uniting the efforts of both clergy and laity, strive, Venerable Brethren, to make men thoroughly know and love the Church; for the greater their knowledge and love of the Church, the more will they be turned away from clandestine societies.

And it is true, the more we know our religion the more we live it, especially our liturgy, the traditional one to which we remain attached and which was once that of the whole Church; the more we will be immunized, so to speak, against all the evil tendencies of Rationalism and against all these errors.

Rationalism Destroys the Liturgy

Confronted with the reformed liturgy of Vatican II, one experiences a sort of sorrow and disgust. One is no longer at ease, because it no longer expresses our faith, our way of thinking, our Christian life. This is a quite normal reaction. Little by little, put off by this transformation, people began to desert the churches.

An example of the penetration of Rationalism in the new liturgy is the fact that its proponents wanted the faithful to be able to understand everything. Rationalism cannot accept something it cannot comprehend: everything must be judged by reason. And of course in the liturgy there are mysterious elements: Latin, the sacred language, the prayers said in a low voice. The priest is turned to the cross and the faithful cannot see what he does. They cannot follow all his gestures. Thus, a certain mystery exists.

This is true; there is a mystery, there is a sacred language. But even if the faithful do not understand this mystery, the consciousness of the mystery of Our Lord is much more profitable to them than for them to hear the prayers of the Mass read aloud in the vernacular. Firstly, even in the vernacular certain passages are difficult to understand, the truths themselves are difficult to grasp. Then one must take into account the inattention of the mind. People are easily distracted; they listen awhile, focus on one phrase and then lose the train of thought. They themselves admit that it is tiring to always hear talking. They cannot be recollected for a moment, and they complain.

Prayer is above all a spiritual action, as Our Lord said to the Samaritan: "...the true adorers shall adore the Father in spirit and in truth. For the Father also seeketh such to adore him." Prayer is more interior than exterior. If there is exterior prayer, it is in order to favor the interior prayer of the soul, spiritual prayer, the elevation of our soul to God. This is the end that is sought: lift up souls to God; whereas the other wearies the soul with its continual noise. There is not a moment of silence. And finally, wearied, the people give it up.

The error thus committed in desiring to transform the liturgy is the result of the rationalist spirit that has held sway in our time. They wanted to adapt everything to the modern man who wants to understand everything; they cannot bear to be spoken to in a language they cannot understand, so they say.

And yet everyone knows that the faithful have always had missals where the Latin and the vernacular translation were set side by side. This kind of missal was in use throughout the world, and it was not difficult to follow the Mass. So the reasoning was absurd. But they wanted to adapt things to the spirit of modern man who does not like mystery, and who cannot bear not to understand everything he hears. Thus they destroyed the mystery, banished the sacred, the divine, from the ceremonies. Conclusion: we must remain attached to our liturgy.

The Third Order of St. Francis

And then, curiously, the Pope recommends something a bit striking: the Third Order of St. Francis:

We use this occasion to state again what We have stated elsewhere, namely, that the Third Order of St. Francis, whose discipline We a little while ago prudently mitigated, should be studiously promoted and sustained: for the whole object of this Order, as constituted by its founder, is to invite men to an imitation of Jesus Christ, to a love of the Church, and to the observance of all Christian virtues; and therefore it ought to be of great influence in suppressing the contagion of wicked societies....

Amongst the many benefits to be expected from it will be the great benefit of drawing the minds of men to liberty, fraternity, and equality of right; not such as the Freemasons absurdly imagine, but such as Jesus Christ obtained for the human race and St. Francis aspired to: the liberty, We mean, of *sons of God*, through which we may be free from slavery to Satan or to our passions, both of them most wicked masters; the fraternity whose origin is in God, the common Creator and Father of all; the equality which, founded on justice and charity, does not take away all distinctions among men, but, out of the varieties of life, of duties, and of pursuits, forms that union and that harmony which naturally tend to the benefit and dignity of the State.

The Pope, then, encourages membership in the Third Order of St. Francis, whose spirit he esteems. And it is true that this Third Order has done an immense amount of good, and has enabled many souls to sanctify themselves.

Restore the Guilds

Among the remedies suggested, the Pope recommends restoring "the associations or guilds of workmen, for the protection, under the guidance of religion, both of their temporal interests and of their morality."

If our ancestors, by long use and experience, felt the benefit of these guilds, our age perhaps will feel it the more by reason of the opportunity which they will give of crushing the power of the sects....For this reason, We greatly wish, for the salvation of the people, that, under the auspices and patronage of the Bishops, and at convenient times, these guilds may be generally restored.

The popes have often pointed to the benefits that accrued from the guilds, or "corporations," which were Christian workers' associations animated by the spirit of religion, the spirit of faith, and which united managers and workers in the love of their craft or trade and in the search for the greatest perfection in their work and in a more equitable division of the profits and goods between them. The corporations were grouped by trade. Each corporation had its own patron saint and its feastdays. The managers and workers were also united by a common faith. And this fostered an atmosphere of peace as well as charity and justice, whereas nowadays the unions are political instruments, veritable combat arms made to aggravate strife between the classes, and to divide workers and managers, rather than enable them to work together.

The unions are the reflection of political factions and the instruments of the parties: Communist unions, Socialist unions, Christian unions, and so on. Because of this their purpose is not the amelioration and perfection of their work. And yet both workers and managers have a stake in the vitality of their company. And so the co-operation of workers and managers is essential for the survival of their own livelihood and profession. But nowadays the unions formulate such exorbitant demands that they condemn the enterprises to failure.

This is the cause of the failure of a number of small enterprises which simply cannot meet the ever increasing demands, whether of the State or the unions. One sees the concentration of workers in enormous industrial complexes where they are like a mass. The human contact no longer exists as it did in the smaller enterprises, which were more natural, because they were situated in the villages. Whereas now thousands of workers have been concentrated in enormous factories in the industrial cities. This is one of the offspring of Socialism. And all of this is in the hands of multinational financial corporations and the big banks which are themselves, in the final analysis, in the hands of Freemasonry. We always come back to them: everything is in their hands. Everything!

The popes have always favored the restoration or continuation of the guilds; and it is necessary to try and understand what this entails. It is useful to read the works that were written at the end of the last century, around 1870, and especially those which narrate the efforts of the workers' circles of Albert de Mun and others, such as the writings of René de la Tour du Pin.[3] They understood very well what the Church was seeking.

The Church has been reproached for having lost sight of the workers and for not having taken sufficient interest in them in the last century. This accusation is entirely false and unjust. It was the Catholic elite that led the fight to re-establish a Christian social order and to ameliorate the condition of the workers. Who destroyed the guilds? It was the Revolution, because these organizations upheld religion even as they created favorable conditions for the exercise of the trades, and so helped Christianize the country. So the Revolution destroyed this edifice in order to reduce all men to the same level, to create a single mass of workers without the former hierarchy and organization that had existed within the corporations. The result was that the workers found themselves helpless before the liberal bosses. Of course they were exploited.

Little by little the Christian owners and managers attempted to re-establish the corporations. But Freemasonry reacted to prevent this, and Socialism, which had already gained an enormous influence, created politicized workers' unions. And now the Socialists pose as the savior of the working class, which is utterly untrue.

Dialectic and Class Warfare

The workers were pushed into a continual fight against their employers, and at the same time the unions instilled in them the spirit of envy, which is utterly contrary to the virtue of temperance. They were pushed to seek uniquely the enjoyment of the goods of this world, to get an ever increasing share of goods, the profits of the consumer society. This is absolutely contrary to the Christian spirit: no more limits, no more moderation. The Socialists and Communists have been quite skilled in profiting from the situation created in order to draw the greatest number possible into this permanent fight, which is in conformity with the Marxist theory

---

[3] A recommended work is the book by Xavier Vallat entitled *La croix, les lys et la peine des hommes*, which recounts the history of the French Catholic social movement.

of dialectic, which affirms that progress can only come by the war between the classes, and from the opposition of citizen to citizen, and citizens to government. Everywhere they have a chance to provoke these confrontations, they do so. But they only act this way in the Christian societies they wish to destroy.

Is the same dialectic practiced in the Communist countries? Of course not. One has only to observe the difficulty the workers encounter when they wish to organize into a union which is not in the hands of the Communist party. Communism cannot allow liberty free reign. In the USSR there are no strikes, or else they are quickly and severely suppressed. Class warfare is no longer possible, because only the government and the workers remain on the scene.[4] There are no problems: the workers have only to work, and the government, to take in the money and pay them a pittance to live on. That is all.

The Church's Social Doctrine:
The Encyclical *Rerum Novarum*

The Popes have taught what they require in several very well developed encyclicals, for example, *Rerum Novarum* by Leo XIII. There are other encyclicals on the social questions and on the benefits that accrue from the guilds. One should not hesitate to refer to them in order to have a point of comparison with the present situation and to be able to understand it.

It is interesting that the Swiss have kept this spirit of Corporatism; in 1927 or 1928 they concluded an accord between owners and workers declaring strikes illegal. This is why there are no strikes in Switzerland. At the same time, they established boards or councils, so that as soon as a problem arises, bosses, workers and representatives of the economic boards of the country meet to study and resolve the disagreement, see if it is possible to increase wages, and finally conclude an agreement. But work goes on, because halting work endangers the enterprise. For if a strike lasts a certain length of time, the competitors profit from the situ-

---

[4] "The ruling caste which constitutes the party is not only the political ruling caste, it is also the sole proprietor and employer." (Jean Madiran, *La vieillesse du monde*, "La technique de l'esclavage," part one, IV.)

ation to lure away the clients of a company paralyzed by a strike. It is absurd that the workers, by acting in such a manner, kill the very thing by which they live. From this point of view, Switzerland is really a model. It is the only country in Europe where the strike is illegal. When this is related in other countries, people answer with incredulity; they cannot believe there is a country left where strikes are prohibited. Yet Switzerland has one of the highest standards of living. This is normal.

Christian Social Order

In the December 1980 issue of *Itinéraires*[5] there was an article about a recently published work on Chile, showing the progress the country had made since the expulsion of Communism. It is the country that has made the most economic progress in the world in the last five years. The same thing happened in Portugal under Salazar, and in Spain under Franco. The living standard improved because there was order, because everyone was working, and the spirit of justice returned under Christian laws. When the Christian spirit takes hold in a society it brings with it the spirit of justice, of mutual aid, understanding and peace. The money becomes stable, and people live in peace and harmony. This is so obvious that the enemies of social justice as the Church understands the term are furious, and seek to destroy the countries that give an example contrary to their own designs.

Another example is Cuba. There people are very unhappy too, but not for the same reasons. It is because they lack everything and go hungry. Disorder reigns, and despite all this, in the Western countries Communism is always presented as the workers' party, the party of progress that defends the unfortunate. Such a representation is incredible, and the offshoot of disinformation and willful blindness. But they do not care, for above all they desire to reject and suppress the Christian spirit. The teaching of the popes on the subject is particularly enlightening.

Finally, Leo XIII proposes another remedy, the society founded under the patronage of St. Vincent de Paul:

---

[5] No. 248, a review by Louis Salleron of the book by Suzanne Labin, *Chili, le crime de résister* (Nouvelles éditions Debresse).

We cannot omit mentioning that exemplary society, named after its founder, St. Vincent, which has deserved so well of the people of the lower order. Its acts and its aims are well known.[6] This is what Pope Leo XIII says about it:

> Its whole object is to give relief to the poor and miserable. This it does with singular prudence and modesty; and the less it wishes to be seen, the better is it fitted for the exercise of Christian charity, and for the relief of suffering.

It is true that now a complex system of insurance exists which has, to a certain extent, diminished the misfortunes. But there are still so many poor, especially in the big cities, many of whom are unknown but whose poverty exists nonetheless. For these cases the Institute of the Brothers of St. Vincent de Paul would have done much good. For it helped to bring not only material relief, but also spiritual help by the many organizations it sustained to help the poor in their different needs. There will always be poor people. Our Lord said: "For the poor you have always with you" (Mt. 26:11).

Protect the Youth from the Sects

The Pope then reminds them of the dangers that threaten youth in the instruction that is given:

> In order more easily to attain what We wish, to your fidelity and watchfulness We commend in a special manner the young, as being the hope of human society. Devote the greatest part of your care to their instruction; and do not think that any precaution can be great enough in keeping them from masters and schools whence the pestilent breath of the sects is to be feared.

---

[6] Here we can cite as an example the Institute of the Brothers of St. Vincent de Paul. They were founded in 1845 by three laymen, the first of whom later received Holy Orders: Messrs. La Prévost, Myionnet and Maurice Maignen. Living the common life, these religious, who had been well instructed in the social teaching of the Church and the on-going fight against liberalism, directed halfway houses, orphanages, groups, credit unions, protective associations for apprentices, and charitable foundations. It was a magnificent work for the regeneration of Christian dignity and the improvement of the condition of workingmen.

Thus, one infers, the Pope is designating the public schools. It is a salutary warning that remains ever opportune, because one often hears parents say, that they still prefer to put their son or daughter in a public school rather than in the Catholic school.

Can this be done? It is true that in certain instances the secular schools are not very hostile to religion or the Catholic faith. Even so, it must not be forgotten that in these secular schools the children are brought up in an atmosphere where God and religion are omitted, and this is very grave. The simple exposure to this atmosphere which is fundamentally atheistic is a grave risk for the children. In the long run they are likely to become completely indifferent as to religion. They may acquire the profound impression that religion is not necessary. Who needs it? What good is it? One goes to school, gets a degree, practices a profession or trade. Religion serves no useful purpose.

The ambiance of the secular school penetrates the minds and hearts of the children. We must found, therefore, integrally Catholic schools.

Prayer for the Combatants in the Fight Against the Sects

Then, quite naturally, as he should, the Pope turns towards prayer, and finishes there:

> We well know, however, that our united labors will by no means suffice to pluck up these pernicious seeds from the Lord's field, unless the Heavenly Master of the vineyard shall mercifully help us in our endeavors. We must therefore, with great and anxious care, implore of Him the help which the greatness of the danger and of the need requires....So vehement an attack demands an equal defense—namely, that all good men should form the widest possible association of action and of prayer.

The Pope enjoins us to have recourse to prayer, for there lies our true help:

> We beseech them, therefore, with united hearts, to stand together and unmoved against the advancing force of the sects; and in mourning and supplication to stretch out their hands to God, praying that the Christian name may flourish and prosper, that

the Church may enjoy its needed liberty, that those who have gone astray may return to a right mind, that error at length may give place to truth, and vice to virtue. Let us take as our helper and intercessor the Virgin Mary, Mother of God....Let us beseech Michael, the prince of the heavenly angels, who drove out the infernal foe; and Joseph, the spouse of the Most Holy Virgin, and heavenly Patron of the Catholic Church; and the great apostles, Peter and Paul, the fathers and victorious champions of the Christian faith. By their patronage, and by perseverance in united prayer, We hope that God will mercifully and opportunely succor the human race, which is encompassed by so many dangers.

And finally, in concluding the important encyclical which summarizes all that his predecessors had said on the subject of the Masonic sects, the Pope gives his apostolic benediction.

Chapter V

THE LETTER *CUSTODI* OF POPE LEO XIII TO THE ITALIAN PEOPLE ON FREEMASONRY
(DECEMBER 8, 1892)

This document is not an encyclical, but a letter Pope Leo XIII addressed to the Italian people. The Pope expresses himself to his people with more spontaneity and vivacity of feeling than he would in a more official act addressed to the ensemble of Christendom. It is worthwhile spending a little time on this letter, for it has retained all its topicality:

> Our country has seen and suffered great evils in such a short span of time, for the faith of our fathers has been made a sign for persecutions of every sort. The satanic intent of the persecutors has been to substitute Naturalism for Christianity, the worship of reason for the worship of faith, so-called independent morality for Catholic morality, and material progress for spiritual progress. To the holy maxims and laws of the Gospel, they have opposed laws and maxims which can be called the code of revolution.

Here the Pope is surely alluding to the "rights of man."

> They have also opposed an atheistic doctrine and a vile Realism to school, science and the Christian arts.

With just sentences like these, one could write a book! The Pope sums up in a few lines all that we have seen unfold before our eyes over the last two hundred years:

> Having invaded the temple of the Lord, they have squandered the booty of the Church's goods, the greatest part of the inheritance necessary for the ministers....In this battle against the Catholic religion, what partiality and contradictions there are! They closed monasteries and convents, but they let multiply at

will Masonic lodges and sectarian dens. They proclaimed the right of association, while the legal rights which all kinds of organizations use and abuse are denied to religious societies. They proclaim freedom of religion and reserve odious intolerance and vexations precisely for the religion of the Italians—which, for that reason, should be assured respect and a special protection.

The Pope goes on:

> We do not wish to exaggerate the Masonic power by attributing to its direct and immediate action all the evils which presently preoccupy Us. However, you can clearly see its spirit in the facts which We have just recorded and in many others which We could recall. That spirit, which is the implacable enemy of Christ and of the Church, tries all ways, uses all arts, and prevails upon all means. It seizes from the Church its first-born daughter and seizes from Christ His favored nation, the seat of His Vicar on earth and the center of Catholic unity.

Having described these actions, the Pope teaches and warns:

> Remember that Christianity and Masonry are essentially irreconcilable, such that to join one is to divorce the other. You can no longer ignore such incompatibility between Catholic and Mason, beloved children: you have been warned openly by Our predecessors, and We have loudly repeated the warning.
>
> Those who, by some supreme misfortune, have given their name to one of these societies of perdition should know that they are strictly bound to separate themselves from it. Otherwise they must remain separated from Christian communion and lose their soul now and for eternity.

The Pope then enumerates the principles for conducting the offensive:

> Masonry has taken control of the public schools, leaving private schools, paternal schools, and those directed by zealous ecclesiastics and religious of both sexes to compete in the education of Christian youth. Christian parents especially should not entrust the education of their children to uncertain schools. Masonry has confiscated the inheritance of public charity; fill the void, then, with the treasure of private relief. It has placed pious works

in the hands of its followers, so you should entrust those that depend on you to Catholic institutions. It opens and maintains houses of vice, leaving you to do what is possible to open and maintain shelters and half-way houses. An anti-Christian press in religious and secular matters militates at its expense, so that your effort and money are required by the Catholic press.

The Catholic press no longer exists. I wonder where one could give his money—if he had any—to the Catholic press. There are a few journals, but there are no more Catholic newspapers. I do not know of any in Italy or France. There used to be the *Catholic France*; but what has it become? *The New Man* is very liberal; and *Avvenire*, in Italy, is horrendous. It is the most revolutionary newspaper. One wonders how bishops can finance such newspapers. *Avvenire* is perhaps even worse than *Le Monde*, because it calls itself a Catholic newspaper; yet it is empoisoned by the same spirit:

> Masonry establishes societies of mutual help and credit unions for its partisans; you should do the same not only for your brothers but for all the indigent....

> May this struggle between good and evil extend to everything, and may good prevail. Masonry holds frequent meetings to plan new ways to combat the Church, and you should hold them frequently to better agree on the means and order of defense. It multiplies its lodges, so that you should multiply Catholic clubs and parochial groups, promote charitable associations and prayer organizations, and maintain and increase the splendor of the temple of God. The sect, having nothing to fear, today shows its face to the light of day. You Italian Catholics should also make open profession of your faith and follow the example of your glorious ancestors who confessed their faith bravely before tyrants, torture, and death. What more? Does the sect try to enslave the Church and to put it at the feet of the state as a humble servant? You must then demand and claim for it the freedom and independence due it before the law. Does Masonry seek to tear apart Catholic unity, sowing discord even in the clergy itself, arousing quarrels, fomenting strife, and inciting insubordination, revolt, and schism? By tightening the sacred bond of charity and obedience, you can thwart its plans, bring to naught its efforts, and disappoint its hopes. Be all of one heart and one mind, like

the first Christians. Gathered around the See of Peter and united to your pastors, protect the supreme interests of Church and papacy, which are just as much the supreme interests of Italy and of all the Christian world.

Unfortunately, in our time those who appear subject to the papacy work against it. Those who seem subject to the bishops work against the Church.

As for us, they say that we have distanced ourselves from the See of Peter and from the Church. Yet it is we who are the best defenders of both, we who are the most ready to defend the Holy See and the bishops in so far as they are the successors of the apostles and the representatives of the Church; but not the Liberalism they profess.

Pope Leo XIII, so you see, urges us to fight.

Part Two

PONTIFICAL DOCUMENTS ON LIBERALISM

The liberal Catholics have not ceased to reply that they have a will to orthodoxy equal to that of the most intransigent, and that their only care is the interests of the Church. The compromise they seek is not theoretical and abstract, but rather practical....

There they go off into a false distinction which they call "the thesis and the hypothesis"!

...This is not a compromise of law but of fact. If their adversaries condemn them, it is because they examine their theories from the point of view of the "thesis," whereas they themselves take the point of view of the "hypothesis" (that is, according to the facts). Their point of departure is practical principle and fact they judge undeniable. This principle is that the Church cannot be understood in the concrete environment where she must accomplish her divine mission without harmonizing herself with it.

It is subtle reasoning: "The Church can never make herself heard in the concrete milieu without chiming with it." But how well? If it entails wedding the errors of the milieu, what is the Church doing there? It certainly is not preaching the faith. The theory, they say, is one thing, and they agree with us on the theory. Truth cannot compromise with error. One cannot mix light and darkness, they agree. But leave that aside, say they. Our concern is the task of the apostolate, a matter of practice. What must we do? We must know how to put ourselves on the same wave-length as others; that is to say, adopt their way of thinking and understanding. That is how one starts to mix error with truth.

The Liberal Catholic Betrays His Religion

The liberals do not have a scholastic mind. St. Thomas teaches that obviously there are principles, and they exist to be put into practice. Thus, as Fr. Berto would say, all practice can be reduced to good Thomistic principles. The principles must guide our action, by the virtue of prudence, of course, which teaches us how to proceed in order to apply the principles. But one cannot say that the principles are one thing, and that they can be dispensed with once you begin to act.

This is the case of the liberal who is a Catholic in his family life. At home, morning prayer and evening prayer are said as a family, they go to Mass on Sunday and respect the pastor. But away from home, in practicing his profession, in politics, and in public life, you will find him aligned with the Socialists and perhaps even with the Communists. He is favorable to all that the enemies of the Church propagate. Then he is no longer a Catholic. He gives his vote to any one or any party; he is in favor of divorce. But he will insist that in his family they are fervent Catholics; outside, he practically goes over to the enemy. He is in a state of perpetual contradiction, because he reasons, that the political domain has nothing to do with the Catholic sphere. The Catholic viewpoint is narrow; whereas his is broader. One must, after all, know how to get along with others, and be able to work with them.

Then, he may reason thus out of ambition, because he desires to become representative or mayor of his town. In this case, it's over. He has an entirely different attitude and a different way of looking at things. It is terrible, because he really betrays his religion.

In the book by Fr. Roussel there are several pages of an extremely interesting bibliography. Unfortunately, the books are out of print and can only be found at the used booksellers or estate sales.

Vatican II: the Triumph of Liberalism

The Church is dying from Liberalism, for ever since the Council it has been penetrated by it. The division between cardinals appeared clearly even when I was a member of the Central Preparatory Commission of the Council. It was comprised of sixty-six cardinals, about twenty archbishops and bishops and the four superior generals of the great religious orders. The Central Commission was presided over by Pope John XXIII, who visited it frequently. All the texts were centralized there. Very quickly, a division between the cardinals was manifested: there were liberal, conservative, and traditional cardinals. Such a division within the Church had never been seen before; it began when Catholic Liberalism was born in order to favor the French Revolution; churchmen wanted to come to an understanding with the Revolution, so as not to be obliged to oppose it.

The popes on the contrary condemned the Revolution and all its bad principles. But the reaction of Catholics like Lamennais, or even Montalembert and others, in France and elsewhere, was that an arrangement had to be made; the fighting could not go on forever. They desired to make a compromise between the principles of the Revolution and Catholicism. In the last analysis, they wanted to wed the Church and the Revolution. Ever since that time a fundamental breach appeared in the Church between those who remained firmly opposed to these principles, and those who wanted to accommodate them.

That this is so is attested by many. In the work *The Post-Catholic Liberal* by Prélot, which retraces the history of Liberalism, one finds a very significant passage:

> Liberalism triumphed at Vatican Council II after a century and a half of fights and condemnations (he means condemnations coming from Rome); finally, after an incessant struggle, the moment came for Liberalism to triumph. This triumph was Vatican Council II.

Here then is a clear and concise testimony, so to speak. It is laymen who make this assessment, like Henry Fesquet in *Le Monde*. All the great liberals have either said or written that, at Vatican Council II, their principles triumphed.

Why was Liberalism able to win at the Council? Because it was a "pastoral" council. Had it been a dogmatic council, the Holy Ghost would have prevented Liberalism from prevailing; but it was a pastoral council that was not intended to define truths. Popes John XXIII and Paul VI asserted this repeatedly. It is the only instance in the history of the Church that a council was "pastoral." The Church had only convened councils in order to define or make more explicit certain truths against the errors that were being spread throughout the world. What the Council Fathers could and should have condemned was Communism, for example. If at the time of the Vatican Council II there was a grave error threatening to dominate the world, it was Communism. Communism should have been studied in depth, and the Church met in council should have condemned it, along with Socialism. It would have been necessary to study the errors in depth, draft the theses, give complete descriptions, and then pronounce condemnations. Then the Council would have been eminently useful. But it was just a "pastoral" council that had no precise goal. One wanted simply to address a message to the whole world. What happened was that the liberal influence held sway, and it was the liberals who dominated the course of the Council. They were able to silence one after the other the conservative cardinals. One felt that events favored the liberals, and that Paul VI upheld them against those who wanted to maintain tradition and keep the faith.

Now that we perceive the disastrous consequences, it is important to understand Liberalism and to see the influence it exercised. From the fact of not wanting, apparently, to fix any precise objective for the Council, one ended by trying to marry error and truth, and engendered total confusion. Such confusion has arisen that people no longer know what they must believe, what they must not believe, how to distinguish virtue and vice, truth and error.

The new catechisms no longer define truth. As for morals, what is being taught, for example, concerning marriage.... Nothing is left, but complete disorder. There are other works that are very helpful in studying Liberalism, for example, the very interesting book by the Deputy Emile Keller, called *Le Syllabus, Pie IX et les Principes de '89*. Another source of information is the treatise on the Church by Cardinal Billot. In tome II of his *De Ecclesia*, "On the Relations of the Church and Civil Society," the author devoted about forty pages to the error of Liberalism. One reads there, for example:

> Liberalism taken as an error in matters of faith and religion is a varied doctrine that more or less aims at freeing man from God, His law, and revelation; and consequently destroys all dependence of civil society vis-à-vis religious society, that is, the Church, who is the guardian, interpreter and teacher of the divinely revealed law.

Cardinal Billot explains Liberalism very well, which he defines as being an incoherence. Why? Because on the one hand the liberal Catholic affirms his faith, but on the other, in action, he does not act according to the faith. He is in a state of perpetual contradiction. It is very striking.

Paul VI: a Liberal Pope

This is the case of Paul VI, who was most certainly a liberal. How many times was it said that he was a man with two-faces. Those who were acquainted with him were struck by this. He was sometimes Catholic, then sometimes very modernist and favorable towards false ecumenism and dialogue with all the religions. Always this two-sidedness, an attitude capable of destroying the Church. It was a kind of incessant dialectic, of internal struggle between Catholicism and false principles, those of Freemasonry and the revolution. The principles of Rationalism and Naturalism against the supernatural, and, ultimately, against Our Lord, have exposed the Church to a kind of incessant hammering, the Church destroying itself. Another sign of this contradictory behavior: Paul VI himself decried the "auto-demolition" of the Church which he himself had done so much to advance. It is intolerable to live in such a state of permanent contradiction; for this reason, at the end of his life, Paul VI was a tormented man. He found himself in a frightful position because on the one hand he perceived the destruction at work in the Church following the very principles he himself had favored and helped to put into operation, and he suffered from it. Yet he continued nonetheless to advance even more the principles that were destroying the Church: freedom of religions, separation of Church and State, understanding with the Communists, the Freemasons, and with all the enemies of the Church. That could only serve to destroy it. On the one hand he pushed, and on the other he was afraid because he saw that he would be responsible. He was a torn man. It was reported a few times that during the night he cried out.

This situation was the fruit of his Liberalism. If they know what they are doing, liberals cannot have a clear conscience. It is impossible. This kind of sickness of desiring to get along with the world and even with the Church's enemies, this "we have to get along, the fighting has to stop, the combat's over" is not only utopian, but it is also contrary to the path which the good God has shown us.

Continual Combat

For it was God Himself who decided that there would be a fight when He said to Satan "I will put enmities between thee and the woman, and thy seed and her seed"—this signifies the Virgin Mary and Our Lord. "Thy seed" signifies in particular Freemasonry and the sects, and in general this whole world which belongs to Satan. Between him and the Blessed Virgin Mary and her seed, that is, Our Lord Jesus Christ and His mystical body, there will be enmity, continual combat. That is why St. Augustine wrote that the two contending Cities have been in opposition from the beginning of mankind. There is a combat, and Our Lord came to fight. He triumphed by the cross, and that is the most splendid act he did. He reigned by the cross.

And the combat continues. That is why we Christians cannot suddenly proclaim that the combat is over, that we must have peace at any price with our enemies, that we will come to terms; that there is no longer any reason to fight. It is not possible, because that would be tantamount to saying that the devil is no longer, that no one is under his influence....The liberal is absolutely obsessed by the search for union, and he will not fight evil. And what happens is that the liberal destroys the forces of resistance within the Church. He seeks to compromise, as, in the nineteenth century, Lamennais did in his newspaper *L'Avenir*. He wrote:

> Many Catholics in France love liberty. (One could say as much for every country.) Let the true liberals then band together with them to demand "an entire, absolute liberty of opinion, of doctrine, of conscience and of cult" and all the civil liberties (...) without privilege and without restriction....Moreover, let the Catholics understand as well that religion "needs only one thing: freedom."[1]

What rubbish! Lamennais himself practically went beyond what the very enemies of the Church were after. But, as Fr. Roussel explains very well in the introduction to the collection of his conferences, the liberal is someone who easily scrambles all his ideas, and words are easily equivocal if not clearly defined; this is particularly the case of the word "liberty."

---

[1] *Dictionnaire de Théologie Catholique*, T. IX, col. 527.

"Liberty of Conscience," an Ambiguous Expression

The Catholic affirms and upholds two principles: the reality of man's *free will*, against the determinists, and his necessary dependence vis-à-vis God, his laws and the authorities who are established by him. Man is both free psychologically, because endowed with a spiritual soul exempt from the determinism of matter; and obliged or compelled morally, because dependent on God and his laws. (...) On the contrary, the liberal begins by confusing these notions and, thanks to the equivocations thus made possible, he does not fail to turn into absolute rights his wishes, wills, and whims. An example will make it possible to better grasp this radical opposition: The liberal, like the Catholic, preaches liberty of conscience.

Notice the ambiguity: What does the Catholic mean by liberty of conscience? That can be understood in two different ways. If one does not define it, if nothing is said, the Catholic will say that he agrees, that, of course, he too claims liberty of conscience. He goes along with the meaning of the other, who does not change his notion.

Fr. Roussel explains the signification that the Catholic attaches to the expression "liberty of conscience":

> By this the Catholic means the right of each to know, love and serve God without hindrance, the right to practice his religion, the Catholic religion, and to see that the laws of his country defend and uphold it, the right of the Church to accomplish its mission in the world: *ut destructis adversitatibus et erroribus universis, Ecclesia tua secura tibi serviat libertate.*

The last part is from a collect: We pray that, once all the errors of the whole world and all that opposes her have been destroyed, the Church may serve God with security. Then the author explains the meaning the liberal gives to the expression "liberty of conscience":

> As for the liberal, he wishes to affirm by that, the complete independence of every man with regard to religion, the freedom to believe what he likes or nothing at all; it is the right to error and apostasy, it is the right to require, moreover, that the laws of his country take into account his skepticism and his unbelief.

Behold how the liberal understands liberty of conscience: his country must accept everything, even atheism, and the laws must acknowledge the right to propagate any and all errors. The true Catholic, on the contrary, cannot mean it in this way, that would be impossible. For him, freedom of conscience means that man is free to follow, according to the dictates of his conscience, what God asks of him by the precepts of religion. The good God has given us a religion by Jesus Christ Our Lord. He founded a Church; He founded THE religion. There are not thirty-six religions, but the one true religion founded by God. So the true Catholic demands the freedom of conscience to be able to obey the commandments of God.

The liberal's position is otherwise: No orders, no constraints; each must have total freedom to do what he wants. Thus, he wants freedom, not only respecting religion and the faith, but also, of course, freedom of thought and morality: total freedom. This is what the liberal means by freedom of conscience. One must take pains, therefore, when using these words, to always define them, otherwise one runs the risk of bringing grist to the mill of our enemies, and falling into the trap that has been set for us. Do not be drawn to say, for want of prudence and from a misplaced impulse of generosity, that "We agree with you, we too desire liberty of conscience and the rights of man...." We would then be totally muddled.

Fr. Roussel points out this radical ambiguity very clearly:

> So, when the Church calls for freedom of conscience, or even better, freedom of consciences, we fail to suspect that beneath the identical formulation, a radical misunderstanding lies. The same words are used, but opposite things are meant.

It is quite typical of Liberalism, Catholic Liberalism, to accept equivocation.

"God, depart!"

Joseph de Maistre also described those who wish to chase away God in the name of liberty. In his *Essais sur les Principes Générateurs des Constitutions Politiques*, he writes:

In France especially, the philosophers' fury knew no bounds, and soon, a single tremendous voice formed from a multitude of voices resounding in unison was heard to cry to God from the midst of guilty Europe: Begone. Must we forever tremble before masters and receive from them the lessons it pleases them to give us. Truth throughout Europe is hidden by the censers' smoke. It is time for it to emerge from this fatal fog.

All that exists displeases us, because your Name is inscribed on all that exists. We want to destroy everything and remake everything without you. Leave our councils, leave our academies, leave our homes. Reason is enough for us; begone.

De Maistre here personified Liberalism perfectly, for it can be summed up in a word: "God, begone!" And so, one is stupefied to behold the ignorance of bishops, priests and many of the faithful, who do not want to recognize the reality of this fight that exists and must exist and continue: God has willed it. He does not want evil, but He permits evil for a greater good.

So important is it to grasp the concepts touched upon in this chapter, that the next is devoted to developing and describing in detail these errors, as well as the arguments necessary to true Catholics, in order to strengthen their faith, and help keep them from succumbing to the seductions of the false ideas of liberal Catholics.

Chapter VII

THE ENCYCLICAL LETTER *LIBERTAS PRAESTANTISSIMUM* OF LEO XIII ON HUMAN LIBERTY AND LIBERALISM
(JUNE 2, 1888)

The incompatibility of Masonry and Catholicism has been established, then, with the help of pontifical texts. It remains to treat of the ideas that govern the entire Masonic organization and which can be called liberal ideas. These ideas are propagated throughout the world and are more or less accepted, even by Catholics. These are the errors that the popes have denounced for more than a century and a half.

An Erroneous Mind

To understand the numerous pontifical documents condemning Liberalism, one can refer to *Liberalism and Catholicism*, by Fr. Roussel (available from Angelus Press, Kansas City, MO). It is an excellent résumé of the errors and studies on Liberalism that Fr. Roussel presented during a series of conferences given in 1926. He treats of Liberalism in general, then he deals with liberal Catholics and finally he expounds all the errors of liberal Catholicism. He describes the liberal mentality very well, its falsified intellect always in contradiction with itself, that affirms one thing and its contrary, and which remains in a state of perpetual incoherence.

From this we can better understand the situation of the Church today: an unthinkable situation that pushes certain distraught members of the faithful to say that there is no pope, that there are no more valid sacraments, nor valid Masses. This is an extreme radicalism that fails to grasp what Liberalism is. One must make more prudent judgments, precisely because liberals are not "absolutists"; they are always between error and truth, they contradict themselves and are, so to speak, hard to nail down. Obviously, they destroy truth, dogma and the faith, but they do not go so far as to accomplish absolutely invalid acts. They know their religion sufficiently well so as not to make statements that would raise an uproar against them; they manage to do things acceptable in principle, at least at the boundaries of orthodoxy and validity, although frankly bad in practice. For example, the rite of the Mass published by the printing presses of the Vatican is one thing, the actual Masses, the translations, and the particular innovations in the actual celebration are another; and it is these latter that permit one to state that often these Masses are invalid.

First Part:
WHAT IS LIBERTY?

The most important document of the magisterium on Liberalism is the encyclical *Libertas Praestantissimum* of Pope Leo XIII. The first part gives a precise definition of liberty, for this is a widely misunderstood notion:

> There are many who imagine that the Church is hostile to human liberty. Having a false and absurd notion as to what liberty is, either they pervert the very idea of freedom, or they extend it at their pleasure to many things in respect of which man cannot rightly be regarded as free.

Why is this accusation of hostility made against the Church? Because the Church upholds the law; and it is the law that guides liberty, orients it by orienting the will. The people who demand total liberty, a liberty without limits, esteem that the Church, being in favor of the decalogue and exact moral laws, is against human liberty. As if the law in and of itself went against liberty! They think that freedom is something absolute and that once it is limited it is no longer freedom. They imagine that liberty is a natural faculty that allows man to do whatever he likes.

Hence the importance of knowing exactly how to define liberty, and why God gave it to us. Liberty is a relative notion, like obedience, in fact; it is good in the measure that it seeks the good. And it is no longer liberty in the measure that it leads to evil. Liberty was not given to us for its own sake, but so that we could pursue the good in a way that is not predetermined.

Psychological and Moral Liberty

Leo XIII begins by distinguishing between psychological or natural liberty (free will) and moral liberty (the good or bad use of free will):

> It is with *moral* liberty, whether in individuals or in communities, that We proceed at once to deal. But, first of all, it will be well to speak briefly of *natural* liberty....

The distinction is made between *moral liberty*, which concerns good and bad acts, and natural liberty, also called psychological liberty, which concerns free acts, acts accomplished without being determined by an internal cause. But as soon as one adds to an act the idea of good or of evil, human liberty must be oriented. Moral liberty cannot permit everything, precisely because it weighs good and evil; it can only choose the good, because if it chose the evil, it would no longer be true liberty but license.

Liberty the Mark of Intelligence

Leo XIII begins by describing the psychological or natural liberty (or free will) of man:

> The unanimous consent and judgment of men, which is the trusty voice of nature, recognizes this natural liberty in those only who are endowed with intelligence or reason....

In fact, only spiritual beings, endowed with a mind or reason, are considered free, and not the animals, who only obey instinct.

> For, while other animate creatures follow their senses, seeking good and avoiding evil only by instinct, man has reason to guide him in each and every act of his life. Reason sees that whatever things that are held to be good upon earth may exist or may not, and discerning that none of them are of necessity for us, it leaves the will free to choose what it pleases.

That is the definition of psychological liberty. The Pope continues:

As the Catholic Church declares in the strongest terms the simplicity, spirituality, and immortality of the soul, so with unequaled constancy and publicity she ever also asserts its freedom. These truths she has always taught and has sustained them as a dogma of faith, and whensoever heretics or innovators have attacked the liberty of man, the Church has defended it and protected this noble possession from destruction....[S]he defended human liberty....At no time, and in no place, has she held truce with fatalism.

Unlike the Moslems, who teach fatalism:

Liberty, then, as We have said, belongs only to those who have the gift of reason or intelligence. Considered as to its nature, it is the faculty of choosing means fitted for the end proposed.

This is the exact definition of psychological liberty.

Moral Liberty

Now, if we consider the end, the ultimate end of man is God Himself. It was God who assigned this end to our life and existence; thus, our liberty must choose between the means that lead to this end and not to another. It is here that the question of good and evil enters in. Our freedom, unlike God's, can lead to evil because of the weakness of our understanding, which can be mistaken about the goodness of particular things. We risk choosing ones that are contrary to our end, we act thus by error because we desire an apparent good that is for us in fact evil.

Since, however, both these faculties are imperfect, it is possible, as is often seen, that the reason should propose something which is not really good, but which has the appearance of good, and that the will should choose accordingly. For, as the possibility of error, and actual error, are defects of the mind and attest its imperfection, so the pursuit of what has a false appearance of good, though a proof of our freedom, just as a disease is a proof of our vitality, implies defect in human liberty. The will also, simply because of its dependence on the reason, no sooner desires anything contrary thereto than it abuses its freedom of choice and corrupts its very essence.

Otherwise one would have to say that God had given us a faculty attached to our will that was bad, namely, the faculty to do evil! And this is impossible. He gave us a will in order to do good, and not evil, obviously:

> Thus it is that the infinitely perfect God, although supremely free, because of the supremacy of His intellect and of His essential goodness, nevertheless cannot choose evil; neither can the angels and saints, who enjoy the beatific vision.

The Capacity to Do Evil a Defect of Our Liberty

If the power to do good and evil were a good, a perfection, we would have the impression of being able to do more than if we could only choose to do good: we would be able to choose evil as well. At first sight, this would seem like a more extensive power. Not so! For if it were a perfection, it would also be a perfection in God who, therefore, could also do evil! Though God is sovereignly free, He possesses freedom to an infinite degree, and yet He cannot do evil. The same holds for the blessed, angels or men.

Yet prior to their trial, the angels were able to commit moral evil, they could sin. When God presented them with something new, either their eventual elevation to the beatific vision or, as some say, having revealed to them the mystery of the Incarnation, God's will to become man, then certain angels rebelled. They refused the possibility of needing to have anything beyond what they already possessed by nature, or else, being pure spirits, they rejected the prospect of being obliged to adore a God-Man, composed of matter, Our Lord Jesus Christ.

Thus, for angels as well as for men, the power to commit evil is not a perfection! This is exactly what St. Augustine pointed out in the controversy with the Pelagians (cited by Pope Leo XIII):

> If the possibility of deflection from good belonged to the essence or perfection of liberty, then God, Jesus Christ, and the angels and saints, who have not this power, would have no liberty at all, or would have less liberty than man has in his state of pilgrimage and imperfection.

That God, the angels and the elect could be less free and less perfect than men is obviously unthinkable. Moreover, it suffices to reflect a bit: To choose evil can only be a defect. Let's compare it to sickness. Which is more perfect: to be able to be sick or to not be able to be sick? If being able to be sick is better than not being able to, then what of the elect, who cannot be sick, whereas men on earth can "choose" between health and sickness. It is thus that one could be more perfect on earth than in heaven! Ridiculous.

To be able to choose evil is a defect, and can only be a defect: one chooses, essentially, one's own destruction; one commits suicide. To seek what is sin is to seek one's own imperfection, that is, non-being. How could God possibly seek his own harm? It is impossible; He would no longer be God. How could the angels and elect, who possess perfect happiness in a state of absolute perfection, destroy themselves by choosing evil? It is impossible.

It is necessary to fix firmly in mind the idea that the power to do evil is a defect of human liberty, a flaw of freedom. This is what condemns Liberalism: For the liberals think, precisely, that we are free, thus we can do good and evil; and if we cannot do evil, then we are no longer free! Such is their argument. And these are the principles that are currently governing our so-called liberal societies: Man is free, he must be able to exercise his liberty to do everything he wants.

What Limits?

Nonetheless there must be a certain limit to this freedom in civil life, otherwise the consequences will be very grave, people will kill, set fires. So they add that there is freedom "within the limits of public order," which can be broadly understood depending on the government. There is, for example, all that is not contrary to public order: unavowed faults like homosexuality, divorce, which nonetheless is against family life, and the natural and moral order. But since that does not bother anyone, it should be free. Behold the current thinking in society. They affirm that that does not disturb public order, yet how can so many crimes be explained, the fact that the crime statistics increase year after year, and that the criminals are younger and younger, seventeen and even fifteen years old. It is because the family has been destroyed: these young people have no family, the parents are divorced or remarried, they have abandoned the children; it is a state of total disorder. These children have no morality, they have seen evil at home; they have no notion of anything.

It must be understood that even to maintain public order, the moral order must be upheld; one must not be permitted to say that if one is not free to do evil then one is not free. Our liberty does not include evil. For that, God will punish us. Now, if the essence of our liberty were to be able to do evil as well as good, then we should not be punished! Yet God will punish us in the measure that we have used this God-given faculty for doing evil. Our merit is to be able freely to choose between means. For example, some young men have chosen to be seminarians and become priests, whereas they could have chosen to marry or to remain celibate, or to practice a profession. They have chosen between goods, and their act is meritorious; they had freedom at their disposition for this, and not for being able to choose between good and evil.

The false principles of Liberalism are thus reduced to nothing. Their great principle is that man is free; whence the freedom of religion: anyone can choose whatever religion he wants. There is neither error nor truth, and one can without limit choose one or the other. This principle applies equally to virtue and vice. The consequence is that the laws become more and more permissive, in accordance with this false definition of freedom, which must be attacked at the root, as Pope Leo XIII has done.

The liberals stop short at the power to choose between the means that are placed at our disposition in life without considering the right end. The Pope, as does true philosophy, gives as the rule "to choose between means that lead not only to what one proposes, but to the right end."

Liberty: Our Faculty to Choose the Means While Respecting the True Order of Ends

Our choice must be delimited by the end. And the ultimate end, beyond our particular purposes, was forever fixed for us by God: the final end of our life is the glory of God and the salvation of our souls. We have no right to use our freedom to stray from this end. We are free for a fixed end, and to choose between the means that lead us there. Do you wish to go to Rome? You have the right to choose between the different routes that lead to Rome, your final destination, but if in the midst of the journey you should decide to change trains and head to Amsterdam, you no longer have the same final destination, the fixed end.

The morality of our acts is constituted by the fact of being oriented towards our final end. And the laws that have been given to us, the ten commandments, are like the wayside signs that indicate the route that leads to the end. It follows that the law is not made to limit our freedom, but to guide it; it is possible to choose the right way thanks to the laws, because they show us how to arrive at our end.

This is what the liberals refuse to recognize: for them, if the goal is fixed one is no longer free. Yet one must know what one wants: either to come to misfortune and eternal punishment; or else to attain the happiness that God has prepared for us if we use our liberty according to His will, the will that He placed in us, that is inscribed in our nature. Hence the importance of the encyclical *Libertas*, perhaps the only one in which the Pope has been determined to define liberty with entire precision, so as to refute all the errors of Liberalism. Further on he says:

> The real perfection of all creatures is found in the prosecution and attainment of their respective ends; but the supreme end to which human liberty must aspire is God.

These are things that people do not want to understand. All those who speak in favor of freedom are given audience; but those who speak of delimiting liberty are rebuffed. Liberty is a kind of mirage. All the electoral campaigns are made in its name; and people refuse to admit that the liberty to do evil leads to the ruin of society. One forgets why the good God gave us this power attached to the understanding and the will. It is because the reason can know the good and compare the means to reach the end to be attained, and having made the choice, to propose to the will to act in a way according to the principles of reason and faith.

Law: A Precious Help to Our Liberty

And what helps us to use our liberty well? The law does. Pope Leo XIII explains:

First of all, there must be *law*; that is, a fixed rule of teaching what is to be done and what is to be left undone. This rule cannot affect the lower animals in any true sense, since they act of necessity, following their natural instinct, and cannot of themselves act in any other way.

It can be said that in a certain way, analogously, the animals also have laws; but this refers to their instincts, which they follow blindly. They do not reflect, they are guided. Even the vegetable kingdom has its laws, those of germination, growth, flowering and reproduction. That is because the good God created the plants for a fixed end, as he did the animals. He gave them laws inscribed in their nature which they follow perfectly. A plant will never turn away from its law, unless it is impeded by an unnatural occurrence, for the seed is meant to germinate, and the sprout to grow.

But as for men, the good Lord who created them, endowed them with understanding so that they could know their own law, which leads to the end, and which, with supernatural grace, guides them to eternal happiness. We shall attain this happiness in the measure that we apply our minds and wills to this law. It is after all incredible that those who possess intelligence, and thus knowledge of the law that governs them, should nonetheless do evil. On the contrary, they should follow this law with more perfection than the plants and animals do theirs. The good God has given us understanding in order to voluntarily put to work the powers he has placed in us, in order to attain the end prescribed for us. And shall we refuse to attain this end?

At first sight, it would seem inconceivable that man should sin; unfortunately, given his constitution and his effectively limited and imperfect knowledge, it is possible for him to become attached to apparent goods that, in fact, lead to death. The object of sin is a false good, a disordered good that is not directed to the end.

Right Reason Is Ordered to the End

For example, drink is good in so far as it is necessary for health, but someone who seeks to become drunk is acting in a disordered manner, he is heading for suicide. He no longer follows the law. It is the same for all the goods to which we become attached in a disordered way: they are all good, but only to a degree, and thus good only in so far as they lead us to the end, which has been established by God.

Hence, everyone needs the law, which is summed up in the law of love: love God and one's neighbor. Someone who ruins his health by drink, for example, harms his own family; he fails to love his family.

What, then, is the definition of the law? Pope Leo XIII gives a definition:

> The reason prescribes to the will what it should seek after or shun, in order to the eventual attainment of man's last end, for the sake of which all his actions ought to be performed. This ordination of *reason* is called law.

It is the road sign on the route that we must follow. It is also what justifies the law. It makes it possible to distinguish between good and bad laws, those that direct our reason well and those that do not. A bad law is not a law: it is no longer an *ordinatio rationis*, because it goes against reason. One must disobey it. We read:

> In man's free will, therefore, or in the moral necessity of our voluntary acts being in accordance with reason, lies the very root of the necessity of law. Nothing more foolish can be uttered or conceived than the notion that, because man is free by nature, he is therefore exempt from law. Were this the case, it would follow that to become free we must be deprived of reason; whereas the truth is that we are bound to submit to law precisely because we are free by our very nature. For, law is the guide of man's actions; it turns him towards good by its rewards, and deters him from evil by its punishments.

Eternal Law, Natural Law, Human Law

In this first part of the encyclical, the Pope applies himself to explain the reason for the law in relation to freedom. It is then that the distinction appears between the eternal law, the natural law, and human law. The natural law is that:

> ...which is written and engraved in the mind of every man; and this is nothing but our reason, commanding us to do right and forbidding sin.

And human law is nothing else but the application of the natural law to society by the authorities. The Pope adds:

> Just as civil society did not create human nature, so neither can it be said to be the author of the good which befits human nature, or of the evil which is contrary to it. Laws come before men live together in society, and have their origin in the natural, and consequently in the eternal, law.

So the natural law depends intimately upon the eternal law, the law that is in God, the supreme legislator:

> It follows, therefore, that the law of nature is the same thing as the *eternal law*, implanted in rational creatures, and inclining them *to their right action and end*; and can be nothing else but the eternal reason of God, the Creator and Ruler of all the world.

The Necessity of Human Law

These considerations are very important, because they establish the necessity of our obedience to law. The law isn't arbitrary;[1] it must always correspond to the superior law, and, consequently, to the eternal law. Human laws, ecclesiastical laws as well as those of the civil authority, must be in conformity with the law of the Creator who made nature itself. This is what must guide our obedience:

> For, what reason and the natural law do for individuals, that *human law*, promulgated for their good, does for the citizens of States.

But there are some enactments of the civil authority:

> ...which do not follow directly but somewhat remotely, from the natural law, and decide many points which the law of nature treats only in a general and indefinite way. For instance, though nature commands all to contribute to the public peace and prosperity, whatever belongs to the manner and circumstances, and

---

[1] Even the eternal law is not the decree of an arbitrary and obscure will, but the work of divine wisdom; the natural law isn't arbitrary, since it corresponds to the good of our nature; neither is human law, as it must be in conformity with the natural law.

conditions under which such service is to be rendered must be determined by the wisdom of men and not by nature itself.

Hence there is a wide domain that must be specified by the authorities, whence the need of a civil code of law, as there is the code of canon law in the Church, which must always be in relation to the fundamental law, which is at once both the natural law and the eternal law. Human law can never prescribe things contrary to the eternal law:

> Therefore, the true liberty of human society does not consist in every man doing what he pleases, for this would simply end in turmoil and confusion, and bring on the overthrow of the State; but rather in this, that through the injunctions of the civil law all may more easily conform to the prescriptions of the eternal law.

Memorize this magnificent definition of moral liberty in society, what civil liberty consists in, and notice the necessary relation between civil law and the eternal law:

> ...The liberty of those who are in authority does not consist in the power to lay unreasonable and capricious commands upon their subjects, which would equally be criminal and would lead to the ruin of the commonwealth; but the binding force of human laws is in this, that they are to be regarded as applications of the eternal law, and incapable of sanctioning anything which is not contained in the eternal law.

This is what makes the force of civil laws:

> If, then, by anyone in authority, something be sanctioned out of conformity with the principles of right reason, and consequently hurtful to the commonwealth, such an enactment can have no binding force of law.

It would not even be a law!

Bad Laws

Consider the current laws concerning divorce, abortion—these laws that destroy marriage and the family. They cannot compel; one must disobey them.

The same thing applies to ecclesiastic laws: if they command things contrary to the good of the Church and the salvation of souls, they are no longer laws, and we cannot submit to them. The same thing pertains with the current reforms: their effects are baneful, yet it was foreseeable because they were contrary to the tradition, to all that had previously been done in the Church. Was it necessary to believe that our predecessors had been wrong for twenty centuries? Impossible! Their laws sanctified souls; how is it possible to make new laws that are the opposite?

It used to be, for example, that a marriage between a Catholic and a Protestant was not permitted unless the two spouses signed an agreement stating that they promised to have the children baptized and brought up in the Catholic religion. Now this is no longer required.[2] Here is something unthinkable and contrary to the Faith: it concerns the salvation of the souls of children! It is inconceivable that the Church could decree such laws in the so-called spirit of ecumenism. One does not barter the Catholic Faith to please Protestants. There have been, clearly, bad legislators in the Church who have caused immense damage.

How, for example, could the *imprimatur* have been accorded to the new catechisms? This is another effect of bad laws. For no one has the right to give children bad instruction such as is found in these modernist manuals, that denature the true religion, call into question the virginity of the Blessed Virgin, and omit original sin. How should we submit to laws and obligations so contrary to the good of society, the Church and souls?

Let's continue the reading:

> If, then, by anyone in authority (the Pope does not limit the statement to the civil authorities only), something be sanctioned out of conformity with the principles of right reason, and consequently hurtful to the commonwealth, such an enactment can have no binding force of law, as being no rule of justice, but certain to lead men away from that good which is the very end of civil society.

The Church was instituted for the salvation of souls. This is the first law. Any law contrary to it is null and void.

---

[2] 1917 Code of Canon Law, canon 1061-1062; New Code of Canon Law (1983), canons 1124-1125.

True Liberty Postulates Law

Therefore, the nature of human liberty, however it be considered, whether in individuals or in society, whether in those who command or in those who obey, supposes the necessity of obedience to some supreme and eternal law, which is no other than the authority of God, commanding good and forbidding evil. And, so far from this most just authority of God over men diminishing, or even destroying their liberty, it protects and perfects it, for the real perfection of all creatures is found in the prosecution and attainment of their respective ends; (It bears repeating: We possess freedom in order to choose between means that are ordered to the true end); but the supreme end to which human liberty must aspire is God.

We have no right to do anything that leads us away from God; should we do so, we would not be exercising our freedom, we would be abandoning ourselves to license. It is necessary to grasp the distinction: license permits itself anything, it means to do as one pleases. Liberty, on the contrary, is the power to act in the order of the good. This is what the Church has always taught, as Pope Leo XIII reminds us:

These precepts of the truest and highest teaching, made known to us by the light of reason itself, the Church, instructed by the example and doctrine of her divine Author, has ever propagated and asserted; for she has ever made them the measure of her office and of her teaching to the Christian nations.

The New Law of the Gospel

Leo XIII does not fail to mention the superiority of the new law promulgated in the Gospel by Our Lord:

As to morals, the laws of the Gospel not only immeasurably surpass the wisdom of the heathen, but are an invitation and an introduction to a state of holiness unknown to the ancients; and, bringing man nearer to God, they make him at once the possessor of a more perfect liberty.

The Pope then chooses a beautiful example of the true liberation ushered in by the law of the Gospel: the gradual abolition of slavery, not by violent revolution, but by the true fraternity of men in Jesus Christ:

> Thus the powerful influence of the Church has ever been manifested in the custody and protection of the civil and political liberty of the people. The enumeration of its merits in this respect does not belong to our present purpose. It is sufficient to recall the fact that slavery, that old reproach of the heathen nations, was mainly abolished by the beneficent efforts of the Church.

There are those who have taught that slavery had not been suppressed thanks to the Church, but only in the 18th century thanks to the revolutionary principle of Liberalism. The truth is that, while the Church could not at once alter the organization of society as it was at the time of the conversion of Constantine, which, unfortunately, had its customs; nonetheless, bit by bit, by its influence the Church delivered men from these inhuman bonds.

For example, in Africa, the custom of buying women exists. Upon first arriving in the country, one is indignant: what a disgrace! But to change things is not so simple. The bishops of Cameroon tried to react against this incredible traffic, by eliciting from Christians, and especially from the catechists, the promise to set a good example; that is, that they marry or marry their sons without paying money to obtain the wife. What happened? The women were so accustomed to being bought, they had such an ingrained feeling that the more one paid the more they were worth and esteemed, that they thought that if their husbands had not paid anything for them, there was no real bond between them. They felt that they were not held in esteem by their husbands, and so at the first quarrel they could leave! The result: the marriages did not endure. The bishops had wanted to do the right thing, but it turned against marriage itself! Such interminable discussions followed. One has to know not to go too fast. In fact, the only thing that can change mentalities is conversion; several centuries of Christianity are necessary.

If one asks why the Church did not suppress slavery from the time of Constantine, it is necessary to realize what would have happened to the slaves, suddenly deprived of their master, who gave them a wife, food, and afforded them a roof and clothing.

They would have been completely lost. Where would they have gone? Many would have returned to their masters! Of course, they worked, they were not free to come and go as they pleased, nor dispose of their own persons; they were absolutely attached to the house, serfs. But to change that, it was necessary to act very gradually, prepare minds, and refrain from giving slaves their freedom until they could exercise it legitimately for their good.

Returning to the consideration of good and bad law, the Pope explains that:

> Moreover, the highest duty is to respect authority, and obediently to submit to just law;...But where the power to command is wanting, or where a law is enacted contrary to reason, or to the eternal law, or to some ordinance of God, obedience is unlawful, lest, while obeying man, we become disobedient to God. Thus, an effectual barrier being opposed to tyranny, the authority in the State will not have all its own way, but the interests and rights of all will be safe-guarded—the rights of individuals, of domestic society, and of all the members of the commonwealth; all being free to live according to law and right reason; and in this, as We have shown, true liberty really consists.

Having thus clearly shown the relationship of law to liberty, Leo XIII can conclude:

> If when men discuss the question of liberty they were careful to grasp its true and legitimate meaning, such as reason and reasoning have just explained, they would never venture to affix such a calumny on the Church as to assert that she is the foe of individual and public liberty.

Second Part: Liberalism

Naturalists and Rationalists, Abettors of Liberalism

The second part of the encyclical on Liberalism now begins; absolute Liberalism and its principles are presented:

> Many there are who follow in the footsteps of Lucifer, and adopt as their own his rebellious cry, "I will not serve"; and conse-

quently substitute for true liberty what is sheer and most foolish license. Such, for instance, are the men belonging to that widely spread and powerful organization, who, usurping the name of liberty, style themselves *liberals*.

This is indeed the definition of Liberalism:

> What *naturalists* or *rationalists* aim at in philosophy, that the supporters of *Liberalism*, carrying out the principles laid down by naturalism, are attempting in the domain of morality and politics.

In the encyclicals on Freemasonry, as we saw, the popes denounced the grave errors of Naturalism and Rationalism. The liberals, thus, are the "partisans" of these errors in the civil and moral orders.

What is the chief principle of the rationalists? The sovereign dominion of human reason! Ultimately, man makes himself god, he only obeys his own reason, he only obeys himself:

> The fundamental doctrine of *Rationalism* is the supremacy of the human reason, which, refusing due submission to the divine and eternal reason, proclaims its own independence, and constitutes itself the supreme principle and source and judge of truth. Hence, these followers of Liberalism deny the existence of any divine authority to which obedience is due.

Duty Precedes Rights

Further on, the Pope says that there are different kinds of liberals, that all are not as radical in their way of thinking, but the root vice of Liberalism is nonetheless present: the denial of authority. It is the same principle underlying the rights of man: there are rights, but no duties, because whoever says duty says obligation, and thus authority, and thus a point of reference above oneself.

Who gives us these duties? Who will judge if we fulfill them? Who will punish us if we neglect them? Obviously, a superior authority! There is the authority of the father of a family, a head of state, the head of the Church; but to what do these authorities report if not to the authority of God? Thus, as soon as one speaks of duties, one is led to God. That is why it is necessary to speak of the decalogue, of the law of God. To preach duty is to exhort the practice of virtue and responsibility. When everyone fulfills his duty, the rights of others will be respected.

The father of a family has the duty to rear his children according to the Christian religion; he guarantees by that fact the rights the children have to a Christian education. And so on: the industrial magnate, if he fulfills his duties, will respect the right of his employees to a just wage; but these also have the duty to do the work that is justly required of them.

Duty precedes rights: it is very important to retain this adage. We are born with duties, and we have rights in order to be able to accomplish them. We are born with the duty to adore God, and that is why no one has the right to keep us from doing so. In the same way, the father of a family has the duty to bring up his children, to feed and shelter them, and it is for this reason that he has rights, for example, the right to a certain amount of private property, and the right to be able to earn by his labor what is necessary to be able to rear them. Let us retain the principle that it is duty that is the basis of rights, and not the inverse, as the rationalists and liberals, for whom man is born with rights, dare to assert.

Democratic Ideology and Moral Positivism

If authority is no longer recognized, necessary consequences ensue. Morality is no longer possible, or else it is replaced by "independent" morality, from which, Leo XIII writes:

> arises that ethical system which they style *independent* morality, and which, under the guise of liberty, exonerates man from any obedience to the commands of God, and substitutes a boundless license.

This is what is called today permissive morality—do as you please. The origin of this laxism is contained in this, that, because it does not come from God, authority is seated in individuals, in the people; it is the law of the greater number, that is, democracy, the ideology that holds that number confers authority. Of course, persons can designate the subject of authority, but it cannot be said that they **give** authority. But the democratic ideology, the Pope explains, claims that:

> the efficient cause of the unity of civil society is not to be sought in any principle external to man, or superior to him, but simply in the free will of individuals; that the authority in the State comes from the people only; and that, just as every man's individual reason is his only rule of life, so the collective reason of the community should be the supreme guide in the management of all public affairs. Hence the doctrine of the supremacy of the greater number, and that all right and all duty reside in the majority.

Thus God, supreme lawgiver, is replaced. It is no longer He who creates duty and right; it is the people or their representatives. They can do whatever they will, because they are the unique source of rights and duties:

> But, from what has been said, it is clear that all this is in contradiction to reason. To refuse any bond of union between man and civil society, on the one hand, and God the Creator and consequently the supreme Law-giver, on the other, is plainly repugnant to the nature, not only of man, but of all created things.

From these abominable principles, by which men forge their own society, Leo XIII draws some of the consequences:

> A doctrine of such character is most hurtful both to individuals and to the State. For, once ascribe to human reason the only authority to decide what is true and what is good, and the real distinction between good and evil is destroyed; honor and dishonor differ not in their nature, but in the opinion and judgment of each one; pleasure is the measure of what is lawful; and, given a code of morality which can have little or no power to restrain or quiet the unruly propensities of man, a way is naturally opened to universal corruption. With reference also to public affairs: authority is severed from the true and natural principle whence it derives all its efficacy for the common good; and the law determining what it is right to do and avoid doing is at the mercy of a majority. Now, this is simply a road leading straight to tyranny. The empire of God over man and civil society once repudiated,

it follows that religion, as a public institution, can have no claim to exist.

Permissive morality, independent morality, positive law, majority rule. All this flows from the democratic ideology, and results in a secular, atheistic society that Leo XIII describes:

> It follows that religion, as a public institution can have no claim to exist, and that everything that belongs to religion will be treated with complete indifference. Furthermore, with ambitious designs on sovereignty, tumult and sedition will be common amongst the people; and when duty and conscience cease to appeal to them, there will be nothing to hold them back but force, which of itself alone is powerless to keep their covetousness in check.

Society's Self-Destruction

Perhaps it will become necessary to assign two policemen to escort every citizen, one to keep him from being killed, and the other to keep him from killing. One is obliged in our day to increase the number of policemen, and this is because morality no longer guides people; because they lack interior discipline, it is necessary to keep them, by an exterior force, from doing whatever they like. This becomes intolerable, and we see police states emerge. For, as the Pope says, force alone is a weak check on the popular passions:

> Of this we have almost daily evidence in the conflict with *socialists* and members of other seditious societies, who labor unceasingly to bring about revolution. It is for those, then, who are capable of forming a just estimate of things to decide whether such doctrines promote that true liberty which alone is worthy of man, or rather pervert and destroy it.

Leo XIII foresaw Communism with its methods of enslaving the masses. What prepares the way is sedition and civil strife. People are now accustomed to this kind of disorder. One day, when things return to normal, future generations will discover the absurdity of our epoch.

The Encyclical Letter *Libertas Praestantissimum* of Leo XIII 151

Let's take the example of vacations. A few years ago,[3] everyone flocked to Spain; bombs went off and everyone went to Italy. But there, cars or suitcases were stolen. The crowd settled upon Portugal, but it became socialist, and nothing went well. Now people seem to be coming to France which, for the moment, is quiet, perhaps because the death penalty[4] makes people hesitate to commit too many crimes. One observes that people are afraid to go to one place or the other. But no one seeks the cause, which is quite simple: there is no code of morality.

Even Switzerland experiences these manifestations. Then the experts study the "profound motives" of these youths; one doesn't want the police to brutalize them. They forget quite simply that these young people have no code of morality, that no one taught them the catechism, that they were allowed to do whatever they felt like. There are even bureaus where the children can go to complain about their parents, and the parents may even be prosecuted by them.

Society has been overthrown: authority is no longer possible. Young people burn cars, break store windows and pillage, wound police and passers-by; others commit suicide. What a beautiful society, a liberal society.

Even Catholics seem not to know what to do. Yet it is simple: return to the religion of all ages, to tradition, to the ten commandments, and stop talking all the time about rights!

Mitigated Liberalism: First Category, Refusal of the Supernatural Order

After having exposed the doctrine of absolute Liberalism and its consequences, the Pope exposes mitigated Liberalism and its various degrees:

> There are, indeed, some adherents of Liberalism who do not subscribe to these opinions, which we have seen to be fearful in their enormity, openly opposed to the truth, and the cause of most terrible evils. Indeed, very many amongst them, compelled

---

[3] Recall that Archbishop Lefebvre gave this course in 1980; he is describing the events of those years.
[4] This was abolished by the Socialists in France in 1981.

by the force of truth, do not hesitate to admit that such liberty is vicious, nay, is simple license, whenever intemperate in its claims, to the neglect of truth and justice; and therefore they would have liberty ruled and directed by right reason, and consequently subject to the natural law and to the divine eternal law. But here they think they may stop, holding that man as a free being is bound by no law of God except such as He makes known to us through our natural reason.

They reject, then, all that is not merely natural, that is, all the supernatural, the Church, all that Our Lord gave us. For the liberals, none of that exists, and, points out the Pope, "In this they are plainly inconsistent." They want to grant the necessity of submitting to the natural law and the decalogue, but not to the Church! not to the precepts of the Church! not to revelation! This is absurd, because if one must obey God to a certain degree, one must obey Him completely:

> Man must, therefore, take his standard of a loyal and religious life from the eternal law; and from all and every one of those laws which God, in His infinite wisdom and power, has been pleased to enact. And the more so because laws of this kind have the same origin, the same author.

It is impossible to see why, in fact, we should make a distinction between laws we obey and those we do not.

Second Category: The Partisans of the Separation of Church and State

Here is another category of mitigated liberals:

> There are others, somewhat more moderate though not more consistent, who affirm that the morality of individuals is to be guided by the divine law (in the family, for instance), but not the morality of the State....

So, families should be subject to the law of God, but not States!

> In public affairs the commands of God may be passed over, and may be entirely disregarded in the framing of laws. Hence

follows the fatal theory of the need of separation between Church and State. But the absurdity of such a position is manifest.

It is, unfortunately, a widespread opinion even among Catholics that the State has no business meddling in religion, that it should let every man free to choose his own, that the State has no interest in spiritual matters, because its role is uniquely temporal. This is not the opinion of Leo XIII:

> Nature herself proclaims the necessity of the State providing means and opportunities whereby the community may be enabled to live properly, that is to say, according to the laws of God. For, since God is the source of all goodness and justice, it is absolutely ridiculous that the State should pay no attention to these laws or render them abortive by contrary enactments. Besides, those who are in authority owe it to the commonwealth not only to provide for its external well-being and the conveniences of life, but still more to consult the welfare of men's souls in the wisdom of their legislation.

It is also the duty of those who rule to protect and uphold the faith of their subjects. Heretics were once prosecuted because the rulers deemed that by propagating their innovations, the heretics sowed the seeds of discord and strife in society and in the State. Today everywhere freedom is given, for example, to the Protestants to spread their errors by means of the sects; we suffer the consequences. It is certain that had the Church, with the help of the States, been able to nip Protestantism in the bud in the 16th century, things would be very different today. For it is Protestantism that ushered in Liberalism and all its false principles that have corrupted society and now are destroying the Church.

According to Leo XIII, the States are obligated to intervene in order to assure that the spiritual welfare of their subjects is fostered:

> And, what is still more important, and what We have more than once pointed out, although the civil authority has not the same proximate end as the spiritual, nor proceeds on the same lines, nevertheless in the exercise of their separate powers they must occasionally meet. For their subjects are the same, and not infrequently they deal with the same objects, though in differ-

ent ways. Whenever this occurs, since a state of conflict is absurd and manifestly repugnant to the most wise ordinance of God, there must necessarily exist some order or mode of procedure to remove the occasions of difference and contention, and to secure harmony in all things. This harmony has been not inaptly compared to that which exists between the body and the soul (thus, the union between the State and the Church) for the well-being of both one and the other, the separation of which brings irremediable harm to the body, since it extinguishes its very life.

Vatican II, Instigator of the Ruin of Good Concordats

These words of Leo XIII absolutely condemned ahead of time what was said the day of cloture of the Vatican Council II, the 8th of December, 1965, in the name of Pope Paul VI, by Cardinal Liénart, who read the first "message" addressed to rulers:

> In your earthly and temporal city, God constructs mysteriously His spiritual and eternal city, His Church. And what does this Church ask of you after close to 2,000 years of experiences of all kinds in her relations with you, the powers of the earth? What does the Church ask of you today? She tells you in one of the major documents of this council (the one on religious liberty). She asks of you only liberty.

This is not what Leo XIII demands! No, liberty alone is not enough, there must be a compact, a union between the two powers.

As for Cardinal Liénart, he continues:

> She asks of you only liberty, the liberty to believe and to preach her faith, the freedom to love her God and serve Him, the freedom to live and to bring to men her message of life. Do not fear her.

This position is false and inadequate: the State should help the Church. Otherwise, it might divest itself of all interest in the Church's affairs, maintenance of buildings, compensation of priests. If from one day to the next the government were to say that henceforth it would cut off all payments to the Church, in what state would the Church find itself? Some say that it is better to be in a state of freedom as in France, where the priests are not paid by the government. Yes, but one has to see the real poverty in which priests often live. In very many countries, tax-exemption is granted to religious groups: if the Church had to pay, that would represent enormous sums.

The situation in Germany is peculiar: the priests are not paid by the government, but by the bishops; even so, all the Germans pay to the State a "worship tax," and must declare their religion. A part of this revenue in proportion to the number of declared Catholics is paid to the bishoprics, and with this the bishops remunerate the priests. That is why in Germany, as well as in certain Swiss cantons which have the same system, the clergy is not poor; the diocesan offices resemble ministries with a sizable administration. That is why the German Church can help South America and send funds for the missions everywhere.

It can even happen that the priests have too much money (good salaries, tax exemption, gifts, mass stipends...) and it certainly isn't good for a priest to be too rich. There is no danger of that happening in France, where they receive no aid whatsoever from the State, and where the bishop can only remunerate them by giving a part of the tithes. In the little dioceses, this means poverty. I remember the diocese of Tulle[5] where the people were not rich and where the collection produced very little: one could only give very little to the priests, but they bore their poverty with courage and great virtue. Even the special collections brought very little! It was true misery.

This allows the French priests to take an independent stance. The traditionalist priests can take advantage of it, as they are supported neither by the State nor the bishops, but by the faithful, while in Germany or Switzerland, as soon as they leave the rectory they lose all their income, and the faithful, accustomed to paying the "worship tax" are not accustomed to supporting their priests. Hence they give proportionately less than the faithful in France. It is sad to say, but the material question always plays a role in life. It requires a great deal of courage to be able to bear to live in poverty. It is approximately the same situation in Italy, where the priests are paid by the State; the day they leave their parish in order to join

---

[5] Archbishop Lefebvre was the Archbishop-Bishop of Tulle for several months in 1962.

a traditionalist group, they know that they next day they will be without an income.

So, there are certain inconveniences in relying upon the State for a living, but that is nonetheless the normal state of affairs![6]

This is why Leo XIII expresses the meetness of the union of Church and State, which can be regulated by concordat. What is abnormal is their separation. It is like the union of the soul and the body, or the union of spouses: they often quarrel, but must one therefore conclude that it would be normal for them to separate in order to avoid quarrels? One falls into the absurd. It is scarcely a good reason to clamor for this separation just because some difficulties arise, as was done in the name of Vatican Council II. At the request of the Church itself, excellent concordats were suppressed. We will suffer the consequences.

For Leo XIII, then, the States must not be indifferent to the spiritual welfare of their citizens; by means of material aid, they must help religion to endure and to develop. As to which religion they must help, the Pope specifies it.

Third Part:
THE MODERN LIBERTIES

First Liberty: Freedom of Worship

In the third part of his encyclical, Leo XIII exposes the different kinds of freedoms that are vaunted nowadays as the conquests of our era:

> To make this more evident, the growth of liberty ascribed to our age must be considered apart in its various details.

The first is the freedom of religions:

> Let us examine that liberty in individuals which is opposed to the virtue of religion, namely, the liberty of worship, as it is

---

[6] Formerly, the priests had a living thanks to the revenues from ecclesiastic benefices, as the Church had the right to own property in her own name without the authorization of the State. And this is the just state of affairs. But as a consequence of the Revolution or the Masonic despoliation of Church property, the clergy was reduced to a state of public beggary, save where a concordat regulated with the State the subvention of the clergy.

called. This is based on the principle that every man is free to profess as he may choose any religion or none.

This is the erroneous principle of Religious Indifferentism. It denies either the obligation to worship God, or else that one religion must be preferred to another. The Pope refuses this error:

> But, assuredly, of all the duties which man has to fulfill, that, without doubt, is the chiefest and holiest which commands him to worship God with devotion and piety.... [R]eligion ... rules and tempers all virtues. And if it be asked which of the many conflicting religions it is necessary to adopt, reason and the natural law unhesitatingly tell us to practice that one which God enjoins, and which men can easily recognize by certain exterior notes, whereby Divine Providence has willed that it should be distinguished.

Sanctity, Mark of the Divinity of the Church

Among the four marks or notes by which the Catholic Church is recognizable as the one true religion, the most evident sign of the divinity of the Catholic Church is holiness. That is why in the measure that holiness disappears, the proof of the divinity of the Church fades. The clergy and the virtue of celibacy of the priests and religious congregations are what chiefly manifest this holiness. Without that, it is difficult to realize that the Catholic religion is the one true one. But today the numbers of priests and religious and nuns are diminishing, and those who remain no longer even wear an exterior sign of their belonging to God, of their oblation to God.

Formerly, when in town one would cross the path of a priest or religious; the churches were vibrant, everything was well ordered, the Blessed Sacrament was manifestly present; one knelt. Anyone could see these things. Such testimonials were found throughout Europe. In the hospitals and clinics, the Little Sisters of the Poor took care of the old people; the Sisters of the Assumption visited the families of the sick. Now the religious have practically been banished: the hospital has become the occupation of laymen—and let no one else interfere! Yet there is a great difference between a sister who helps the sick to bear their sufferings, and who shows true charity, and a simple nurse who can be very good, very gentle, but who cannot have, in general, this religious character, this note of charity. When her shift is over, the nurse leaves; the religious does not; she remains beside the patient at night if need be. This total devotion to the sick profoundly permeated the atmosphere of the hospitals and clinics. They made the sisters go, and often it was the priests of Catholic Action who told them: "You are taking bread out of the mouths of the nurses." And so the vocations of hospitaller religious were ruined.

The contemplative life has also disappeared: it is better to devote oneself to action, isn't it? And so they broke the grills and the sisters came out of their cloister; there is no more contemplative life. And the result: no more vocations.

What priests have done and said since the Council in order to destroy the religious life, and thus the sanctity of the Church, is unimaginable. And this is without counting the priests who have married, and the worker-priests. How can people whose faith is unsteady still be encouraged to believe that the Catholic religion is the one true one? They hear Protestants speak who are very respectable, deaconesses who are very devoted, and even Moslems who are more pious than we. They do not know what lies behind the Islamic mask: the enslavement of the woman, and the immorality of Islam. But they lose their faith and no longer step into a church.

Hence the importance of the holiness of the Church, this visible sign that, as Pope Leo XIII says, makes her recognizable.

The Duty of the State in Regard to Religion

Let's continue the reading:

> This kind of liberty, if considered in relation to the State, clearly implies that there is no reason why the State should offer any homage to God, or should desire any public recognition of Him; that no one form of worship is to be preferred to another, but that all stand on an equal footing, no account being taken of the religion of the people, even if they profess the Catholic faith. But, to justify this, it must needs be taken as true that the State has no duties towards God....

This is, then, the Religious Indifferentism of the State. How denatured it is, that so many should hold that men united in society have no duties towards God, as if they did not have any individually!

> Wherefore, civil society must acknowledge God as its Founder and Parent, and must obey and reverence His power and authority.

It is, then, a duty of the civil society to worship God, be-cause, like the family, it is a creature of God. The State itself, the civil authority, owes public worship to God Who is its author. And it is here that Leo XIII specifies once again what religion is meant:

> Since, then, the profession of one religion is necessary in the State, that religion must be professed which alone is true, and which can be recognized without difficulty, especially in Catholic States, because the marks of truth are, as it were, engraven upon it. This religion, therefore, the rulers of the State must preserve and protect, if they would provide—as they should do—with prudence and usefulness for the good of the community.

"Rights" for All Religions

It follows, then, very clearly that the freedom of religion is a false freedom. A century after Leo XIII, this false freedom has become an accepted principle. Few even are the Catholics who understand that one has the duty to interdict the expansion of a false religion in a country; this goes to show how deeply errors have penetrated minds.

To avoid being poisoned, let us always return to true principles. Everywhere it is asserted that it is better for the State to let everyone free in regard to religion, and yet this reasoning is absolutely contrary to what the good God desires. When He created men and societies, it was so that religion would be given scope to act, and not just any religion!

But consider the declaration of Vatican II on religious liberty: "religious groups" (*D.H.*, I, 4) are spoken of under the heading "The General Principle of Religious Freedom":

> Religious communities are a requirement of the nature of man and of religion itself. Therefore, provided the just requirements of public order are not violated, these groups have a right to immunity so that they may organize themselves according to their own principles. They must be allowed to honor the supreme Godhead with public worship....[7]

What "groups" are meant? Mormons? Scientologists? Moslems? Buddhists? And where is Our Lord Jesus Christ amongst them all? Who is the "supreme Godhead"? The Great Architect?

> [They must be allowed to] help their members to practice their religion and strengthen them with religious instruction, and promote institutions in which members may work together to organize their own lives according to their religious principles.

You have indeed read correctly "according to their religious principles." This is unheard of. Let us recall, though, that this was only a "pastoral" council, and that the Holy Ghost was not present:

> Religious communities have the further right not to be prevented from publicly teaching and bearing witness to their beliefs by the spoken or written word.

"Their beliefs"? But this is what is contrary to the Catholic faith. Should the States, then, guarantee to these groups the power to write, to spread their errors, and propagate their teaching by means of institutions? Unthinkable.

It is not only a question of errors. One must also consider the consequences, for this does not remain within the speculative realm: each religion has its doctrinal convictions, but also its moral practices. The Protestants accept divorce and contraception; the Moslems have a right to polygamy. Must the States permit all of this so that the "religious communities" can "organize their own lives according to their religious principles"?

If so, how can any limits be set? Why not human sacrifice? One might object, because that is against the public order. But

---

[7] Austin Flannery, O.P., ed., "Declaration on Religious Liberty," *Vatican Council II: The Conciliar and Post Conciliar Documents* (Collegeville, MN: The Liturgical Press, 1975), p. 802.

would a father who sacrificed his child really disturb the public order? This is what one comes to! And then, why not euthanasia? Killing old folks in the hospitals would deliver society from a crushing, costly burden. A shot and it's over, and without disturbing the public order. The ramifications are truly horrendous to consider. In the name of the enunciated principles, "the right of all not to be prevented from publicly teaching and bearing witness to their beliefs," everything and anything is allowed.

The conciliar declaration adds:

> However, in spreading religious belief and in introducing religious practices everybody must at all times avoid any action which seems to suggest coercion or dishonest or unworthy persuasion especially when dealing with the uneducated or the poor. Such a manner of acting must be considered an abuse of one's own right and an infringement of the rights of others.

These are affirmations that turn against us. One writes that there must be limits to propaganda so as not to impose upon people incapable of distinguishing truth from error (against, for example, the Jehovah's Witnesses and the Adventists, who go from door to door and dispose of much money...). But then they come to us and say not to try to convince people to make them leave their religion and convert to the Catholic religion. If all the "religious groups" have a right to exist, then what will Catholic missionaries do in the missions? If everyone possesses a natural right to have his own religion, it isn't worth trying to convert them, we do not even have the right!

The declaration continues:

> Also included in the right to religious freedom is the right of religious groups not to be prevented from freely demonstrating the special value of their teaching for the organization of society and the inspiration of all human activity.

What special value? That of the Moslems with their polygamy and slavery?

> Finally, rooted in the social nature of man and in the very nature of religion is the right of men, prompted by their own religious sense, freely to hold meetings or establish educational, cultural, charitable and social organizations.

And after all, since everyone has the right to be able to meet freely, why not the Freemasons as well?

All this is absolutely contrary to the teaching of the popes of the nineteenth and the first half of the twentieth century. If truth exists, the good God cannot give to error the right to be propagated like the truth. It is impossible. To speak thus is tantamount to insulting God.

Second Liberty: Freedom of Speech and of the Press

Having thus dealt with freedom of religion, Leo XIII says:

> We must now consider briefly *liberty of speech*, and liberty of the press.

On one occasion when I happened to meet him, I pointed out to Pope Paul VI that on this point the teaching of the Council is contrary to the teaching of Leo XIII. I said, "Who must be obeyed? You tell us that we disobey. But if I obey what Vatican Council II says, then I must disobey Pope Leo XIII, Pope Pius IX, Pope Gregory XVI, and Pope Saint Pius X; in short, I must disobey all the popes who taught one and the same thing: that there is no right to error. You tell me that error has rights, that people are free to have their religion and to make known everything they want by means of the press. They can do this freely, and the State has no right to prevent them, no matter what the religious group, no matter what the religion, no matter what the principles. Pope Leo XIII states the contrary. There is no right to freedom of the press; there is no right to diffuse error by means of the press. That liberty does not exist. There can be no right to freedom of speech and freedom of the press."

Who must be obeyed? I said: "I obey the popes who have always used the same language, and who have always said the same thing for twenty centuries. I deem that I must obey them, and not the Vatican Council II which affirms the contrary."

Paul VI replied, "Oh, we haven't got time to discuss theological questions." Granted that it is a theological question. The Pope sensed that he had no tenable reply. What could he have answered?

Cardinal Seper wrote to me: "You must submit to the magisterium of the Church and to the current magisterium, thus, to

Vatican Council II." But, precisely, it is because I do submit to the magisterium of the Church that I refuse certain parts of the magisterium of the Second Vatican Council; submissive to the magisterium of the Church, I cannot admit that what was officially taught by the popes be contradicted by a "pastoral" council. Because there would be no reason for a subsequent council not to teach the opposite of this one! There would be no truth. If every fifty years the truths and dogmas are changed, then there are no more dogmas, there is no magisterium. It is out of veneration for the magisterium that we cannot accept its being despised and changed.

When we say this to the champions of Vatican II, they do not know what to reply.

Leo XIII, then, treats here of freedom of speech and the press:

> It is hardly necessary to say that there can be no such right as this, if it be not used in moderation, and if it pass beyond the bounds and end of all true liberty. For right is a moral power which—as We have before said and must again and again repeat—it is absurd to suppose that nature has accorded indifferently to truth and falsehood, to justice and injustice.

Yes, only truth, only justice have rights, because right is founded upon God himself, and God is Truth and Virtue. What opposes God is contrary to truth and justice, and can have no right.

Some pretend that it is ridiculous to say that truth and justice have rights, and that error and vice have no rights; only persons have rights, and not ideas. But when one says that truth has rights, one thinks of God, hence of a person, of persons, of the Blessed Trinity, and not of abstract truth, of course!

When a government is overthrown, the first thing claimed by the self-styled sovereign people is freedom of the press. One knows that this is often just a manner of speaking. In the lands of "liberty," the so-called people's democracies, there is really the tyranny of democracy. There is no longer question of truth or error, there is only one press in power. Those who deplore it protest that liberty must be allowed, for if liberty is granted to all, then surely truth will triumph over error. But experience has shown the contrary: it is easier to do evil than good, it is more in conformity with the disorder in human nature. That is why, when one grants this liberty, it is error that gains. It suffices to count the number of really Catholic newspapers remaining in each country. What press organ can one rely upon? Newspapers like *L'Avvenire* in Italy and *La Croix* in France can scarcely be called Catholic. There is no longer a truly Catholic press. This is what happens when liberty is allowed. Error takes the upper hand. And the press exerts considerable influence—and Pope Leo XIII had no inkling of television!

> The excesses of an unbridled intellect, which unfailingly end in the oppression of the untutored multitude, are no less rightly controlled by the authority of the law than are the injuries inflicted by violence upon the weak. And this all the more surely, because by far the greater part of the community is either absolutely unable, or able only with great difficulty, to escape from illusions and deceitful subtleties, especially such as flatter the passions. If unbridled license of speech and of writing be granted to all, nothing will remain sacred and inviolate; even the highest and truest mandates of nature, justly held to be the common and noblest heritage of the human race, will not be spared. Thus, truth, being gradually obscured by darkness, pernicious and manifold error, as too often happens, will easily prevail.

The Pope remarks that weeds are always more abundant than good and useful plants. Leave a field fallow and untended, and soon the nettles and thistles will smother the rest of the vegetation:

> Liberty will ever be more free and secure in proportion as license is kept in fuller restraint. In regard, however, to all matters of opinion which God leaves to man's free discussion, full liberty of thought and of speech is naturally within the right of every one.

Clearly, one can leave men free to discuss matters that do not pertain to faith and morals.

Third Liberty: Freedom to Teach

Leo XIII moves on to another liberty, graver still, the freedom of teaching, which extends to the formation of youth:

> A like judgment must be passed upon what is called liberty of teaching. There can be no doubt that truth alone should imbue

the minds of men, for in it are found the well-being, the end, and the perfection of every intelligent nature; and therefore **nothing but truth should be taught**....

Here is an evident principle, the golden rule of teaching:

> For this reason it is plainly the duty of all who teach to banish error from the mind, and by sure safeguards to close the entry to all false convictions. From this it follows, as is evident, that the liberty of which We have been speaking is greatly opposed to reason, and tends absolutely to pervert men's minds, in as much as it claims for itself the right of teaching whatever it pleases—a liberty which the State cannot grant without failing in its duty. And the more so because the authority of teachers has great weight with their hearers, who can rarely decide for themselves as to the truth or falsehood of the instruction given to them.

> Wherefore, this liberty, also, in order that it may deserve the name, must be kept within certain limits, lest the office of teaching be turned with impunity into an instrument of corruption.

If we glance at the teaching currently administered in the schools, and even in self-styled Catholic schools, we cannot help but be horrified by the constant evolution in the teaching which is teaching no longer. And this is true at every level. It is the students who propound ideas and discuss them; the professors guide the conversation, but teach nothing. A counterfeit education is installed, and every new year brings a lowering of the standards. Audio-visual aids can be helpful in certain cases, but they exercise the visual memory rather than the intellect. The children accumulate impressions, but they do not assimilate, reflect, reason; the rational faculty is weakened. A pope like Leo XIII would make a serious critique of modern education:

> Now, truth, which should be the only subject matter of those who teach, is of two kinds: natural and supernatural.

That is, truth known by reason and truth known by faith. Both sciences must be taught:

> ...On this, as on a firm basis, morality, justice, religion, and the very bonds of human society rest.

The Benefits of Christian Philosophy

The Pope continues by saying that the Church has received especially the mission of teaching: "Go and teach all the nations" (Mt. 28:19). The governors should take this into consideration, for the universities built over the centuries, where eminent professors taught, were truly admirable, and added immeasurably to the glory of the Church and Christian civilization.

Imagine what the Sorbonne must have been at the time of St. Albert the Great and St. Thomas Aquinas, of St. Ignatius and St. Francis Xavier. Imagine the saints like St. Bonaventure, who went to the Sorbonne, who were formed by these universities, and who studied there true philosophy, the true faith! Now what is taught at the Sorbonne? A couple of friends at the University report that at the most there are two or three professors of philosophy who are not communists! And this in a university founded by the Church and sanctified by her for so many centuries! The communists have come to roost there like cuckoos, birds that intrude in the nests of other birds.

The revolutionaries have taken over everything, the bishoprics, the schools, the buildings, the hospitals. They are set up in handsome edifices that they did not build, even if, subsequently, they developed them.

In a free, anti-communist Catholic university like that of Guadalajara in Mexico, where there are more than 30,000 students (10,000 Mexicans and 20,000 foreigners), there is no department of philosophy or theology. What kind of anti-Communism can be taught in such conditions? It must be very rudimentary: news about worldwide Communism, meetings, congresses. But all this lacks the philosophical foundation. For want of chairs of philosophy and theology, it is not possible to make known the ideal that should exist and replace Communism, which is precisely the social reign of Our Lord Jesus Christ. If the faculty does not present that which gives society a normal life, a veritable morality, the natural law, social law, what are they doing? With what will they replace totalitarian society, if they do not know what a Christian society is, and even, philosophically, what society is, and what laws ought to govern the natural social order?

This is what we have come to: an educational void. Hence the importance of our seminaries! The priests we are forming will soon be the only persons to know the true philosophical principles, which are not our principles, nor those of Fr. So-and-so, nor of some professor or other, but those of the Church.

Thomist philosophy has been rejected, despite the incessant reminders of the popes that the Church has made it her own, to such a degree that one speaks of St. Thomas Aquinas as the Common Doctor. It is philosophy by the light of faith in accord with truth; it is to this doctrine that most encyclicals refer. If we want to know reality, the world, the essence of things, all that God has created, we must immerse ourselves in the philosophy of St. Thomas, the philosophy of commons sense.

How admirable this philosophy is, and nowadays how rejected! It is rejected even in Rome at the Gregorian, at the Angelique, and at the Lateran. What will the future priests and bishops know in truth? They are going to be modernists from the start, for in the seminaries they are taught Freud, Marxism, evolution, relativity, and they know longer know what truth is! It is truly frightening to consider.

Hence the importance of our seminaries. The priests who emerge should be pillars of truth. It will be held against them that they have been formed according to the doctrine of St. Thomas, they will be attacked all the more because of the light of truth and common sense they will possess; they will not be pardoned for having the truth, the truth against which all the errors clash.

Hence the importance of founding universities near our seminaries. I hope that one will be able to be founded in each country.[8] If at the beginning they are as simple as can be, at least the professors will teach the truth, not only to future priests, but also to laymen called to hold important positions in society. Thus formed, these will possess such a power of reasoning and of persuasion as to be able to convince all opposition. Thanks to the clarity of their ideas, they will be able to exert an influence in society. But if Thomism is no longer taught in the universities, nor Catholic

---

[8] Two now exist in France: The Institute of St. Pius X, 21 rue du Cherche-Midi, 75006 Paris; and the Institute of St. Gregory the Great, 56 rue d'Inkermann, 69006 Lyon.

doctrine in the seminaries, where will one go to find the light of truth?

Numerous are the pontifical documents written about the doctrine of St. Thomas; it is truly the philosophy of the Church, hence the philosophy of God, that by which every reasonable man and every Christian should live. Pope Leo XIII writes:

> To [the Church] He entrusted all the truths which He had taught, in order that it might keep and guard them and with lawful authority explain them; and at the same time He commanded all nations to hear the voice of the Church, as if it were His own, threatening those who would not hear it with everlasting perdition. Thus, it is manifest that man's best and surest teacher is God, the Source and Principle of all truth; and the only-begotten Son, Who is in the bosom of the Father, the Way, the Truth, and the Life, the true Light which enlightens every man, and to Whose teaching all must submit: "And they shall all be taught of God" (Jn. 6:45).

Unfortunately, the liberals, who demand freedom of teaching while they allow any kind of teaching to be taught, multiply obstacles for the Church. One could add that in our day it is against us that the obstacles are multiplied. It is after all unheard of that, under the very eyes of the pope and the cardinals responsible for the teaching of the Church, a teaching that is not Catholic should develop. One should not be surprised at what is happening in other universities. Clearly, the first step in a reform would be to give true professors to these universities. How can it be that rabbis and Protestant pastors teach at the Gregorian University of Rome?

Moreover, the teaching has become eclectic. One wants to know everything about everything; encyclopedias are compiled on everything men think, about anything except the truth. I have seen the curriculum for the seminaries in France: Thomism, for example, is not longer the principal doctrine taught in philosophy, but it is studied as one system among others. What will these seminarians become? It is said that some seminaries have more seminarians than others, but what formation do they receive? They will become priests who will think as they like, for whom truth and error are relative. What conviction will they have in preaching? For it is in the truth that we find the courage to speak with authority; if there is no truth, if truth is an opinion like others, then no real preaching is possible. They will talk about political or social events, of revolution here or there, but they will no longer have a grasp of the true priestly vocation.

Fourth Liberty: Liberty of Conscience

Finally, Leo XIII treats of liberty of conscience, taking care to distinguish, for words, if they are not defined, are always ambiguous:

> If by this is meant that everyone may, as he chooses, worship God or not, it is sufficiently refuted by the arguments already adduced. But it may also be taken to mean that every man in the State may follow the will of God and, from a consciousness of duty and free from every obstacle, obey His commands. This, indeed, is true liberty, a liberty worthy of the sons of God, which nobly maintains the dignity of man and is stronger than all violence or wrong—a liberty which the Church has always desired and held most dear. This is the kind of liberty the Apostles claimed for themselves with intrepid constancy, which the apologists of Christianity confirmed by their writings, and which the martyrs in vast numbers consecrated by their blood.

A Culpable and Fatal Ambiguity

Nowadays ambiguities are tolerated. A few years ago, during the canonization of some Irish martyrs Paul VI gave a discourse riddled with ambiguities. He played on the phrase "freedom of conscience" as if these martyrs had manifested the necessity of this freedom, as if they had died for it. But these martyrs understood freedom of conscience as Pope Leo XIII was to define it: the freedom to affirm the truth and to adhere to it. But if it is a question of defending the freedom of every religion or of every thought, that is a completely different matter. It is not for this that they went to be martyred. They refused to become Protestants because that is error. Thus they were massacred for truth's sake, and not for the sake of the freedom of every opinion. To play upon the blood of these martyrs who manifested their attachment to the true faith, in order to make it seem that they died to defend the freedom of all religions is inadmissible.

Nowadays people demand freedom of religion without defining it; but here one must make oneself clear. To defend a certain freedom, the freedom of individuals so that there are no unwarranted investigations by the State into what persons believe and which might be followed by persecutions, is very good. It is also good to prevent people from being invaded in the privacy of their home because they profess a false religion, Moslem or Buddhist, for example.

But to give the impression that the Church defends the freedom of all religions is inadmissible, because she cannot defend the freedom of error. To demand freedom for all religions to be able, like the Catholic religion, to disseminate their doctrine, have a press, institutions, schools and temples is to enter a dangerous terrain. Because soon one will see temples and mosques everywhere,[9] and the Catholics will not be able to say anything, since they themselves wanted to grant freedom to error.

True Tolerance

Later on Pope Leo XIII speaks of tolerance. That this should be necessary in States is understandable. But it is one thing to tolerate, and another thing to admit a right. One tolerates evil, but one does not approve it. A parallel can be drawn to ourselves: we are sinners, we have evil tendencies, but we are not going to kill ourselves because we cannot tolerate our vices; we must bear with ourselves, to a certain degree, without, however, approving our vices. We bear them while trying to combat them and re-establish order within ourselves. The same thing is true of societies: they are sick; to want to suppress every evil would make social life impossible; one is not going to kill society! The States are thus obliged to tolerate certain things.

Formerly, for example, they used to call "houses of toleration" what were nothing other than houses of prostitution. The State deemed it necessary to tolerate these, because by wanting to suppress these houses entirely, the consequence would have been

---

[9] In 1993, there were more than one thousand mosques in France.

for prostitution to spread everywhere clandestinely, which would have been worse than regulating it. It is the duty of the State to decide if it must tolerate something or not; thus, Catholic States and Catholic princes, who prosecuted vice and public sin, tolerated these houses. Yet it was a very restricted liberty.

About tolerance Pope Leo XIII writes:

> Yet, with the discernment of a true mother, the Church weighs the great burden of human weakness, and well knows the course down which the minds and actions of men are in this our age being borne. For this reason, while not conceding any right to anything save what is true and honest, she does not forbid public authority to tolerate what is at variance with truth and justice, for the sake of avoiding some greater evil, or of obtaining or preserving some greater good.

The Pope recalls that God Himself permits evil without willing it. He cannot will evil, but He permits it for the sake of a greater good or to avoid a greater evil.

To Tolerate Does Not Mean to Recognize a Right

Prior to Vatican II, two schemas were drafted, the one by Cardinal Bea on religious liberty, and the other by Cardinal Ottaviani which spoke of "*de tolerantia religiosa*." They were in violent opposition, and in the midst of a meeting Cardinal Bea raised his voice to proclaim: "I do not agree with this schema at all!" Yet religious toleration is truly the traditional doctrine of the Church, for whom it is entirely impossible to speak of freedom of religions. In certain cases error is tolerated, but it is never admitted to be a natural right.

For example, in countries like Germany where there are equal numbers of Catholics and Protestants, it is impossible to suppress Protestantism. But in completely Catholic States like Spain, where there were very few Protestants, laws favored Catholicism and impeded the development of Protestant institutions: and this was the policy until Franco, under pressure from the Vatican, at last granted freedom to the sects. Consequently, the Protestants became more numerous, and the Jehovah's Witnesses arrived on the scene.

The same thing happened in Latin America, where the countries were ninety-five percent Catholic. The heads of State followed the principles declared by the popes and considered it an obligation to protect their Catholic people from the errors that would have destroyed the faith. This is quite normal when one believes in Our Lord Jesus Christ, and it was beautiful to see the faith officially professed in these countries: in the processions and the official religious ceremonies representatives of the civil authority were always present. It was a great example for the population.

But this was suppressed. These States have become "laic," and subsequently an invasion of the sects has followed. In Chile temples crop up everywhere, Mormons, Adventists, the Salvation Army. As soon as the Church lacks firmness in upholding her principles, and the clergy lacks the courage of its convictions, the Catholic faith is encroached upon, the faithful abandon it and join the sects.

It is normal for the Church, then, to tolerate what it cannot prevent, as in a place where there is a majority of non-Catholics. But the heads of State can only offer the dissidents tolerance, they cannot admit their possession of any natural right:

> But, to judge aright, we must acknowledge that, the more a State is driven to tolerate evil, the further is it from perfection; and that the tolerance of evil which is dictated by political prudence should be strictly confined to the limits which its justifying cause, the public welfare, requires....One thing, however, remains always true—that the liberty which is claimed for all to do all things is not, as We have often said, of itself desirable, inasmuch as it is contrary to reason that error and truth should have equal rights. And as to "tolerance," it is surprising how far removed from the equity and prudence of the Church are those who profess what is called Liberalism.

Fourth Part:
DEGREES OF LIBERALISM

Having finished the third part, the Pope recapitulates:

> And now to reduce for clearness' sake to its principal heads all that has been set forth with its immediate conclusions, the sum-

ming up in this briefly: that man, by a necessity of his nature, is wholly subject to the most faithful and ever-enduring power of God; and that, as a consequence, any liberty, except that which consists in submission to God and in subjection to His Will, is unintelligible. To deny the existence of this authority in God, or to refuse to submit to it, means to act, not as a free man, but as one who treasonably abuses his liberty; and in such a disposition of mind the chief and deadly vice of Liberalism essentially consists.

Here the Pope puts his finger on the wound: the evil is to refuse to recognize the sovereignty of God, the laws of God. One no longer wants God to intervene in human affairs, as He did by Our Lord Jesus Christ. But one must submit oneself to this intervention of Jesus Christ, one must recognize his reign. Such is the fundamental principle that the Pope reiterates.

The Deadly Sin of Liberalism

In the fourth and last part of the encyclical, the Pope identifies more precisely what the capital sin of Liberalism consists in. It is, he says, this disposition of the soul that leads a man to deny the sovereignty of God and to refuse to submit to it.

This is, in fact, the essence of Liberalism. When one glances at the moral and social consequences of such a stance, one is frightened with good reason. Yet it is also well to remember that for at least twelve centuries after the period of persecutions, the good God was served and recognized in the great majority of the European States. And with the conversion of the Indians of South America, there was a hope that the entire world would submit to Our Lord Jesus Christ, to the Truth, and thus live by a supernatural spirit as God wanted!

The break occurred at the time of the Protestant revolt, but even before, with the Renaissance, the cult of man had appeared on the scene with the cult of pagan civilization. All this developed like a cancer on a body. Soon the revolt became generalized, sometimes bloody, and how many Catholics were the victims of it! Then society became laic, without God, against God, secularized. What is meant by the word "secularized," if not the complete loss of faith? In a totally profane society, the dimension of the faith disappears, and everything that the faith commands also disappears. Then, logically, necessarily, this spirit was to penetrate inside the Church, and it too, especially since the Council, became secularized. Priests lose their faith in grace and in the sacraments; the inward reality disappears behind the exterior rites become purely formalistic.

Who has helped spread these errors? It was, precisely, the liberal Catholics, who were fascinated by these ideas of liberty. Liberty against the authority of God! We are witnessing now the destruction of civil society, the family and the Church. It behooves us to find out the cause, and it is this deeply ingrained error of Liberalism which is, basically, the same error as Protestantism, and which developed by the action of Freemasonry.

Liberalism, as with every disease, has diverse degrees, but it is always a serious illness. Once one calls into question the authority of God over men and society, there is no reason to stop or draw a line. If one denies to Our Lord Jesus Christ a certain domain, the others will soon be contested as well.

First Degree: Absolute Liberalism

Pope Leo XIII then precisely identifies the various degrees of Liberalism:

> ...In more ways than one can the will depart from the obedience which is due to God or to those who share the divine power. For, to reject the supreme authority of God, and to cast off all obedience to Him in public matters, or even in private and domestic affairs, is the greatest perversion of liberty and the worst kind of Liberalism; and what We have said must be understood to apply to this alone in its fullest sense.

This first degree is doctrinaire Liberalism, such as the Freemasons espouse, and the complete putting into practice of which is envisaged by Socialism and Communism.

Second Degree: The Church Despoiled or Reduced in Status

> Next comes the system of those who admit indeed the duty of submitting to God, the Creator and Ruler of the world, in-

asmuch as all nature is dependent on His Will, but who boldly reject all laws of faith and morals which are above natural reason, but are revealed by the authority of God.

These, then, accept natural religion, but not supernatural religion. They reject revelation, and so doing they reject the Church, which represents revelation, the deposit of faith, and the transmission of that deposit. Ultimately, this is also to reject Our Lord, Who instituted the Church as distinct from the State. Among those who are against the influence of the Church in civil society, the Pope distinguishes two attitudes.

There are those who refuse categorically to recognize the Church as a society which must exert an influence in civil society. For them:

> ...they would pay no more regard to the Church than if she did not exist; and, at most, would allow the citizens individually to attend to their religion in private if so minded.

In short, theirs is an attitude of complete contempt of the Church and of revelation, the putting into act of which results in the despoliation of the Church and the suppression of her institutions.

There is also the attitude of those who agree to consider the Church as a society, but as no different from other societies; thus, as a religious association without any exclusive prerogative, and without the nature of a perfect society with the right to own property, to administer and govern her members, and to teach freely:

> They aggrandize the power of the civil government to such extent as to subject the Church of God to the empire and sway of the State, like any voluntary association of citizens.

This is, in fact, what happens to the Church in many countries. In France, for example, the State does not recognize the Church as a society with right of ownership; it only recognizes it to cultural associations which can own the property in each diocese. Even the Society of St. Pius X was obliged to create cultural associations in order to legally own its property.

The liberals find this normal, because there are also associations of Adventists, Jehovah's Witnesses, etc. In the States with which a concordat is in effect, as in Germany and Italy, the Church is recognized as a society owning the diocesan property, but not as the one true religious society founded by Our Lord. There is no longer any State whose constitution states that only the Catholic religion is publicly, officially recognized by the State; the last State to have suppressed such a clause was Ireland.

Third Degree: Liberal Catholics

There remains one last category, that of liberal Catholics. These are practicing Catholics who think they do well by saying that the Church should march in step with the times; they do not all approve of the separation of Church and State, but they think that it is necessary to bring the Church:

> ...to adapt herself to the times and conform to what is required by the modern system of government.

This is how the Pope judges this proposition:

> Such an opinion is sound, if it is to be understood of some equitable adjustment consistent with truth and justice; in so far, namely, that the Church, in the hope of some great good, may show herself indulgent, and may conform to the times in so far as her sacred office permits. But it is not so in regard to practices and doctrines which a perversion of morals and a warped judgment have unlawfully introduced. Religion, truth, and justice must ever be maintained; and, as God has entrusted these great and sacred matters to the care of the Church, she can never be so unfaithful to her office as to dissemble in regard to what is false or unjust, or to connive at what is hurtful to religion.

The liberal Catholics make a rule of the exception: by the very fact they destroy the rule. The Church concedes that temporarily she cannot act otherwise when she cannot go against the State; she accepts a concordat, and she maintains relations with a State even if it does not consider the Catholic religion as the only recognized religion. But nonetheless, as soon as possible she must seek the means to be in a situation that accords with the truth; she only tolerates provisionally being placed on a par with other religions.

As for the liberal Catholics, they find this situation to be normal. It is impossible to regain the influence that was enjoyed during the Middle Ages, they say. It is quite acceptable for society to be secular. Here one finds the theory of Jacques Maritain that society must develop. Once it was religious, but with time and progress and the change of mind-set, it is normal that society should become irreligious. Behold how the combat is abandoned, whereas it is as necessary as ever to affirm and uphold the social reign of Our Lord Jesus Christ, without which there can never be peace or liberty or the salvation of souls. So it is, and there is no room for beating about the bush.

Without the Grace of Jesus Christ, No Society Is Normal

Never forget that without grace we are incapable of acting in a manner perfect and holy. We cannot even keep natural goodness for long, because original sin has introduced disorder into our very nature. If one says that Our Lord need not reign over society, men will be left to themselves and little by little they will fall into bad habits and sin. That is why grace is necessary for a society to be truly Christian.

Of course everything does not collapse over night. After the Revolution, society did not fall immediately into barbarism. Many people were still Christian, and a certain goodness remained in the social order. People lived, one could go out without fear of being murdered, immorality did not penetrate everywhere. Then came the separation of Church and State. Could it be said that because there were still good people even without a public cult being offered to Our Lord, that it is possible to do without public worship and remain just? The reply is that after a certain length of time, it became apparent that the worm was in the fruit, and that everything was spoiled. We are now witnessing the ultimate consequences of the removal of the Christian religion from schools, universities, the State. Society is profoundly corrupt: divorce, destroyed families, children left to themselves. These are the consequences of Naturalism, of the rejection of the royalty of Our Lord.

One day in Mexico, the journalists asked me, "What do you think of the progress of society? How should society evolve in order to bring about greater justice and a more equitable distribution of goods?" I answered: "There are not thirty-six viable systems, there is only one, the reign of Our Lord Jesus Christ. As long as this reign is not re-established, as long as the laws of Our Lord are not observed, as long as grace does not vivify souls, it will be utterly futile to seek to obtain justice, peace, and normal social life. Grace alone regenerates souls and begets true virtue; grace alone makes of men sons of God, and along with charity infuses the social virtues without which envy alone develops. This is easily observed: to-day people are incited to envy and to claim rights. Men are set against each other; all must obtain the same thing! But envy creates hatred, and hatred engenders civil discord: civil wars ensue, and men devour one another.

If, on the contrary, souls are transformed in Christ, those who exercise authority in the State and the rich owners of goods and lands will be more just. Animated by the virtue of justice, they will understand that they have duties towards their subordinates. And the latter will understand that they must work, and accept their condition with resignation, for we are not on earth uniquely to make a fortune. They will understand that supernatural life is worth much more than all the riches of earth.

Communist Society

The journalists asked me, "Then you do not believe that Communism is the solution for social progress?" I answered: "Go and ask those behind the iron curtain; go and spend some time there. Ask the Vietnamese, who built rafts, and huddled their families and a few possessions on them and put out to sea, of whom tens- and maybe hundreds of thousands perished while fleeing from Communism. Think of all those who were killed trying to flee from behind the iron curtain, machine-gunned or electrocuted. And what of the Polish? Why did the Polish workers revolt, since Communism is said to be the liberator of the working class? They take the bread out of their mouths to send it to Russia where people are dying of hunger.[10]

It is extraordinary that journalists could ask such a question. It goes against common sense. But the communists have such skill

---

[10] Recall that Archbishop Lefebvre was giving this course in 1980, at a time when the Poles were in an uprising against the Communist regime.

at making people think that they are the only ones interested in an equitable distribution of goods, in progress and in liberty. People let themselves be taken in as long as they are not actually under the communist rod. Certainly, the communists have succeeded in increasing wages in certain cases, but that could have occurred as well without them, by means of existing organizations. Think of the example of Chile: under the Communist regime of Allende, to get a little sugar or bread it was necessary to stand in line for hours, and often it was only to hear that there was none left. Behold communist happiness.

So, the liberals are people who let themselves be taken in by all the modern errors; they abandon Our Lord, and consequently can no longer work towards the good of society.

True Liberty and Coups d'Etat

The Pope continues by recapitulating his condemnation of modern errors:

> From what has been said it follows that it is quite unlawful to demand, to defend, or to grant unconditional freedom of thought, of speech, of writing, or of worship, as if these were so many rights given by nature to man.

Here is truly the conclusion of the encyclical. In this sentence, the Pope condemns ahead of time the *Declaration on Religious Liberty*, which demands these liberties as a right conferred by nature. Who is right? It is impossible to reconcile the two affirmations:

> For liberty is to be regarded as legitimate in so far only as it affords greater facility for doing good, but no farther.

Hence, there is no freedom for error. Then follow some considerations on the different forms of government. We should retain these very strong affirmations:

> Whenever there exists, or there is reason to fear, an unjust oppression of the people on the one hand, or a deprivation of the liberty of the Church on the other, it is lawful to seek for such a change of government as will bring about due liberty of action.

In such cases, an excessive and vicious liberty is not sought, but only some relief for the common welfare.

And a little farther, this passage:

Neither does the Church condemn those who, if it can be done without violation of justice, wish to make their country independent of any foreign or despotic power.

Moreover, one must conclude that the Church grants that one can recognize as legitimate a regime that issues from a legitimate use of force.

The Forms of Government

As to what concerns the different forms of governments, I do not say that Pope Leo XIII was a democrat, but he conceived more readily than his successor St. Pius X that democracy is a legitimate form of government, all the while condemning the ideology:

Again, it is not of itself wrong to prefer a democratic form of government, if only the Catholic doctrine be maintained as to the origin and exercise of power. Of the various forms of government, the Church does not reject any that are fitted to procure the welfare of the subject; she wishes only—and this nature itself requires—that they should be constituted without involving wrong to any one, and especially without violating the rights of the Church.

This is somewhat the case of Switzerland, which has had this regime for centuries without being any the worse for it, although, bit by bit, it is sliding towards Socialism.[11] As for St. Pius X, he clearly expressed his esteem for monarchy as being the most natural form of government, and the most in conformity with the nature of society; whereas democracy requires of its citizens greater virtue, difficult to find, which makes democratic governments more prone to slide into anarchy or Socialism.

---

[11] On the contrary, in France the Republic was founded from its inception according to the democratic, Masonic ideology condemned by Leo XIII; the Catholic doctrine on the origin and exercise of power is denied. How then could Catholics rally to this regime without accepting the ideology? This was the snare that not even Leo XIII was able to avoid when he ordered French Catholics to rally to the Republic four years later.

The encyclical is finished:

These things, Venerable Brothers, which, under the guidance of faith and reason, in the discharge of Our Apostolic office, We have now delivered to you, We hope, especially by your co-operation with Us, will be useful unto very many. In lowliness of heart We raise Our eyes in supplication to God, and earnestly beseech Him to shed mercifully the light of His wisdom and of His counsel upon men.

If only men had listened to the Popes more, we would not be in the situation in which we are now. God knows, though, that they did not keep quiet.

Chapter VIII

THE ENCYCLICAL *MIRARI VOS* OF POPE GREGORY XVI CONDEMNING LIBERALISM, INDIFFERENTISM, AND FREEDOM OF CONSCIENCE
(AUGUST 15, 1832)

We are going to study in succession the encyclicals of the two 19th century popes who were the first to seriously attack Liberalism very specifically: *Mirari Vos* of Gregory XVI, and *Quanta Cura* of Pius IX.

The first thing to note is that it was the writings of Felicity de Lamennais, a priest, in which he set forth his liberal ideas, as dangerous as they were widespread, which led Pope Gregory XVI to intervene by publishing *Mirari Vos* on August 15, 1832. In fact, he did not name Lamennais, but Lamennais understood that if the Pope had written this encyclical it was in fact to condemn him and the perverse ideas he propagated.

I highly recommend a book entitled *L'Eglise Occupée*, in which the author, Jacques Ploncard d'Assac, devotes an entire chapter to the liberalism professed by Lamennais. Another work, by Fr. Emmanuel Barbier, on liberal Catholicism presents numerous considerations showing the pernicious influence exerted by Lamennais during the first half of the 19th century. Lamennais had founded a newspaper, *L'Avenir*, which initially attracted the collaboration of eminent men who were far from being liberals, at least at heart, such as Dom Guéranger, who wrote for the first issue, but who quickly realized that he was amongst bad company, and withdrew his collaboration.

What are the main points that we should retain from this encyclical? The first two pages express the situation that Pope Gregory XVI found himself in at the beginning of his pontificate.

It happens to be his first encyclical. Reading what the Pope writes, one cannot help but draw a parallel with our own circumstances. One wonders how things could have reached such a state as early as the era at which he wrote, that is, in 1832. It has been a century and a half since the encyclical was written, and matters have only grown worse. What might this Pope have said had he lived now?

The Pope describes the perversity of morals, the youth corrupted by the lessons and examples of their masters, and disorders in religion:

> Abyss of bottomless miseries, which these conspiring societies have especially dug, in which heresy and sects have, so to speak, vomited, as in a sewer, all that their bosom holds of license, sacrilege, and blasphemy.

It is frightening. He addresses the bishops: what does he ask them to do?

> ...for the salvation of all the people, let Us unite Our vigilance and efforts. This you will do perfectly if you watch over yourselves and your doctrine, as your office makes it your duty.

It is really striking that he asks of the bishops the same thing that St. Pius X exhorted: "Watch over your doctrine." The Pope uses turns of phrase and expression that are quite relevant for our own time.

Immutability of Dogmatic Formulas

How should they watch over their doctrine?

> ...[by] repeating incessantly to yourselves that every novelty attempts to undermine the Universal Church.

Here he is paraphrasing the holy Pope Celestine:

> *Universalem Ecclesiam quacumque novitate pulsari.*

If only this adage of St. Celestine, imbued with great wisdom, had inspired the Conciliar Fathers at Vatican II, then they would not have engaged the Church in the path of all the reforms that have led to such an upheaval.

The Sovereign Pontiff also quotes Pope St. Agathon:

"Nothing that has been regularly defined can bear diminution, or change, or addition, and repels every alteration of sense, or even of words."

Not only must one not change the meaning of what has been defined, but not even the expression can be modified.

But now they want to make new creeds under the pretext of adapting the formulas of the *Creed* to modern times, to modern man. This is absolutely contrary to what Pope Gregory XVI demands, by citing the same affirmation of his holy predecessors.

One must not change the expression once it has been defined. It is the terms themselves that have been defined. If they are changed, the doctrine is ruined. For example, the fact of having introduced novelties into the translation of the *Credo*, which was altered thereby, by substituting "of the same nature" for "consubstantial" was an enormity. They removed the word by which the Arian heresy had been destroyed. They replaced it again by the very expression that had been called into question by the Arian heresy, because, so they alleged, "consubstantial" is a word no one understands any more; a "scholastic" word that people nowadays can no longer understand. Whom are they kidding?

So, this clarification made by the Pope is very important. Then he accuses the innovators:

> It is the height of absurdity and outrage towards [the Church] to pretend that a restoration and regeneration have become necessary to secure its existence and its progress; as if it could be believed that it was thus subject either to faintness, darkness, or other alterations of this kind.

Restoration, regeneration, *aggiornamento*. It was by using these terms denounced by Gregory XVI that everything was perpetrated by Vatican II. Of course it is true that in the Church the faithful always need to renew themselves according to the doctrine of the Church and by the grace of the Church, by the supernatural and spiritual benefits of the Church. But it is something else entirely to dare to say that the doctrine of the Church, the sacraments, the Church's institutions and structures need restoration and renovation.

For who is the author of the institutions of the Church, and who created the doctrine of the Church, who instituted the sacraments, who inaugurated the holy sacrifice of the Mass? It was indeed Our Lord Jesus Christ. Can one then say to Our Lord Jesus Christ, All that you instituted has aged, everything must be restructured and renovated, because it is no longer suitable for our times?

It is just like those who wanted to draft an ecumenical bible, and who censured the Holy Ghost. The Vulgate was recognized by the Council of Trent as substantially representing the Scriptures as they were given by the Holy Ghost. Now they transform these texts, truncate them and adapt them; they changed the passages that displeased the Protestants. Unbelievable! And now it is sold everywhere, in all the churches, and it is recommended by the bishops.

When we are told that we disobey Rome, that we refuse to accept what Rome promulgates, our reaction is this: But where is Rome? What does Rome say? And it is at this point that we must refer to what the popes have said on the irreformability of the Church's doctrine. This is what I replied to Pope Paul VI when he told me that I should accept the Council.

The Liberal Mentality: Perpetual Incoherence

Religious liberty was condemned by Pope Gregory XVI, by Pope Pius IX and by all the popes until Vatican II. With whom must we side?

Must we disobey the popes prior to the Council? Must we now obey the current pope? It is impossible to accept the contrary of what the magisterium of the Church always taught before the Council.

"Ah," Pope Paul VI said to me, "there isn't time now to discuss theological questions."

We completely, totally and absolutely obey all the popes who taught prior to Vatican II, when the Liberalism they condemned infiltrated the Church. Even now, the Pope is troubled by the liberalism from which he has not been able to disentangle himself. The liberals are in a state of constant contradiction, incoherence, hesitation. In his latest directives, the Pope made reprimands.

He significantly reaffirmed that it is necessary to make an act of adoration before receiving Holy Communion. This is exactly what we require; not only do we require it, we do it. Whereas in all the ceremonies since the Council, there is no act of adoration. People come forward to receive Holy Communion in the hand or on the tongue, but there is no act of adoration. If the Pope does not use sanctions, his words remain a dead letter. If in practice he lacks the firmness he displays on paper, he is acting in a typically liberal manner.

We Fight Liberalism: We Are Anti-Liberals

It is against Liberalism that we fight, for it is corrupting and destroying the Church. We refuse it, and we maintain that we are perfectly obedient to the Church, and in a certain measure, obedient to what the Pope would desire. It is because he hasn't the courage or the strength to fight against them, because he is a liberal. We are with him to the extent that he is anti-liberal, that he himself desires to combat the Liberalism in the Church. It can be hoped that one day Rome will count on us and find in our work a support in order to return to what the popes prior to the Council have always demanded.

It is impossible to read the encyclicals of these popes, like that of Gregory XVI, and be in agreement with what is being done today and which has always been condemned. How many times have I heard bishops say that, realistically, it is impossible to express the faith today as it was expressed one hundred years ago or at the time of the Council of Trent. Their language completely contradicts what Gregory XVI affirms.

Is it necessary, then, to side with Gregory XVI and all the popes who have expressed with equal vigor the irreformability of Catholic doctrine and have denounced all the evils that menace it, popes like Pius IX, Leo XIII and Pope St. Pius X? Or must we side with those who want to change the expression of our faith? To change the formulation of the faith is to change the faith; unfortunately, we observe this today.

Indifferentism: Death of the Missionary Spirit

One of the main themes Gregory XVI stresses is Indifferentism:

> We now come to another and most fruitful cause of the evils which at present afflict the Church and which We so bitterly deplore; We mean Indifferentism, or that fatal opinion everywhere diffused by the craft of the wicked, that men can by the profession of any faith obtain the eternal salvation of their souls provided their life conforms to justice and probity. But in a question so clear and evident it will undoubtedly be easy for Us to pluck up from amid the people confided to your care so pernicious an error. The apostle warns us of it: "One God, one faith, one baptism." Let them tremble then who imagine that every creed leads by an easy path to the port of felicity; and reflect seriously on the testimony of our Savior Himself, that those are against Christ who are not with Christ.

This condemns all the schemas, all the documents concerning the non-Christian religions elaborated during the Council. Reading them, one would think that all the religions are means of salvation, which is unthinkable. It is truly Indifferentism. Ever since then, one speaks of "the three monotheistic religions," but the Jewish and Islamic religions are against Christ because they are not with Him. It is clear. How is it possible to use such an expression as "the three monotheistic religions"? We are with Christ, our God, the others are against Him. The Jews are manifestly against Christ. The Moslems are also against Him, that is also clear; they say that we are idolaters because we adore a man, Jesus Christ, whereas they only adore one God. If they are against Christ, they are not with Our Lord, and so they cannot be with God. One could cite the words of St. John: "Whosoever denieth the Son, the same hath not the Father. He that confesseth the Son hath the Father also" (I Jn. 2:23).

Yet we read in *Nostra Aetate* (the *Declaration on the Relation of the Church to Non-Christian Religions*):

> The Church has also a high regard for the Muslims. They worship God, who is one, living and subsistent, merciful and almighty... (§ 3);

The Catholic Church rejects nothing of what is true and holy in these religions. (§ 2).

Such affirmations completely destroy the missionary spirit. What could missionaries who are convinced by these conciliar documents on the relations of the Church with non-Christian religions possible think, if not, "What am I doing here if it is possible for people to be saved in all the religions, provided that they be good? I needlessly disturb consciences."

On the contrary, if one is convinced that there is no salvation outside the Faith of Our Lord Jesus Christ, then one would ardently desire to be everywhere at once in order to cry out, "For heaven' sake, believe in Our Lord Jesus Christ!" The missionary spirit consumes the souls of priests and pushes them to travel throughout the world to go and preach the gospel, to preach Our Lord and convince the adepts of false religions to be converted to the one true religion. What happened at the occasion of the Council was overwhelming.

"Freedom" of Conscience: Freedom of Error

Gregory XVI develops the theme:

> From this poisoned source of indifferentism flows that false and absurd, or rather extravagant, maxim that liberty of conscience should be established and guaranteed to each man—a most contagious error, to which leads that absolute and unbridled liberty of opinion which for the ruin of Church and State spreads over the world, and which some men, by unbridled impudence, fear not to represent as advantageous to the Church. "And what more certain death for souls," says St. Augustine, "than the liberty of error!"

The phrase "liberty of conscience" must be correctly understood, of course; for we also demand liberty of conscience, so that no one can force our consciences to adopt error; we demand not to be tortured as were the martyrs, in order to force them to adore idols. For us, liberty of conscience means the freedom of the soul to adhere to the truth.

But when freedom of conscience is taken to mean that everyone is entitled to his own morality and his own faith, that he can do as he pleases and believe what he wants, this is unacceptable. A Moslem will say, "For us polygamy is normal, my conscience tells me that polygamy is good. You say that that is not so, but that is your own affair; as for me, I say yes." And so on with all immorality, whatever can be thought of. Such a position is inadmissible.

The same holds for the religions: It is not correct to say that everyone can have the religion he wants. But in *Dignitatis Humanae* (the *Declaration on Religious Liberty*), the contrary is expressed.

Recently, in getting ready for the visit of the Pope to Paris, *Le Figaro* devoted an entire page to Archbishop Lefebvre and his work. After a relatively accurate exposé by John Bourdarias on the Society and its development, there were two other articles, one by Michael de Saint-Pierre, and one by a priest. The one by Mr. Saint-Pierre was good, interesting; essentially, it defended us. But the one by the priest was against us: "Archbishop Lefebvre is against freedom of conscience," whereas he, the author, is for it, that is to say, for freedom of all religions, all opinions, and even all philosophies.

Nothing is more irritating to the advocates of the freedom of all religions than the opposition we make basing ourselves upon the acts of the magisterium. And this is a very Masonic reaction. As soon as you attack them on this point, they react violently, and they accuse us of being intolerant. That is scarcely an argument.

What happened at the Council was very serious, because it was effected by the penetration of liberal ideas within the Church. Presently at Rome they do not know how to extricate themselves. The Catholic religion cannot exist in such an oppressive atmosphere. Truth cannot be mixed with error. Error is always against the truth and ends by devouring it, that is, by making it disappear. On the contrary, if they would affirm the truth once again with vigor, the errors would disappear. But without having recourse to the firm declaration of the truth, it is error that wins, at least apparently and for a limited time, for ultimately, only the truth will triumph.

This is why it seemed important to me to carefully emphasize certain points expressed by Gregory XVI in his encyclical *Mirari Vos*.

Chapter IX

THE ENCYCLICAL *QUANTA CURA* OF POPE PIUS IX
CONDEMNING NATURALISM, LIBERALISM, INDIFFERENTISM, COMMUNISM AND SOCIALISM
(DECEMBER 8, 1864)

The importance of this encyclical is really that it constitutes the preamble of the *Syllabus* in which Pope Pius IX set forth a summary of the modern errors that he had condemned or that had been formally condemned by his predecessors. It is a subject of special interest to us today. The stir that the publication of this document caused even among Catholics is well known. To recall to mind truths in an encyclical is passable, but to draw up a precise catalogue of condemned propositions is something else.

The Liberals' Reaction to the *Syllabus*

The liberal Catholics reacted violently. For them, the Holy Father exaggerated, it was unacceptable. The *Syllabus* was not suitable to modern times, for the Pope did not take into account the society of the times and the evolution of ideas, etc. In short, they said exactly what the Modernists and Progressives say today about adaptation to the world, *aggiornamento*, etc. The Bishop of Orleans, His Excellency Dupanloup, became the spokesman of the discontented Catholics. The Pope wanted to clarify certain points, pronounce condemnations, yet the key is to know how to interpret them....In short, take some and leave some! And so the liberal Catholics were appeased. Bishop Dupanloup was not condemned, and this is what caused Pope Pius IX's attempt to rectify this situation to fail. By explaining away, interpreting, and seeking formulas in order to by-pass the condemnations, the liberal Catholics succeeded in destroying the effects of these acts of the magisterium.

The Progressives and the Modernists cannot even bear to hear the name of the *Syllabus*. They are infuriated by it, they hold that the document is without authority, that it was an idea of Pope Pius IX, that it was never confirmed and moreover was never applied. But this is false; on the contrary, the *Syllabus* was confirmed by the bishops, by the popes, and, as we have seen, by Leo XIII in his encyclical *Immortale Dei*. The *Syllabus* therefore takes on a very great worth. And Pope St. Pius X in his various writings often reiterated in a very explicit manner the condemnation of the denounced errors. But, as Leo XIII was to observe, the popes were not heeded, and the evil has continued to spread.

The encyclical *Quanta Cura* is very beautiful, for it exposes the situation as Pope Pius IX saw it, and it corresponds in an uncanny way to what the Church has known since Vatican II. It is frightening!

Condemnation of Naturalism in Politics

>...We, to the extreme grief of Our soul, beheld a horrible tempest stirred up by so many erroneous opinions, and the dreadful and never enough to be lamented mischiefs which redound to Christian people from such errors; and We then, in discharge of Our Apostolic Ministerial Office, imitating the example of Our illustrious Predecessors, raised Our voice....We condemned the monstrous and portentous opinions, which prevail especially in the present age, to the very great loss of souls, and even to the detriment of civil society, and which are in the highest degree hostile, not only to the Catholic Church, and to her salutary doctrine and venerable laws, but also to the everlasting law of nature engraven by God upon the hearts of all men, and to right reason; and out of which almost all errors originate.

Pius IX confirms the same condemnation pronounced by Pope Gregory XVI which we cited earlier. He continues:

>For you know well, Venerable Brethren, that at this time there are found not a few who, applying to civil intercourse the impious and absurd principles of what they call *Naturalism*, dare teach

"that the best form of Society, and the exigencies of civil progress, absolutely require human society to be constituted and governed without any regard whatsoever to Religion, as if this [Religion] did not even exist, or at least without making any distinction between true and false religions."

The False Religions: The Devil's Invention

Nowadays if one says that the other religions are false religions the progressives are furious. They cannot bear to hear it. "Then you condemn all the other religions? Are all the other religions are bad?" they ask accusingly. It is a visceral reaction on their part, and this reaction is in conformity with the fundamental principle of Liberalism, that is, all religions are good. "You think that only the Catholic religion is good and is able to do good in society, but consider the piety of the Moslems or the Buddhists," they say.

The popes were not liberals, they remained firm in the Faith, and always deliberately distinguished the true from the false religions. For from what spirit do the false religions come? Do they come from the spirit of God, or do they come from Satan? If they are false, then they take their origin from the spirit of error, the spirit of lies, and the father of lies and of error is the devil. The false religions were invented by the devil expressly in order to separate entire peoples and entire countries from Our Lord, and to impede them from becoming Catholic, and from hearing the Truth. There is no doubt about it. It is thus that it is virtually impossible to convert the Moslems.

Islam Imprisons Millions of Souls in Error

For fifteen years at Dakar I found myself in the midst of three million Moslems, one hundred thousand Catholics, and four hundred thousand animists, and if during these fifteen years I saw the conversion of ten Moslems, that was surely the maximum. (I mean real conversions, the conversion from Islam to Catholicism.) I don't mean to say that there was not a certain influence thanks to our schools, where we had enrollments of ten to fifteen percent Moslems. I didn't want a greater percentage, or else that would have imposed Islam on our schools. Once they are strong enough, they assert themselves and take control, and seek to convert others. When they are weak, they listen and keep silent.

The young people in our schools certainly were influenced, and perhaps some of them desired baptism (baptism of desire)— this is quite possible. But it is very difficult for a young man to convert practically to Catholicism, for he is banished from his family, and he knows that he risks being poisoned. Only university students succeed in converting because they are independent. They know their future is assured and so they no longer need their families and can leave for Europe where they can convert. But it is practically impossible to convert someone within his family. By inspiring the Islamic religion, the devil truly succeeded in preventing the conversion of millions of men.

It was relatively easy to convert the Protestants. There were always many Protestants who converted before the Council. But now there aren't many of these conversions any more. This is understandable because the Church no longer presents herself as an ideal the Protestants should desire, as the Church herself has become protestantized. She now holds little attraction for them. Some Jews have converted, but there is a danger there, because it is not guaranteed they have truly converted, or if they only do so in order to keep or facilitate their material interests or their position. It is very difficult to discern. Certainly, it is a fact that a number have converted.

The State's Duty: Repress Religious Error

Pope Pius IX continues:

> Contrary to the teachings of the Holy Scriptures, of the Church, and of the Holy Fathers, these persons do not hesitate to assert, that "the best condition of human society is that wherein no duty is recognized by the Government of correcting, by enacted penalties, the violators of the Catholic Religion, except when the maintenance of the public peace requires it."

Yet this is exactly the position that was affirmed by the *Declaration on Religious Liberty*; to be opposed to all coercion, even public, is tantamount to pronouncing oneself against the Catholic State. But a Catholic State is one that affirms that the Catholic religion is the public religion of the State, and that it is the only one recognized by the government. By doing so it protects the truth, it protects the true religion. And it is evident that as far as possible (but without having recourse to measures that would be extreme and unlivable), it should keep errors from spreading, and prevent Protestantism and the sects from coming and, little by little, undermining the unity of the Catholic faith of the country. For if it did not, that would end not only by destroying the Church, but also by overthrowing the Catholic government of the country. This is what has happened in many countries because of the weakness of the governments, which let the sects and false religions into the country. One fine day the government was overtaken and overturned. Or else, if a Catholic head of State acts against error, he is suppressed: such was the history of the president of the State of Ecuador, Garcia Moreno. His enemies assassinated him.

It is the duty of the State to protect the faith of the Catholic faithful against errors, as it is its duty to prevent immorality from spreading.

A Right to Freedom of Error

All of this, which had been affirmed by Pius IX, was denied by the *Declaration on Religious Liberty*:

> From this totally false notion of social government, they fear not to uphold that erroneous opinion most pernicious to the Catholic Church, and to the salvation of souls, which was called by Our Predecessor, Gregory XVI, the insanity; namely, "that the liberty of conscience and of worship is the peculiar (or inalienable) right of every man, which should be proclaimed by law, and that citizens have the right to all kinds of liberty, to be restrained by no law, whether ecclesiastical or civil, by which they may be enabled to manifest openly and publicly their ideas, by word of mouth, through the press, or by any other means." But whilst these men make these rash assertions, they do not reflect or consider, that they preach the liberty of perdition,[1] and that, "if it is always free to human arguments to discuss, men will never be wanting who will dare to resist the truth, and to rely upon the

---

[1] St. Augustine, Epistle 105, al. 166.

loquacity of human wisdom, when we know from the command of Our Lord Jesus Christ, how faith and Christian wisdom ought to avoid this most mischievous vanity."[2]

Yet the text of the *Declaration on Religious Liberty* (*Dignitatis Humanae*, section 2) affirms that "this right of the human person to religious freedom must be given such recognition in the constitutional order of society as will make it a civil right."[3] It also claims that every religion has the right to be publicly organized in civil society, and have its own schools, newspapers, and to teach by the spoken or written word. All of this is clearly contained in *Dignitatis Humanae*. One reads there: "...these groups have a right to immunity so that they may organize themselves according to their own principles. They must be allowed to honor the supreme Godhead with public worship..." (*ibid.*, p.802).

Religious Liberty or Toleration? Bea *vs.* Ottaviani

It is for this reason that during the meetings of the Central Preparatory Commission of the Council, Cardinal Ottaviani was so vigorously opposed to Cardinal Bea, who absolutely wanted to see the Council adopt religious liberty. He had written at the head of his schema *De Libertate Religiosa*, whereas Cardinal Ottaviani had written *De Tolerantia Religiosa*. The difference is quite clear: error is tolerated to the degree that it cannot be suppressed, but if one can, one should. The goal is always to pursue and destroy error and confront it with the truth. But in certain States, there comes a moment when, because of the circumstances or the number of Catholics, that is no longer possible, when public order could no longer be assured, and peace would be endangered. The Church has always recognized this. Pope Leo XIII stated this in his encyclical *Libertas*: toleration is a legitimate course of action.

But *De Libertate Religiosa*, as meant by Cardinal Bea, is freedom accorded in principle to all the religions, freedom of opinion, freedom for all to publicly express whatever they will. Such a view exactly contradicts what Pope Pius IX proclaimed in his encyclical *Quanta Cura*. It is unthinkable!

---

[2] St. Leo, Epistle 164, al. 133, sec. 2, Boll. ed.
[3] *Vatican Council II: The Conciliar and Post Conciliar Documents*, p.800.

Decisive Influence of Fr. John Courtney Murray, S.J.

One of the principal driving forces behind the *Declaration on Religious Liberty* was Fr. John Courtney Murray, an American, who was one of the dominant members of the commission entrusted with its preparation. In his book *The Rhine Flows into the Tiber*, Fr. Ralph Wiltgen devoted an entire page proving the influence of Fr. Murray in drafting this text on religious liberty.

In the book which he should publish on religious liberty[4] Michael Davies could well reveal what he found out in America, documents prior to the Council, which condemned Fr. Murray because of his doctrines. In the archives of his diocese, Michael Davies found the transcripts of lengthy conversations between Murray, the Holy Office, and the theologians.[5] His doctrines were condemned at that time. The Holy Office forbade him to defend them and to continue writing.[6] He lightly shrugged it off, and so it was he who was chosen[7] to draft the text of the *Declaration on Religious Liberty* adopted by Vatican II. It is unthinkable! For, naturally, he insinuated his own ideas! It is nonetheless interesting to know that he had been previously condemned by the Holy Office for his ideas, and had been forbidden to publish them.

Then who is right now? Is it the Holy Office that condemned Fr. Murray, by founding its decision on the traditional doctrine of the Church, or is it Fr. Murray, whose ideas have been adopted by the Council?

Council "Experts" Under Condemnation of the Holy Office

I am accused of being against the Council; but this is inexact. I am not against the Council *per se*, but against the influence of Liberalism that clearly infiltrated the Council. It is impossible

---

[4] *The Second Vatican Council and Religious Liberty* Angelus Press, Kansas City, MO).
[5] In particular, Mgr. Joseph C. Fenton, editor-in-chief of *The American Ecclesiastical Review; cf. Davies, op. cit.,* chap. I.
[6] Davies, *op. cit.*, chap I.
[7] Murray was an expert at the Council as early as the second session, and his collaboration in the drafting of the successive schemas on religious liberty was decisive. Cf. Davies, *op. cit.*, pp.109, 117, 125, 137.

to deny this penetration. It is obvious that people who had been condemned by the Holy Office were chosen to be experts at the Council: Fr. Edward Schillebeeckx had been condemned, and he was an expert at the Council.[8]

During a meeting of the Central Preparatory Commission with seventy-seven cardinals and about thirty bishops and superiors of religious congregations gathered, I asked the following question: "Cardinal Ottaviani just said that the experts chosen must not have been condemned by the Holy Office; yet I know three of them who have been: how is it that they appear on the list of experts?" The Cardinal did not reply at that moment, but on leaving the meeting he passed by me, and took me by the arm and said: "I know it well, but it's the boss who wants them there."

This was just the style of John XXIII. For him, there was never any evil. "Oh, no, he is a good guy, you'll see. When he is with everyone he will see the light; all will be well." Meanwhile, it is they who won.

Let's return to the study of the encyclical *Quanta Cura*.

Condemnation of Freedom of All Religions

Introducing the *Syllabus* in the encyclical, Pope Pius IX begins, as we have seen, by particularly condemning the fact that many want to:

> ...apply...to civil intercourse the impious and absurd principles of what they call Naturalism....

Not a few, then, were to be found in his epoch:

> ...who dare teach "that the best form of Society, and the exigencies of civil progress, absolutely require human society to be constituted and governed without any regard whatsoever to Religion, as if this [Religion] did not even exist, or at least without making any distinction between true and false religions." Contrary to the teachings of the Holy Scriptures, of the Church, and of the Holy Fathers, these persons do not hesitate to assert, that "the best condition of human society is that wherein no duty is

---

[8] Fr. Yves Congar, O.P., had also had "difficulties" with Rome because of his book, *Chrétiens désunis*. (Cf. Eric Vatré, *La droite du Père*, Guy Trédaniel, ed., 1994, p.115).

recognized by the Government of correcting, by enacted penalties, the violators of the Catholic Religion, except when the maintenance of the public peace requires it."

This article was the object of very lively discussions. Yet this is exactly what the Vatican II *Declaration on Religious Liberty* says.[9] One finds oneself faced with a problem that must one day be resolved: the Church cannot let what Pius IX explicitly taught be contradicted by a text of the Council.

This is the heart of our opposition to the Modern Rome. In his last letter, Cardinal Seper[10] wrote to me: "You should agree to stop criticizing the Council documents." He does not want us to point out that certain passages do not correspond at all to the doctrine of the Church. When we sent dossiers to Rome explaining our position, most notably a half-a-dozen pages published as a booklet by the journal *Itinéraires*, "Archbishop Lefebvre and the Holy Office," we received no reply. If no one answers us, it is because they are incapable of refuting our arguments.

But be assured, one day Rome will admit that in the Council documents there are unacceptable statements that will have to be changed. What is very serious is that we are seeing come to pass the very continuation of the trend condemned by the popes in the last century. Pius IX, like Gregory XVI in 1832, denounces those who:

> ...from this totally false notion of social government, fear not to uphold that erroneous opinion most pernicious to the Catholic Church, and to the salvation of souls, which was called by Our Predecessor, Gregory XVI (lately quoted), the insanity, namely, "that the liberty of conscience and of worship is the peculiar (or inalienable) right of every man, which should be proclaimed by law..." (*Mirari Vos*).

---

[9] With the sole difference that the exigencies of "the objective moral order," the limit to religious liberty recognized by *Dignitatis Humanae*, are stricter than "the public peace" of *Quanta Cura*. According to *Dignitatis Humanae*, a religion that professes immorality should be repressed, yet immorality is not necessarily contrary to public peace.

[10] Cardinal Seper, who had succeeded Cardinal Ottaviani, was then Prefect of the Congregation for the Doctrine of the Faith.

Yet that is what the Council affirms: everyone can practice his religion. So who is right? As for us, we hold to the doctrine expressed by Gregory XVI and Pius IX, reiterated by Leo XIII, and then by St. Pius X and Pius XII. When we are told that we are going against the magisterium of the Church, we answer that, on the contrary, it is because we are attached to the magisterium of all the popes that we cannot accept the errors that are being taught today. For, if we are told, "The magisterium belongs to its time; Pius IX's is over, that was more than a century ago..," then there is no magisterium left. If the magisterium of Pius IX is now worthless, then so is that of his predecessors, as well as his successors. Today's magisterium will be worthless in ten years. To what should one adhere? Where is the truth?

The Occupied Church

For twenty centuries the Church always affirmed the same thing, faithful to its message and to tradition. But for three or four centuries, Liberalism has succeeded in getting hold of society, then in the twentieth century it entered the Church, and has now won over the hierarchy. Essentially, the devil and the Freemasons have succeeded in penetrating the Church to the highest level, and in making her teach things she had formerly condemned. Of course the Church itself cannot err, cannot change; but she has been infiltrated by men who do not belong to the Church. They have invaded the Church, and occupied the highest offices, but they do not constitute the Church. We are witnessing a veritable occupation, as the writer Ploncard d'Assac perceived by entitling his book *L'Eglise Occupée*.

It's true; Rome is occupied. Weak popes, themselves more or less liberal, let themselves be controlled by these enemies. They no longer have the courage to react; they hesitate because their own doctrine is not solid. And so the evil continues to spread and to wreak havoc. Even Pope John Paul II, who seemed energetic, has not had the necessary courage. He expresses desires, but he doesn't manage to bring them about or to impose them. He is afraid of the people at Rome who say that Tradition is finished. As long as the Pope does not expel them from Rome, there is no hope of a change. We are undergoing, and the Church is undergoing, a veritable passion. We have come to that.

To understand the evil, it is worthwhile to reread *L'Histoire du Libéralisme* of Fr. Emmanuel Barbier. All this helps us to understand the current crisis. The crisis didn't happen in the space of a decade; it began in the sixteenth century, when men rebelled against God and decided to laicize the States, to chase the Church from civil society, and to banish Our Lord. This secularization of society has now entered the Church itself: the altars, the Mass, and all the ceremonies have been secularized. This is very apparent in the new Masses, where the sense of the supernatural, of holiness, and of mystery have disappeared. It is empty, hollow; it's theatrical, everything remains external. In Mexico a priest said recently: "The progressive religion is a mask; there is nothing behind it."

Let us then attach ourselves to the truths taught by popes who were courageous in their time.

Liberation Theology

The error that consists in pushing aside religion from civic life has consequences, which Pius IX points out:

> Religion has been excluded from civil Society, and the doctrine and authority of divine Revelation, or the true and germane notion of justice and human right have been obscured and lost, and material or brute force substituted in the place of true justice and legitimate right.

The substitution of brute force in the place of moral and spiritual force is what we are witnessing in the socialist countries today:

> But who does not see and plainly understand, that the Society of man, freed from the bonds of Religion and of true justice, can certainly have no other purpose than the effort to obtain and accumulate wealth, and that in its actions it follows no other law than that of the uncurbed cupidity, which seeks to secure its own pleasures and comforts?

Behold the ideas that have gained a foothold in the Church. Liberation theology is an example: envy is breathed into hearts and souls by talk of the division of wealth, of a "standard" of living, as if that were paramount. They put religion at the service of this envy; priests only preach that the same opportunities, the same pleasures are everybody's due.

Who speaks, then, of eternal life? What is this false terrestrial paradise that will never exist? That there are injustices and that we should decry them in order to recall everyone to his duty, amen. But let us not forget that the modest societies, far from modern civilization, have the best way of life. It strikes us as too poor, as too miserable: no radio, no television, few changes of clothes. But they work, they have their own fields, the forests, the wood; they build their houses, perhaps not quite so comfortable, without reclining sofas in the American mode...but those people live well, they are happy and know how to open themselves to the realities of religion, being little attached to material things. Unfortunately, often fetishes replace religion, but if one succeeds in driving them out and teaching the people the Catholic religion, then the result is balanced, happy people. The essential is not to seek riches and comfort.

Destruction of Religious Orders and Christian Education

Pius IX continues:

> For this reason, also, these same men persecute with such bitter hatred the Religious Orders, who have deserved so well of Religion, civil Society, and Letters; they loudly declare that these Orders have no right to exist, and, in so doing, make common cause with the falsehoods of the heretics. For, as was most wisely taught by Our Predecessor of illustrious memory, Pius VI, "the abolition of Religious Orders injures the state of public profession of the Evangelical counsels; injures a mode of life recommended by the Church, as in conformity with Apostolical doctrine; does wrong to the illustrious founders whom we venerate upon our altars, and who constituted these societies under the inspiration of God" (Letter to Cardinal de la Rochefoucauld, March 10, 1791).

Evidently, these religious orders dwelt in simplicity, in poverty, in the renunciation of the goods of this world. But this was so contrary to the principles of modern society, that it was necessary to get rid of an example so bothersome for the propagation of modern ideas.

Unfortunately, now it is the orders that are destroying themselves. Since the Council, many have practically suppressed poverty, obedience, sometimes chastity. There is not even the consolation of being able to blame the enemies of the Church! Hence the necessity of restoring the religious orders: Benedictines, Franciscans, Dominicans, in order to give anew the example of holiness which the world needs so much:

> Not content with abolishing Religion in public Society, they desire further to banish it from families and private life. Teaching and professing these most fatal errors of Socialism and Communism, they declare "that domestic society, or the family, derives all its reason of existence solely from civil law, whence it is to be concluded that from civil law descend and depend all the rights of parents over their children, and, above all, the right of instructing and educating them.

Hence, too, the right to divorce! And also, the right to take away from parents and the Church the education of youth in order to corrupt it, says the Pope.

The Infallibility of *Quanta Cura*

Having thus exposed the errors, Pope Pius IX concludes, not without having made clear that he speaks in virtue of his apostolic mandate. There has been much discussion as to whether this encyclical bears the mark of infallibility. It is clear that, to introduce his *Syllabus*, the Pope not only invoked his apostolic authority, but also used the terms used by the popes when they wished to proclaim a doctrine infallibly. All of the conditions have been fulfilled for the text of this document to bear the seal of infallibility.[11]

Let us read what Pius IX then writes:

---

[11] Since Vatican I (*Pastor Aeternus*) these criteria are: invocation of the pope's apostolic authority, a doctrine concerning faith or morals, precise definition of the doctrine in question, and the intention of obligating all the faithful to assent (cf. DS 3074, Dz. 1839). Pope Pius IX himself placed quotation marks in his text around all the passages that were covered by the seal of infallibility.

> Amid so great a perversity of depraved opinions, We, remembering Our Apostolic duty, and solicitous before all things for Our most holy Religion, for sound doctrine, for the salvation of the souls confided to Us, and for the welfare of human society itself, have considered the moment opportune to raise anew Our Apostolic voice. Therefore do We, by our Apostolic authority, reprobate, denounce, and condemn generally and particularly all the evil opinions and doctrines specially mentioned in this Letter, and We wish that they may be held as reprobated, denounced, and condemned by all the children of the Catholic Church.

The Pope then encourages the bishops to remind the faithful of what he has said, and then he calls for prayer:

> We have therefore judged it right to excite the piety of all the faithful, in order that, with Us and with You all, they may pray without ceasing to the Father of lights and of mercies, supplicating and beseeching Him fervently and humbly, and in the plenitude of their faith they may seek refuge in Our Lord Jesus Christ, who has redeemed us to God with His blood, that by their earnest and continual prayers, they may obtain from that most dear Heart, victim of burning charity for us, that it would draw all to Himself by the bonds of His love....

> We have thought it good to open to Christians, with Apostolic liberality, the heavenly treasures of the Church confided to Our dispensation, so that the faithful, more strongly drawn towards true piety, and purified from the stain of their sins by the Sacrament of Penance, may more confidently offer up their prayers to God and obtain His mercy and grace.

The Pope declares a year of jubilee:

> We grant to all and each of the faithful of both sexes throughout the Catholic world a Plenary Indulgence, in the manner of a Jubilee, during one month, up to the end of the coming year 1865.

This makes clear the importance Pius IX wanted to attach to this encyclical, which now is considered as backwards and outmoded.

Chapter X

THE SYLLABUS OF ERRORS OF POPE PIUS IX
(DECEMBER 8, 1864)

In studying the encyclical *Quanta Cura* of Pope Pius IX, we mentioned the *Syllabus*, which is a continuation of the letter. There the Pope denounces "the principal errors of our time," and which since the Council have also become those of our own times, because they have now penetrated the Church, thus opening the most grave and devastating crisis that the Church has known.

The first part is devoted to Pantheism, Naturalism, and Absolute Rationalism. Of the seven condemned propositions, let us look in particular at propositions five and seven.

Rationalism

Proposition 5: Divine revelation is imperfect, and therefore subject to a continual and indefinite progress, corresponding with the advancement of human reason.

The Church teaches, rather, that divine revelation ended with the death of the last apostle, St. John. The Church's task ever since has been to transmit the deposit of the faith, explaining it, naturally, but without either adding or deleting anything. Thus it is absolutely contrary to the doctrine of the Church to speak of the evolution of dogma in keeping with the passage of time or the progress of science.

Proposition 7: The prophecies and miracles set forth and recorded in the Sacred Scriptures are the fiction of poets, and the mysteries of the Christian faith the result of philosophical investigations. In the books of the Old and the New Testament there are contained mythical inventions, and Jesus Christ is Himself a myth.

Those who today deny the resurrection of Our Lord act exactly in this manner.

The second section targets Moderate Rationalism. Seven propositions are condemned, of which several are worth pointing out:

> Proposition 13: The method and principles by which the old scholastic doctors cultivated theology are no longer suitable to the demands of our times and to the progress of the sciences.

Even if this error is not openly preached, it is practiced today in the seminaries, and even the great Roman universities, where the method and principles of St. Thomas have been jettisoned. It suffices to read *Sì Sì No No*[1] to become aware of the atrocities that are believed in the Roman universities. The news is so well reported that this newsletter has become the terror of the professors. Some cardinals circulate it in their offices, and the clergy begins to be enlightened, but it will take time for corrective measures to be taken. With Cardinals Garrone and Villot, the progressives are well placed. One finds oneself before an unbreakable wall. And it is impossible to dispel the administrative torpor.

The Pope is the Pope: a word would suffice for everyone to be compelled to obey him. One wonders if he made a promise at his election not to change anything. He himself says it: he carries on Vatican II; therefore he cannot at the same time end the current disorders. His reproaches to the religious, the Jesuits, are futile in practice, because the people in charge are allowed to keep their posts, and are free to continue as before.

Religious Indifferentism

The third section focuses on Indifferentism and Latitudinarianism. The four condemned propositions are quite pertinent:

> Proposition 15: Every man is free to embrace and profess that religion which, guided by the light of reason, he shall consider true.

---

[1] Available from Angelus Press–*Ed.*

Stated otherwise, everyone has his own conscience and is free to choose his religion![2] This is to deny the existence of a unique true religion, its motives of credibility, and the need for grace to be able to adhere to it. This condemned proposition is to be found exactly in the *Declaration on Religious Liberty* (*Dignitatis Humanae*). Our critics will retort that it contains a sentence affirming that only the Catholic religion possesses the truth, but this sentence was added by Paul VI at the last minute to gain the votes of the 250 bishops who refused to sign the declaration. And it is contradicted by the rest of the document, as is the sentence, also added at the last minute, referring to tradition. By these two additions, Paul VI succeeded in reducing the number of opponents from 250 to 84:

> Proposition 16: Man may, in the observance of any religion whatever, find the way of eternal salvation, and arrive at eternal salvation.

---

[2] In his work *Les principes de la Théologie Catholique*, Card. Ratzinger expressed himself on the subject of the radical reversal of the position taken by the Church on the modern errors: "The one-sided attachment, conditioned by circumstances, to the positions taken by the Church in the initiatives of Pius IX and Pius X against the new period of history opened by the French Revolution had largely been corrected *via facti*, but a new fundamental determination of the Church's relationship with the world as it had come to be after 1789 was still lacking" (p.247, French edition). "In fact, in the countries with a large Catholic majority, the outlook prevailing prior to the Revolution still held sway. Almost no one denies today that the Spanish and Italian concordats sought to retain too many aspects of a conception of the world that no longer corresponded to the reality. Likewise, almost no one can deny that to this attachment to an outmoded conception of the relations between Church and State corresponded similar anachronisms in the domain of education and in the attitude to be taken towards the modern historical method" (p.427). Alluding to the text of the *Pastoral Constitution on the Church in the Modern World* (*Gaudium et Spes*), the Prefect of the Congregation for the Doctrine of the Faith adds: "Let it suffice to say that the text plays the part of an anti-*Syllabus* in the measure that it represents an attempt at the official reconciliation of the Church with the world such as it has become since 1789" (p.427). Confronted by the vigorous reaction his words provoked amongst those who had still retained some notion of the opposition of truth and error, Card. Ratzinger tried to minimize their import. But they had been written down in black and white, and, in a certain measure, this admission reflected for the first time a certain frankness.

Evidently, certain distinctions must be made. Souls can be saved *in* a religion other than the Catholic religion (Protestantism, Islam, Buddhism, etc.), but not *by* this religion. There may be souls who, not knowing Our Lord, have by the grace of the good Lord, good interior dispositions, who submit to God—God in so far as these people can conceive Him—and who want to accomplish His will.[3] There certainly are not many such persons, because these people, not being baptized, suffer more than Christians the consequences of original sin. But some of these persons make an act of love which implicitly is equivalent to baptism of desire. It is uniquely by this means that they are able to be saved. Implicit baptism means the Church: by the very fact that baptism of desire is found implicitly in their act of charity and submission to God, these persons belong to the Church. They are saved by the Church, by Our Lord Jesus Christ.

For there is baptism of water, baptism of blood, baptism of explicit desire (that of catechumens), then baptism of implicit desire, which is contained in an act of true love of God. How many are saved by this form of baptism? God alone knows. It is a great mystery for us.[4]

---

[3] Cf. Pius IX, encyclical letter *Quanto Conficiamur* of August 10, 1863 (DS 2865, Dz. 1677); Letter of the Holy Office to Cardinal Cushing, Archbishop of Boston, August 8, 1849 (DS 3870).

[4] The magisterium has exactly clarified Catholic doctrine concerning persons who, living outside the visible limits of the Catholic Church, have nonetheless the "implicit desire" to belong to it. The letter of the Holy Office to Cardinal Cushing, Archbishop of Boston, of August 8, 1849 (DS. 3870-3872) recapitulates the teaching of Popes Pius IX in his letter *Iam Vos Omnes* of September 13, 1868, to Protestants and other non-Catholics, and Pius XII in his encyclical letter *Mystici Corporis* of June 29, 1943: The Church reproves two opposite errors, that of those who exclude from salvation souls that, "adhere to the Church solely by implicit desire," and on the other hand, the error of those who "falsely assure that men can equally be saved in every religion." In brief, say these two Popes, these souls, while "ordered to the mystical body of the Redeemer by a certain desire or unconscious wish," are nonetheless separated from the visible Church, and thus "in a state in which no one can be assured of his salvation." The letter of the Holy Office specifies that the "implicit desire" to belong to the Church, in order to produce its effect, must contain "supernatural faith" and be "informed by perfect charity." Hence not just any kind of desire suffices.

One cannot say, then, that no one is saved in these religions, but if he is saved, it is always by his attachment to the mystical body which is the Catholic Church, even if the persons concerned do not know it. In any case, salvation is never by their false religion, bereft of foundation and invented by men! One cannot be saved by a religion contrary to the Holy Ghost, who is the Spirit of Truth and cannot dwell where error is lodged.

Outside of the Church No Salvation

This is then what Pius IX said and what he condemned. It is necessary to understand the formulation that was so often employed by the Fathers of the Church: "Outside the Church there is no salvation."

When we say that, it is incorrectly believed that we think that all the Protestants, all the Moslems, all the Buddhists, all those who do not publicly belong to the Catholic Church go to hell. Now, I repeat, it is possible for souls to be saved in these religions, but they are saved by the Church, and so the formulation is true: *Extra Ecclesiam nulla salus*. This must be preached.

It is necessary to preach it, so that people, knowing this, will be drawn to conversion. If we allow any doubt to cloud the subject, we let them believe that the Protestants, for example, are saved as we are, by their religion. This would be to deceive the Protestants themselves, and give them a good conscience and leave them in their error. They could think that, if even the Catholics say that one can be saved by being Protestant, then it is not worth the trouble to convert.

Such an idea would ruin the missionary spirit. If one grants that men can be saved in any religion whatsoever, why go to the missions? Why cross the seas? Why go and expose oneself to the diseases of those insalubrious regions, or to the rebellions of religious groups? How many Franciscans, Dominicans and others have been killed for having tried to convert the Moslems! Then why? Uselessly? If they could be saved in the Moslem religion shouldn't they have left them alone?

But if we are convinced that there is no salvation outside the Church, then we feel a considerable responsibility before this enormous multitude who do not know Our Lord Jesus Christ.

They run the risk, living in error, of going to hell. It is necessary to tell them so, it is necessary to disturb them. It is necessary to preach them the Gospel as the Church has done century after century, by sending her missionaries everywhere. Even at the very beginning, the apostles were killed. Recall the first missionaries of the African Missions of Lyons who died in the first months following their arrival: malaria, hepatitis. In our cemeteries on the tombstones were etched "dead at 25 years," "arrived one year ago," "a year and a half ago." They left home braving death, and their death certainly served those who followed them and who were able to convert and save many of these people—people who lived in error and vice—for even when these religions have an attractive appearance, it suffices to scratch a little to find a world corrupted by all the vices.

The following proposition of the *Syllabus* condemned by Pius IX practically says the same thing:

> Good hope at least is to be entertained of the eternal salvation of all those who are not at all in the true Church of Christ.

We should *wish* their salvation, of course, but we cannot *hope* it. We must *not* entertain a good hope of their salvation, because that would result in not being preoccupied with evangelization nor the salvation of their souls. It is not possible to be saved when one "is not at all" in the Church, not even by baptism of implicit desire. These are, unfortunately, very widespread ideas which the majority of Catholics express without any reticence.

The Situation of the Protestants: Ecumenism

Proposition eighteen draws from the preceding ones an application to the Protestants:

> Protestantism is nothing more than another form of the same true Christian religion, in which form it is given to please God equally as in the Catholic Church.

At this point it isn't superfluous to refer to what is said, if not explicitly then at least implicitly, in the *Declaration on Religious Liberty* of Vatican II: Each man is free to profess the religion which, by the light of reason, he considers as true. It is not even formally affirmed that the Catholic religion, possessing the truth, is the only true religion.

Were it published today, the condemnation made in proposition eighteen would infuriate a lot of people, because the condemned proposition means that one should not try and convert the Protestants.

Of course, individually, it is possible for Protestants, in certain circumstances, to receive particular graces from the good God. But when one looks at the situation, it is not adequate to think that among them are nice people, likable, kind, friendly. Let us look behind the facade at the domain of morality. It was Protestantism that brought on all the evils from which the Catholic countries now suffer: divorce, contraception, broken families, or families with only a few children. And this is not to consider the lack of faith, the destruction of religion, piety diminished, formal and external. So many people who are living in an irregular situation, and who no longer obey God's laws: how can they be saved? Of course, it is the good Lord who will judge, but still it is necessary to see things as they are and to retain the missionary spirit.

Ecumenism is much talked about. It began about 1920-25; it was then a way of approaching the Protestants in order to convert them, and to get them to return to the Church. Both Pope St. Pius X and Pius XI wrote letters on the subject. Now it is different: the Protestants are approached for the sake of mutual understanding and to be enriched by the values that each religion possesses, to exchange ideas on religion. There is no longer any question of conversion. In short, it is the contrary of what the Church has always taught.

This is grave. Today, we are everywhere confronted with multiple religions. In Africa I knew the pagans and Moslems, but with the migrations of peoples taking place in our epoch, this occurs everywhere; it is in France, in Italy and Germany that one encounters not only Protestants, but also Moslems and members of a multitude of sects, the Jehovah's Witnesses for instance.

What Must Be Said

Therefore we must have very precise ideas and always express the Church's judgment. We can speak to the people of these diverse religions, and answer them when they ask for explanations. What must we tell them?

Should we leave them with a tranquil conscience? tell them not to bother, that they have a very beautiful religion which, at the root, is equal to ours? That would be to commit a crime, because these souls were perhaps expecting from us the truth, and we would have kept it from them. From that moment they would never convert.

Some young Protestants invited me one day to Lausanne to give them a conference; they wanted to hear me speak about Ecône. I told them: "I am speaking to you as a Catholic bishop, and I think that that is why you invited me. Do not be surprised then if I tell you exactly what I think about Protestantism."

I made it clear that for us there is only one true religion, and that Ecône represents this conviction, for one cannot be saved outside the Catholic Church. That is why we are traditionalists; that does not mean that we despise the others, but the Protestant religion is for us an error.

Well, in the days following, these young Protestants wrote me to congratulate me. They told me that that was what they had wanted to hear; they knew that a Catholic is a Catholic and that he cannot admit that Protestantism is the true religion. So they were not surprised.

If, on the contrary, I had spoken as the ecumenists do, if I had said that at Ecône we love the Catholic Church, of course, but that we are the friends of Protestants, and find their religion lovely. If I had spoken thus, I think that, first of all, they would not have been happy; they would have thought that I was flattering them, and trying to ingratiate myself with them, but that at heart I did not really believe what I was saying. I would have made them miss an occasion to reflect seriously about converting.

All this is serious, and we Catholics have to constantly face such situations. Let us be of service to these souls, let us always think of their salvation. If I do not speak correctly, if I do not transmit the truth, there will perhaps be souls who shall not be saved, whereas they might have been. Certainly, the good God can act directly, without intermediary in order to convert the whole world. Nevertheless, he wanted to use priests and missionaries.

He counts on us; it is we who must be the occasion of conversion for these souls. It is then that we must think of the grace of God, who profits from our preaching, or a conversation, or conferences to open the souls of these Protestants. He can then give them the grace of conversion, for, of course, it is He who converts souls.

Biblical Societies

In the fourth part of the *Syllabus*, Pius IX refers to the encyclicals and allocutions in which he reproved "in the strongest terms" these "plagues" which are Socialism, Communism, the secret societies, Biblical societies, and clerico-liberal societies. Socialism is condemned, for it is a system that rejects God, refuses His authority in the State, in the family, over individuals, in education. Communism is the same thing, with the same principles. The secret societies are similar, without truth, without dogmas and without morality.

The case of the Biblical societies is more difficult to apprehend, because at first glance these societies are constituted to diffuse the Gospel, the Bible: can this be bad? It is necessary to understand why the popes condemn these societies: It is because they propagate texts of the Sacred Scriptures, edited or translated in the Protestant spirit of free examination, as if it were the right of individuals themselves to interpret Sacred Scripture. The Church has always said that Holy Scripture must be taught by the magisterium of the Church; we must then listen to how the Church interprets a chapter or a parable. It is for this reason that she did not want to disseminate the Bible. Of course, in her preaching, the Church has always been founded upon the Gospel, but she has wanted to safeguard people from the occasion of erring in the interpretation of Scripture and the Gospel.

The Protestant spirit denies tradition and rejects the magisterium. The Holy Ghost, they say, directly inspires the person reading, sometimes differently for the same text from person to person, but it is always the Holy Ghost who breathes where He will. But the Scripture was placed by God into the hands of the Church. Tradition and the magisterium existed before the Scriptures. The sacred writers had not yet written the Gospels, the Acts of the Apostles, the Epistles, when the magisterium existed. The Scripture, which came later, gave a considerable support and a treasure to the Church, but it was the tradition that received Scripture, and must interpret it for the faithful. Hence the reticence of the Church to distribute or to diffuse the Bible.

Unfortunately, a kind of error in the likeness of the Protestant error has entered the Church. Cardinals, bishops and priests have set about distributing the Bible, allegedly to counteract the Protestant Bibles, as if the Church had been wrong not to do so sooner and with as much zeal as the Protestants! And so it is necessary to correctly read what the popes have said about the Biblical societies; they wanted to prevent Sacred Scripture from being interpreted in fanciful ways, as is being done now.

In 1564 Pope Pius IV drew up the formulation of a "profession of Catholic faith" which had to be sworn by all those who received an office: ordinands, bishops, cardinals, professors. Among other things it said:

> I acknowledge the Holy Scripture in the sense that was and still is that of our Mother the holy Church, to whom it belongs to judge the veritable meaning of holy Letters; and I shall never receive and interpret it other than according to the unanimous assent of the Fathers.[5]

Yet, by means of the Council and the penetration of Liberalism in the Church, every theologian today interprets Scripture as he likes, even the miracles. They had even wanted to include in the texts of the Council that, in Sacred Scripture, only those things pertaining to faith and morals were inspired by the Holy Ghost, as if the history of Jesus, the facts, and the miracles were not inspired! A real fight was necessary in order to expunge such a sentence from the Council texts: it was changed, but not completely. It is a very dangerous spirit, because by it one could say that the narrative of the infancy, with its three kings and the shepherds, is but a legend.

The Council of Trent was formal: The Scripture is the word of God, the sacred writers are but the instruments of the divine thought; intelligent instruments, of course, and each book is

---

[5] This oath was still in vigor until Vatican II when it was replaced by Paul VI in 1967, then by Pope John Paul II in 1989, with very vague formulations. (Cf. *Fideliter*, no. 70, p.26.)

marked by the style of each of the writers. But nonetheless it is God who is the author of Sacred Scripture, which is entirely inspired. How is it possible to have the right to pick and choose among the passages of which God himself is the author? Such a thing is unheard of, but this is how far things have gone.

And they have gone farther still, to the point of drafting an ecumenical Bible, both Protestant and Catholic, the "ecumenical translation of the Bible." This is the epitome of their error. They suppressed passages displeasing to Protestants, they inserted passages like those of the Protestant Bible, and this new Bible is now recommended by the bishops. Do they still believe that God is the author of Scripture?

The Rights of the Church

The fifth section of the *Syllabus* treats the errors on the Church and her rights. For example, proposition nineteen expresses an error fairly common in our day:

> The Church is not a true and perfect society, entirely free; nor is she endowed with proper and perpetual rights of her own, conferred upon her by her Divine Founder; but it appertains to the civil power to define what are the rights of the Church, and the limits within which she may exercise those rights.

During the Council and after, theologians and priests circulated leaflets demanding the suppression of religious marriages. According to them, marriage should depend uniquely upon the State. Then, because the State made the marriages, it would also be able to break them easily.

The Catholic Church, the One True Religion

Let's consider proposition twenty-one:

> The Church has not the power of defining dogmatically that the religion of the Catholic Church is the only true religion.

This is what most upsets the Freemasons. As soon as one speaks of it, there are reactions in the press. That is why there was such a strong desire to have the Council draft the *Declaration on Religious Liberty*, which implicitly states that the Catholic religion is not the sole true religion. When we point this out, they retort that, at the end of the first section of this declaration there is a sentence that speaks of the true religion and the unique Church of Christ. Yes, but it is Paul VI who had this sentence added *in extremis*, as I have already had occasion to mention, whereas elsewhere this affirmation is contradicted by demands that "religious groups" (read: the non-Catholic religions) are "not to be prevented from freely demonstrating the special value of their teaching for the organization of society and the inspiration of all human activity."[6] This is tantamount to saying that all the religions are equal.

Analysis of the Council's *Declaration on Religious Liberty*

Let us examine more attentively the *Declaration on Religious Liberty*. In the first chapter, "The General Principle of Religious Freedom," one reads:

> This right of the human person to religious freedom must be given such recognition in the constitutional order of society as will make it a civil right.[7]

Thus, this natural right to religious freedom must be recognized in society as a civil right; this right is to seek the truth.

A "Right to the Free Search for Truth"

> It is in accordance with their dignity that all men, because they are persons, that is, beings endowed with reason and free will and therefore bearing personal responsibility, are both impelled by their nature and bound by a moral obligation to seek the truth,....

If it is human dignity that obliges them to seek the truth, parents cannot impose the truth upon their children; one cannot teach the catechism because it is necessary to wait until the children possess their personal responsibility, until they are adults and can then themselves seek the truth!

---

[6] *Vatican Council II*, p.802.
[7] *Ibid.*, p.800.

...especially religious truth. They are also bound to adhere to the truth once they come to know it and direct their whole lives in accordance with the demands of truth.

They do not specify which truth! Everyone looks for his truth! These passages are unbelievable. Following in the next section (3) comes the following explanation:

> The search for truth, however, must be carried out in a manner that is appropriate to the dignity of the human person and his social nature, namely, by free enquiry with the help of teaching or instruction, communication and dialogue. It is by these means that men share with each other the truth they have discovered, or think they have discovered, in such a way that they help one another in the search for truth. Moreover, it is by personal assent that men must adhere to the truth they have discovered.[8]

A Right Contrary to the Gospel

This is entirely unacceptable and contrary to the mission of the Church. They say that it is not an obligation, one cannot constrain, one cannot say quite simply: behold the truth; this is the truth and you are obliged to believe it. But rather, everyone must seek his own truth, and when he is conscious of having found it, then he must firmly adhere to it.

This is entirely contrary to all that Our Lord Jesus Christ said: Go and teach the Gospel; go and teach the truth to the utmost confines of the earth. He who believes will be saved; he who refuses belief will be condemned. It is simple, it is not at all complicated. If one does not wish to be condemned, he must absolutely adhere to the truth that Our Lord taught. It is both simple and without alternative:

> It is through his conscience that man sees and recognizes the demands of the divine law.[9]

The conscience can be mistaken, whereas the divine law must be communicated to us by the Church, which must remain faith-

---

[8] *Ibid.*, p.801.
[9] *Ibid.*, p.801.

ful to the decalogue and teachings generously given us by Our Lord:

> He is bound to follow this conscience faithfully in all his activity so that he may come to God, who is his last end. Therefore he must not be forced to act contrary to his conscience.

No matter what his conscience suggests to him, he must follow it, and no one should constrain him not to act against his conscience. This is absolutely unthinkable!

> Nor must he be prevented from acting according to his conscience, especially in religious matters.

In religious matters, there is practically no obligation, no constraint, not only for individuals, but also for groups.[10]

The Council Professes Religious Relativism

In section four we read:

> The freedom or immunity from coercion in religious matters which is the right of individuals must also be accorded to men when they act in community. Religious communities are a requirement of the nature of man and of religion itself.

But what religion is meant? It is never specified!

> Therefore, provided the just requirements of public order are not violated, these groups have a right to immunity so that they may organize themselves according to their own principles. They must be allowed to honor the supreme Godhead with public worship....[11]

Yes, as unthinkable as it may seem, it is in the text of the *Declaration on Religious Liberty*: the supreme Godhead. It is not Our Lord Jesus Christ!

> [They must be allowed to] help their members to practice their religion and strengthen them with religious instruction, and promote institutions in which members may work together to organize their own lives according to their religious principles.

---

[10] *Ibid.*
[11] *Ibid.*, p.802.

Hence the Moslems, according to the Moslem principles, the Buddhists according to theirs, the Mormons according to Mormon principles, the Moonies according to Moon's. It cannot be. We have seen in the encyclicals of the popes we have studied, with what unanimity they condemn religious indifferentism. Well, today the *Declaration on Religious Liberty* affirms the opposite:

> Religious communities have the further right not to be prevented from publicly teaching and bearing witness to their beliefs by the spoken or written word.[12]

What faith, what religion is it a question of? It is not specified. It is normal to take into account that a religion is always accompanied by a morality. There is no religion without faith and morals, and consequently behavior is also concerned. According to the doctrine of the *Declaration on Religious Liberty*, the Protestants, then, can freely disseminate their morals, their moral freedom which has practically no law. For the Moslems, the same applies, and they can profess polygamy, slavery, and everything else that makes up their religion; the same applies to the Buddhists concerning their religious habits:

> Also included in the right to religious freedom is the right of religious groups not to be prevented from freely demonstrating the special value of their teaching for the organization of society and the inspiration of all human activity.

Is there in these religions a singular efficacy of their doctrine to organize and vivify all human activity? What of the grace of Our Lord Jesus Christ, the sacraments and the Holy Sacrifice of the Mass?

Is Our Lord Jesus Christ God?

Is Our Lord Jesus Christ God, or is He not God? This *Declaration on Religious Liberty* is unacceptable, because it is fundamentally contrary to the doctrine of the Church, and, as we have seen, absolutely contrary to what the popes have taught. It is unbelievable. If one believes in Our Lord Jesus Christ, if one believes that Our Lord Jesus Christ is God, that He truly founded

---

[12] *Ibid.*, p.803.

the Christian religion with all its prescriptions and institutions, if one believes that it is impossible to be saved outside of Him, how can one write such things? It is absolutely contradictory and irreconcilable.

It is for this reason that in their homilies and sermons they cannot bring themselves to pronounce the name of Our Lord Jesus Christ. They cannot, because the mere fact of pronouncing the name of Our Lord Jesus Christ is tantamount to saying: there is only one God, Our Lord Jesus Christ. And from this all the consequences follow; namely, you must obey Our Lord Jesus Christ, and you must accept His reign. But they can no longer, because that does not coincide with the *Declaration on Religious Liberty*, nor with the *Declaration on the Non-Christian Religions*, for, according to these documents, men no longer accept that.

In the Council documents, practically all the non-Christian religions are praised in nearly the same way as the Catholic religion; one seeks to find in them whatever there may be that is beautiful and good. During the discourse of Pope John Paul II at Bourget, France, it was remarked that a great part of it was consecrated to the glorification of man. The name of man was invoked unceasingly.

As soon as one accepts a declaration like the one on religious liberty, the Catholic religion can no longer be imposed. Then what religion can be imposed? One can try to make man more religious, speak of the deity, of religious sentiment, but one cannot speak of Our Lord; that is impossible. What becomes of the Catholic religion?

After this brief study of *Dignitatis Humanae*, let us now examine another proposition of the *Syllabus of Errors* concerning the rights of the Church:

> Proposition 24: The Church has not the power of using force, nor has she any temporal power, direct or indirect.

Clearly, it is the Inquisition that is targeted here. In fact, in the temporal domain the Church possesses a power uniquely for the protection of the Faith, and not for a temporal purpose as have the civil authorities. Not only does the Church have the right to own the temporal goods necessary for teaching, worship, religious life, etc., and to have the civil authorities respect this right; not only does she have the right to inflict spiritual sanctions (e.g., excommunication) against her guilty members, with all the temporal consequences that that implies; but she also has the right to have recourse to the assistance of the State to defend the Faith. The Church herself does not employ force, the sword, but she calls upon the secular arm, the temporal sword. She must have, then, a certain temporal power, albeit indirect. If the Church did not have the right to use force, then St. Pius V would have been wrong when he commanded the kings as his sons to come to the aid of Christendom, and to fight Islam; then St. Joan of Arc would have been wrong.

The Union Between Church and State

The sixth section deals with the errors about civil society, considered both in itself and in its relation to the Church. The error condemned here is that of Caesarism ("regalism"). This has existed from the time that certain kings wanted to dominate the Church. Now Caesarism exists especially in the Communist and Socialist countries which create national churches as in China, Hungary and Czechoslovakia, where even Catholic bishops accept to be at the service of the State. All these "priests for peace," the priests of the *Pax* movement, serve the Communist State. They do it, perhaps, with the idea that if they did not accept it, they would be persecuted more; that does not alter the fact that, publicly and practically, they are at the service of the Communist government, while those who resist are persecuted and expelled from their parishes.

President Salazar of Portugal was accused of Caesarism. I heard this accusation from the very mouth of the apostolic nuncio at Lisbon. Nevertheless, at the beginning he had admired Salazar, who as a good Catholic, helped the Catholic Church in every field—in the Universities, in the missions—and who thus, in Portugal, in Angola, and Mozambique, helped the Church to expand considerably. But at the time of Pope Paul VI and Cardinal Villot, the nuncio undoubtedly was pressured to oppose Salazar, to thwart his power and to undermine his popularity. It was then that he told me: "Salazar is a Caesarist." Why? Because he opposed the nomination of certain bishops who were probably acting as revolutionaries.

One day Salazar said to me: "I do all I can for the Church. I do not know what will happen afterwards, but as long as I have the power, I want to help the Catholic Church as much as possible." And he added: "I sometimes have the feeling, though, that the bishops do not understand me; they do not see that if they helped me more, we could accomplish even greater progress. For example, at the university I would like to see the truths of the Catholic Faith disseminated; so I would like the Church to appoint professors capable of teaching these truths. I do not feel that I am supported by the bishops."

It was admirable to see this head of State truly desirous of working for the expansion of the Catholic religion. He had asked me to come see him because I had visited the missions of the Holy Ghost Fathers in Angola. He was truly a simple and dignified man. When I think that he was scarcely received by Pope Paul VI when he went to visit Fatima! When heads of State are Catholic, it is they who are persecuted by Rome. It is the Communist heads of State who receive the best reception at the Vatican.

Shortly before his death, Franco said that one of the greatest sorrows he had known was not to have been received at the Vatican for the entire time that he was in authority. Yet Pius XI was not hostile to Franco, far from it; but even then a mood of hostility reigned at the nunciature. On the contrary, King Juan Carlos was received immediately by the Vatican. But does he truly work for the Catholic Church? The world is upside down.

The Error of Separation

In fact, if one reproached Salazar and Franco for concerning themselves too much with matters pertaining to the Church, it is because one has a false notion of the relations that should exist between Church and State. Separation is desired, and yet it is concord that is the most natural in Catholic States. We have seen that not only Pius IX, but also Gregory XVI and Leo XIII said: Governments have received authority not only to direct political, economic and material affairs, but also to help people on the spiritual plane and, consequently, to help the Church. Evidently they must let the Church direct spiritual things, but they must help the Church accomplish her work, and give her all possible means to do so. This is why the Church has always signed concordats, as, for example, with Franco; it included the right of the head of State to veto certain episcopal nominations. If this practice were truly bad, Pius XII would not have said that the concordat signed with Spain was one of the best. It is normal that there should be perfect accord between the Church and the State. When the head of a Catholic State is Catholic, for the good of the Church and his people, he may feel obliged to object to the nomination of certain bishops; he has a right not to let revolutionaries be picked.

When all the bishops are against him, a chief of State is in a very difficult situation. In Chile, for example, a single bishop upheld Pinochet; the others averred that the referendum had been fixed, and united their voices with the foreign governments and the progressive European press, thus lending a hand to the revolution. The same thing has happened in Bolivia, Venezuela. The question of the relation between Church and State is falsified by progressive tendencies: The idea that there must be a separation, that the State has no interest in religious questions is an absolutely false idea.

Hence, section six condemns "errors about civil society, considered both in itself and in its relation to the Church." For example:

> Proposition 50: Lay authority possesses of itself the right of presenting bishops, and may require of them to undertake the administration of the diocese before they receive canonical institution, and the Letters Apostolic from the Holy See.

Here is an abuse of power on the part of the State. The same is true of the following proposition:

> Proposition 51: And, further, the lay government has the right of deposing bishops from their pastoral functions, and is not bound to obey the Roman pontiff in those things which relate to the institution of bishoprics and the appointment of bishops.

And here is the last proposition of this section:

Proposition 55: The Church ought to be separated from the State, and the State from the Church.

This proposition is clearly condemned, and yet it is separation that prevailed at Vatican II! When Pope Paul VI said: "The Church only demands freedom," that meant, effectively, that the Church be left alone, that each power be occupied with its own business, and that there be no longer any relations between them...

Natural and Christian Moral Law

Chapter VII bears upon the "Errors Concerning Natural and Christian Ethics," the ideas according to which the ten commandments and the laws of God are at the disposition of the State:

Proposition 56: Moral laws do not stand in need of the divine sanction, and it is not at all necessary that human laws should be made conformable to the laws of nature, and receive their power of binding from God.

Practically speaking, this means that the law is completely independent, that as soon as the government enacts a law, *ipso facto* it is right and must be obeyed. Well, all the current laws imposed by the States contrary to the moral law do not oblige anyone, because they are contrary to the natural law and the ten commandments; no one is obliged to carry them out. Chapter VII also targets everything that the anti-clerical and masonic governments lay claim to:

Proposition 59: Right consists in the material fact. All human duties are an empty word, and all human facts have the force of right.

Errors on Christian Marriage

Section VIII condemns the "Errors Concerning Christian Marriage," errors still quite frequent in our day:

Proposition 65: The doctrine that Christ has raised marriage to the dignity of a sacrament cannot be at all tolerated.

With regard to the sacraments, many things have come to us from Tradition and are not explicitly to be found in Scripture, but the Church has always interpreted the presence of Our Lord at the wedding feast of Cana, the first manifestation of his public life, as signifying the consecration of marriage and its institution as a sacrament. There are also the words pronounced by Our Lord. But who is entitled to interpret these things? The Church, Tradition.

Take another example, that of the sacrament of penance. In Scripture there are many allusions to sin and to confession. They must be recognized, but who can determine exactly what the sacrament of penance consists in, or say that it was truly instituted by Our Lord? It is the Tradition, what was instituted by the Apostles and which has been transmitted by the Church from generation to generation:

> Proposition 67: By the law of nature, the marriage tie is not indissoluble, and in many cases divorce properly so called may be decreed by the civil authority.

Proposition 71 goes farther still:

> The form of solemnizing marriage prescribed by the Council of Trent, under pain of nullity, does not bind in cases where the civil law lays down another form, and declares that when this new form is used the marriage shall be valid.

Recall that prior to the Council of Trent, only the presence of witnesses was necessary; the presence of a priest was not necessary for the validity of the contract made between the spouses. Because of this there were abuses and grounds to contest the contract, which is why the Council of Trent prescribed that henceforth only those marriages would be valid that were celebrated before the Church's delegate—a priest, having the authority to delegate to other priests. There was only one exception to this rule: the case where the engaged couple could find no priest in their country. This happens nowadays when the engaged couple cannot find a priest who agrees to celebrate according to the traditional rite. At the end of a month, they can marry before witnesses, and if a priest is in the neighborhood, even if he is not delegated, he must attend the wedding. This case is similar to that of a couple stranded in a desert where no priest could possibly happen to come. Canon Law states that if the situation is likely to last for a month, they can choose witnesses and marry right away; the marriage will be valid. This is the only exception.

Now the idea has spread that marriage is not definitive. Many questions come to mind. Before the Council, in the dioceses the engaged couple was given a questionnaire to sign showing that they understood the essential elements of Catholic marriage, especially indissolubility. Now one finds oneself before young Catholics who have had little Catholic instruction or even none, and who are inclined to contract a marriage that would not necessarily be considered indissoluble: if the two agree to separate, they will separate...and then remarry. Such a marriage is invalid. This is equally true of one in which the fiancés would say that they do not want to have children, or only one or two, or that they will use contraceptives. Marriage exists for having children. To refuse to have any is grounds for nullity. How many marriages, then, are still valid? This is an essential matter, and a question that priests must bring up to the engaged couple.

The Pope, Chief of State

We come to section IX entitled "Errors Regarding the Civil Power of the Sovereign Pontiff." It bears upon the possibility that the pope might have a State and be head of State:

> Proposition 75: The children of the Christian and Catholic Church are divided amongst themselves about the compatibility of the temporal with the spiritual power.

Pius IX condemns this proposition because the matter is above discussion. If the popes have accepted this government, and exercised it for centuries, it was in order to be free to exercise the spiritual power. This does not signify the desire to appear as a head of State, but that of having more liberty. Today, ever since the Lateran accord between Pius XI and Mussolini, the Pontifical State has been reduced to the Vatican City. Nonetheless the principle remains, recognized by all the States, even secular and Freemasonic, that the pope is chief of State. He has ambassadors, Nuncios, who take precedence over other ambassadors. This honor is a small detail, but it is nonetheless extraordinary that the States recognize the Nuncios. Despite Liberalism and the idea of the separation of Church and State, to the present day the Vatican has not wished to suppress the nunciatures. It can be easily understood how important it is to have a representative to the various States for the relations with the governments overseeing the liberty of Catholics and for the continuation of the Church's work.

Many think this should be suppressed. It is according to this sentiment that the current popes have refused to wear the tiara; they suppressed what signified their rank as head of State: the protocol, the Palatine Guard, the police. Only the Swiss Guard remains. It is a bit ridiculous, because either the pope is really head of State and can have the attributes of one, or else he is no longer head of State, and he should then suppress the nunciatures.

It has been affirmed that if Liberalism was able to penetrate the Church so easily, it was because it no longer has a civil power. It can no longer defend itself. The infiltration was all the more possible because many of the offices, the secretariats, most of the Congregations and the embassies are situated outside Vatican City.

The Vatican administration is thus in constant contact with outsiders. To think that Rome has a Communist mayor and that the Masonic lodges have headquarters there! If Rome had remained the city of the Sovereign Pontiff, the lodges and the Communists would have infiltrated the Church much less.

Liberty Favors Error

The last chapter, bearing the heading "Errors Having Reference to Modern Liberalism," is still very pertinent:

> Proposition 77: In the present day it is no longer expedient that the Catholic religion should be held as the only religion of the State, to the exclusion of all other forms of worship.

Nonetheless, since Vatican II, the Church has not ceased to ask this of the States. The *Declaration on Religious Liberty* practically says the same thing. Cardinal Seper reproached me for a letter I had written for *Cor Unum* and which was also published in *Fideliter*, in which I said that one was obliged to acknowledge the fact that Pope Paul VI was a liberal. I had already said that before, by citing Cardinal Daniélou, who was his bosom friend and who explicitly wrote as much in *Mémoires du cardinal Daniélou*, a book published by his sister: "Yes, it must be recognized that Pope Paul VI was a liberal."

At my last audience, Cardinal Seper reproached me for that. "How can you say that Paul VI was a liberal?" I replied that it was perfectly true, such was the position of Paul VI concerning the separation of Church and State and religious liberty. "But what do you want us to do now?" he replied. It is not a question of practice and of knowing what to do here and now, it is a question of principle, I answered. Was the Pope in favor of the separation of Church and State, or was he not? Cardinal Seper did not want to reply. "How do you expect us to do anything else?"!

Yet it is they themselves who actively follow the principle enunciated in the *Declaration on Religious Liberty*, and request that States adopt the separation of Church and State so that all sects can be admitted; and finally, they accept the position that it is no longer in the Church's or the States' interest that the Catholic religion be recognized as the only religion of the State to the exclusion of all other forms of worship (proposition 77).

What was condemned by Pope Pius IX has been professed and practiced since Vatican II. We come to the following proposition:

> Proposition 78: Hence it has been wisely decided by law, in some Catholic countries, that persons coming to reside therein shall enjoy the public exercise of their own peculiar worship.

The condemnation of this proposition is quite clear, and yet it is what has now come to pass. The "peculiar worship" has always been considered by the Church to be an error, made up of false doctrines that give rise to a false morality. For these doctrines bring on not only the diversity of worship, but also the behavior that accompanies them: divorce, contraception, pornography, even polygamy and the contempt of women. All of this is absolutely contrary to the principles of the Church.

Yet now they affirm that it is a question of a right of the human person, hence a natural right. This is false. Pope Leo XIII said that, in certain cases, when the State cannot do otherwise, it can regulate the free exercise of worship by decree or law. But, in such an eventuality, it would be legislated in virtue of the principle of tolerance, which the Church has always accepted. The Church accepts the case in which the State promulgates a law of toleration when it cannot do otherwise. But Pope Leo XIII formally affirmed that the exception can never be made by accepting the justification that it proceeds from a natural right. It is absolutely impossible. And this has remained the indestructible position of the Church until Vatican II.

The next proposition treats of the question of the "pest of Indifferentism":

> Proposition 79: Moreover, it is false that the civil liberty of every form of worship, and the full power, given to all, of overtly and publicly manifesting any opinions whatsoever and thoughts, conduce more easily to corrupt the morals and minds of the people, and to propagate the pest of Indifferentism.

There are those who maintain that if liberty is allowed, truth will ultimately triumph. But in our era, error and vice are more attractive than truth. Truth is so constraining! That is why it is often undesirable to participate in public debates between Catholics and the enemies of Catholicism. Truth is difficult to defend and to practice; true morality is demanding. It is easier to defend freedom; the people prefer to hear this kind of talk. So to give equal rein to good and evil is tantamount to letting evil dominate. This is obvious. Even within ourselves, if we were to abandon our efforts to keep evil from growing within us, and if we gave free rein to our instincts, what would we become? It is the same thing in the family and in society.

Liberalism Has Sapped the American Catholic Church

The United States has often been presented to us as a model, although this was one of the scandals of our epoch. In the United States there is complete freedom of worship. Everyone does what he wants; anyone can settle where he will; in certain streets every fifty yards there is some sect or other with its temple; and the Catholic Church is flourishing.

Yet it would take almost nothing for it to disappear completely, to crumble and collapse, because it was founded on the liberal principle of granting freedom to all the sects. In the American mentality, it was almost impossible to find the conviction that the

Truth of the Catholic Church is unique, and that the Catholic religion is the one true religion. The American bishops contributed heavily to the preparation of the text on religious liberty adopted by the Council and presented, as I already said, by Fr. Murray. Now the American Catholics are paying the consequences of this religious freedom which has brought with it moral freedom, a liberty of morals that has infiltrated the Catholic religion. Freedom of faith leads fatally to moral freedom. These two elements are so united that it is inevitable, they cannot be separated. One cannot say that freedom of doctrine is allowed but not freedom of morals, because to each doctrine a particular morality corresponds. Corruption has become an endemic evil, atrocities increasingly occur, and inconceivable deeds are done.

There was a time, evidently, before the Council, when one had the impression that Catholicism in America had an enormous power to develop. There were extraordinary material organizations, enormous seminaries, universities, highly structured diocesan administrations; churches and cathedrals were being built; there were numerous novitiates and Catholic schools. When one came across all that, one was stupefied, in awe before this unimaginable development of the Catholic Church; many people, and many Protestants converted, as was also happening in Europe.

Unfortunately, the doctrine that animated this extraordinary expansion was founded on a fundamentally liberal principle which ended by ruining the Church in the United States. That is why a much higher proportion of priests and religious abandoned their vocations in the United States than anywhere else.

The Americans used to criticize Europe for always being in a fighting stance, almost in a state of religious war, whereas in America the atmosphere was much more relaxed, because of liberty, symbolized for them by the Bartholdi statue which dominates the port of New York. In America, they are free! Whereas in Europe, one always has the feeling of regulations, of dangers: Protestants, Freemasons, anti-clericalism. There is such a feeling of antagonism that one does not truly have the feeling of being free, of enjoying a great liberty.

Unfortunately, all that has been abandoned in Europe, and now disaster reigns everywhere.

The Conciliar *Aggiornamento* Condemned Ahead of Its Time

Let's look at the last proposition, which well describes the spirit that animated the Council and which has led us to the triumph of Modernism and integral Liberalism:

> Proposition 80: The Roman Pontiff can, and ought to, reconcile himself, and come to terms with progress, Liberalism and modern civilization.

That is to say, come to terms with the civilization that is informed by all the principles that issued from the Revolution of 1789, liberty, equality, fraternity. "Progress" is used here in the modernist sense of evolution. Modern civilization is the fruit of this evolution, of this Liberalism in every domain.

With the conclusion of the study of the *Syllabus of Errors* ends the study of the greatest encyclicals of the Popes of the 19th century against the modern errors. We see more than ever in our epoch how useful and precious it is to review all these truths of good sense unceasingly recalled by the Roman Pontiffs, who never ceased to fight for the triumph of truth.

Undoubtedly inspired by God, Pope Pius IX denounced and condemned the errors that the Freemasons and all the enemies of the Church had drawn up in a program to penetrate the Church and by them destroy the Catholic religion; errors that the Liberals, the Modernists and the Progressives succeeded in introducing into the texts of Vatican II. Frequently described as just a "pastoral" Council and not a dogmatic one, as all the preceding Councils had been, it most surely was not inspired by the Holy Ghost. It is unthinkable and even blasphemous to suggest that the Holy Ghost could have inspired it smothering truth with error, but getting away with it, by his omnipotence.

It is with great sorrow that we observe today the bitter fruits of the conciliar and post-conciliar reforms: "The good tree brings forth good fruit." But confronted with the most serious crisis that the Church has ever known since its institution by Our Lord Jesus Christ, let our prayers, our hope, and our confidence turn towards God, who can do all, even when all seems lost.

We must not then give way to discouragement, nor lessen the combat that we wage to contribute, according to our means but with all our strength, to the re-establishment of the reign of Our Lord Jesus Christ over hearts, souls, families, and nations. And thus will be restored Christian civilization, because He Himself has given us the assurance: "The gates of hell shall not prevail against her" (Mt. 16:18).

Finally, let us turn to the Virgin Mary, our good Mother in heaven, and implore her intercession, that she obtain from her divine Son that he grant us to see an end put to the Church's passion.

Chapter XI

OUR APOSTOLIC MANDATE[1]: LETTER OF POPE SAINT PIUS X TO THE FRENCH BISHOPS ON THE SILLON
(AUGUST 25, 1910)

In a letter addressed to the bishops of France, the 25th of August, 1910, Pope St. Pius X condemned the Sillon. This association was born on French soil, and consequently it is to the archbishops and bishops of France that the Pope addresses himself.

The Sillon [i.e., The Furrow] was founded by Marc Sangnier who was somewhat the forerunner of what later became Catholic Action. A good Catholic in private, he entertained certain notions which more and more identified themselves with Liberal and Masonic ideas. Moreover, the Pope himself alludes to this. At its beginning the Sillon was a sentimental student movement. Marc Sangnier visited the high schools and colleges, where he would make impassioned speeches. A brilliant orator, very sentimental, he could awaken an extraordinary enthusiasm in his audience. But he proved himself to be dangerous because he preached a false notion of charity, as the Pope explains very well. At the beginning the bishops themselves were quite favorable to the movement, because its members were Catholics who manifested a desire to extend the reign of Our Lord, to develop the Church, and to renew Christianity. But slowly Sangnier strayed completely, and the Pope had to intervene severely, and quite simply, he condemned the Sillon.

Marc Sangnier submitted; but the ideas of the Sillon tenaciously remained. And it can be said that a good number of the

---

[1] *Our Apostolic Mandate: Letter of Our Holy Father Pope Pius X to the French Archbishops and Bishops on the "Sillon,"* translated by Yves Dupont (Victoria, Australia: Instauratio Press) 1990.

French archbishops and bishops and even cardinals, like Cardinal Gerlier, Cardinal Liénart and others who still lived not long ago, were profoundly marked by the ideas propagated by the movement and which influenced them when they were young men still in school. Cardinal Gerlier, for example, was one of those who lent much support to the concepts of the Sillon in the diocese of Lyons, where he was named archbishop in 1937. Finally, this movement caused considerable ravages, which were to ultimately manifest themselves in our own day.

This letter of Pope St. Pius X is all the more interesting in that in the description of the movement that he paints, one finds extraordinarily depicted the very ideas that are currently being propagated. The Pope targets the people who call themselves Catholic, but who have completely deviated:

> Our Apostolic Mandate requires from Us that We watch over the purity of the Faith and the integrity of Catholic discipline. It requires from Us that we protect the faithful from evil and error; especially so when evil and error are presented in dynamic language which, concealing vague notions and ambiguous expressions with emotional and high-sounding words, is likely to set ablaze the hearts of men in the pursuit of ideas which, whilst attractive, are none the less nefarious. Such were not so long ago the doctrines of the so-called philosophers of the 18th century, the doctrines of the Revolution and Liberalism which have been so often condemned; such are even today the theories of the Sillon which, under the glowing appearance of generosity, are all too often wanting in clarity, logic and truth. These theories do not belong to the Catholic, or for that matter to the French spirit.

(This last comment is a little incense wafted to the French, so that he can pound a little harder on the theories of the Sillon.)

The Heyday of the Sillon

> We have long debated, Venerable Brethren, before We decided to solemnly and publicly speak Our mind on the Sillon. Only when your concern augmented Our own did we decide to do so. For we love, indeed, the valiant young people who fight under the Sillon's banner, and We deem them worthy of praise and ad-

miration in many respects. We love their leaders, whom We are pleased to acknowledge as noble souls on a level above vulgar passions, and inspired with the noblest form of enthusiasm in their quest for goodness. You have seen, Venerable Brethren how, imbued with a living realization of the brotherhood of men, and supported in their selfless efforts by their love of Jesus Christ and a strict observance of their religious duties, they sought out those who labor and suffer in order to set them on their feet again.

This was shortly after Our Predecessor Leo XIII of happy memory had issued his remarkable Encyclical on the condition of the working class. Speaking through her supreme leader, the Church had just poured out the tenderness of her motherly love over the humble and the lowly, and it looked as though she was calling out for an ever growing number of people to labor for the restoration of order and justice in our uneasy society. Was it not opportune then, for the leaders of the Sillon to come forward and place at the service of the Church their troops of young believers who could fulfill her wisdom and her hopes? And in fact, the Sillon did raise among the workers the standard of Jesus Christ.... This was the heyday of the Sillon; its brighter side accounts for the encouragement, and tokens of approval, which the bishops and the Holy See gave liberally when this religious fervor was still obscuring the true nature of the Sillonist movement.

Appearance of Disturbing Tendencies

For it must be said, Venerable Brethren, that our expectations have been frustrated in large measure. The day came when perceptive observers could discern alarming trends within the Sillon; the Sillon was losing its way. Could it have been otherwise? Its leaders were young, full of enthusiasm and self-confidence. But they were not adequately equipped with historical knowledge, sound philosophy, and solid theology to tackle without danger the difficult social problems in which their work and their inclinations were involving them. They were not sufficiently equipped to be on their guard against the penetration of liberal and Protestant concepts on doctrine and obedience.

One could say that something similar happened during and even before the Council. The liberals are Catholics, of course. And one sees priests, bishops, and even cardinals who are full of good intentions recommend union with all the religions, and all the ideologues, in order to end disputes and discord, and do away with fights. Such language may seem noble, but it is vain.

All the ideologues lack what St. Pius X identified as the knowledge of history, sound philosophy and firm theology. They let themselves be taken in by idealists who led them outside the Church. They did not know how to resist Liberal and Protestant errors:

> They were given no small measure of advice. Admonition came after the advice, but, to Our sorrow, both advice and reproaches ran off the sheath of their elusive souls, and were of no avail.

This description of their souls, "their elusive souls," is curious. It is still true of liberal Catholics today. It is futile to place them before the truth and make them notice the reality....No, nothing can be done! For five years we have been discussing with the liberals at Rome and trying to make them face the truth. They will not answer our questions. They do not reply to the problems that we bring to their attention. They flee. Whatever we say flows like water off a duck's back. It flows but it does not penetrate. And they repeat the same thing over and over: You must submit—submission. But submission to what?

The situation is the reverse of what St. Pius X knew, because now it is the liberals who occupy Rome. Now it is they who want to impose their ideas, and it is the traditionalists who appear disobedient to the Church. You might say that those people are Sillonists. Everything that Pope Pius X was so clear-sighted as to denounced concerning the Sillon is exactly what they think, believe, say and do:

> We owe the truth to Our dear sons of the Sillon who are carried away by their generous ardor along a path strewn with errors and dangers. We owe the truth to a large number of seminarians and priests....

Those who became bishops, cardinals and who influenced the Council were, precisely, seminarians at that moment: Cardinal Gerlier, Cardinal Liénart, to speak only of the French:

> ...who have been drawn away by the Sillon, if not from the authority, at least from the guidance and influence of the bishops. We owe it also to the Church in which the Sillon is sowing discord and whose interests it endangers.

The Pope then defines certain points of the Sillonist doctrine that he condemns. In the first place, it is the pretension of the Sillon to escape the jurisdiction of ecclesiastical authority. That is the first point. The second is that the Sillon is carried away by a misguided love of the weak. And thirdly, that the Sillon has a way of understanding human dignity that does not conform to the way the Church understands it. It has the noble concern for human dignity, but misunderstood.

First Error: Independence From Authority

The Pope brings to bear his judgment upon these tendencies of the Sillon. The first is "the pretension of the Sillon to escape the jurisdiction of ecclesiastical authority":

> The leaders of the Sillon claim that they are working in a field which is not that of the Church; they claim that they are pursuing aims in the temporal order only and not those of the spiritual order...

They seek the good of the poor, the workers, of society:

> ...[They claim] that the Sillonist is simply a Catholic devoted to the betterment of the working class and to democratic endeavors by drawing from the practices of his faith the energy for his selfless efforts. They claim that, neither more nor less than a Catholic craftsman, farmer, economist or politician, the Sillonist is subject to common standards of behavior, yet without being bound in a special manner by the authority of the Church. To reply to these fallacies is only too easy: for whom will they make believe that the Catholic Sillonists, the priests and seminarians enrolled in their ranks have in sight in their social work, only the temporal interests of the working class? To maintain this, We think would be an insult to them. The truth is that the Sillon-

ist leaders are self-confessed and irrepressible idealists: they claim to regenerate the working class by first elevating the conscience of Man; they have a social doctrine, and they have religious and philosophical principles for the reconstruction of society upon new foundations; they have a particular conception of human dignity, freedom, justice and brotherhood; and in an attempt to justify their social dreams, they put forward the Gospel, but interpreted in their own way; and what is even more serious, they call to witness Christ, but a diminished and distorted Christ. Further, they teach these ideas in their study groups, and inculcate them upon their friends, and they also introduce them into their working procedures. Therefore they are really professors of social, civic, and religious morals; and whatever modifications they may introduce in the organization of the Sillonist movement, We have the right to say that the aims of the Sillon, its character and its action, belong to the field of morals which is the proper domain of the Church. In view of all this, the Sillonists are deceiving themselves when they believe that they are working in a field that lies outside the limits of Church authority and of its doctrinal and directive power.

Clearly, one cannot pursue justice without stepping into the domain of morals, and from the domain of morals into the domain of the Church.

Second Error: Ill-conceived Love of the Poor

But, as We have already said, the evil lies far deeper: The Sillon, carried away by an ill-conceived love for the weak, has fallen into error.

All of this is quite topical. For example, liberation theology is based, its proponents say, upon the love of the poor. They must be liberated; they are slaves. What kind of liberation is meant? What do they intend to do in order to ease the miseries of these people?

The Sillon proposes to raise up and re-educate the working class.

At the time the working classes were the object of concern. Pope Leo XIII had written the encyclical *Rerum Novarum*. Today it is the needs of the rural and third world populations that are addressed. They want to devote themselves to the betterment and regeneration of the rural classes, the *campesinos* of South America. Pope Paul VI visited them to encourage them in their demands, their spirit of revolt against their oppressors.

Liberation Theology

This is very serious, because it instills in the hearts of these people the vice of envy, for otherwise they are not animated by it. If one were to question them individually, one would learn that most of them are not animated by the spirit of class struggle, no more so than by the desire to steal from their neighbor because he has more than they. They live simply on their little coffee plantations and farms. They sell their produce, or a few animals that they raise. They live poorly, it is true, in very simple cabins. But these are happy people, and who generally have many children. The little children run about everywhere, in the cabin, in the fields, in the sugarcane fields, the coffee orchards. They have eight, ten, twelve, fifteen children. These people are not at all animated by the sentiments that are imputed to them or that the revolutionaries seek to inspire in them, that is, that because they are poor they are unhappy. The subversives want to make them unhappy and instill in these good simple people, who do not think of it at all, a revolutionary spirit, blaming the rich and the government for whatever miseries they may endure.

They want to turn them into revolutionaries. It is atrocious. They try to rally them together and persuade them that the Church is on their side, and that these poor people should fight for social justice, even by force if necessary. It is frightful. The result is that they incite them to join the guerrillas, who burn and kill everywhere. This results in a more miserable condition for the rural peoples than ever before. In the countryside they are raided by the guerrillas, for when these bandits come to their dwellings, they take everything they need to eat, as well as any money they can find. And so then these rural folk are really reduced to a state of misery. And by doing this the instigators pretend to liberate these people! It is quite simply criminal folly and pure wickedness. It is truly a diabolic spirit that drives these self-styled liberators.

I had the opportunity of seeing the *campesinos* in Columbia and Peru when I visited our priests and missionaries who lived in the midst of these people. Certainly, they were poor, but they manifested no rancor and expressed no hatred against anyone. One could see that despite their simple life they were happy. Undoubtedly the governments should do what they can to elevate their standard of life a little, and enable them to own their own modest properties so that they can remain in the country and cultivate their fields, and sell their goods at a fair price.

Instead of pursuing such a policy, they attract them to the cities where they find themselves grouped in enormous agglomerations, and much more miserable than when they lived in the country, where they had some goods at their disposition. They become utterly destitute, and truly what are called proletarians. Grouped in enormous masses around the cities, living in shanty towns called *favellas*, they ultimately constitute a danger, because, grouped as they are, it becomes easy to sow the spirit of revolt amongst them. Thus massed, they could easily provoke a revolution.

In South America, the cities have become enormously spread out, a third of the population of a country huddles there. They number millions of inhabitants. And this has undoubtedly come about because not enough efforts were made to sustain agriculture.

And then, it is also the power of seduction of the cities, which fascinate them. If one of them succeeds in finding a job and getting a little salary, right away he spends it to buy clothing or a camera or a hat...and that becomes his entire fortune. When he returns to the village and displays his wealth to his brothers and sisters, they are wide-eyed, and all those who had stayed in the country suddenly desire to head for the city and follow the one who earned a little money and could dress a little better than they. They have one thought, to go and rejoin the one who has seen the city with its television, the stores, its wonders. The city's power of attraction is horrendous.

And so seduced by what they imagine, they in turn set out for the city, where most of them do not find work. Then they fall into real misery, or else they attach themselves to one or two who work and have a reasonable salary, and they all live on that. There are as many as fifteen or twenty who depend upon one who works and who cannot do otherwise than support them. Their whole salary is absorbed. They cannot possibly save anything. And all this causes very great problems.

And what is more, all this upheaval is willed. The people are being deliberately turned into a proletariat. These people own nothing, and a man who no longer owns anything is ripe for revolution. On the contrary, a man who has a small holding, even if it is not much, it is at least a house, a few cocoa trees, a few banana trees, some sugarcane on which he can live. He can live off his own land. He is attached to the place where he finds himself, and he has no desire to foment revolution. He can at least live.

But those who have gone to the city and have nothing are idle all day long. What do they do to pass the time? Either they steal or they loiter...and become the prey of all the vices.

Clearly there is a profound malaise. But the danger comes from inspiring the spirit of revolt in these poor souls instead of giving them the idea of work, of property...and helping them meet the difficulties they encounter. No, deliberately, they are knowingly led to such a condition that they become rebels. If, on the contrary, they had been given an interior equilibrium by means of spiritual goods, they would no longer have the same frame of mind.

These reflections and examples that I have related because I have observed them, do not distance us from the motives that led Pope Pius X to condemn the Sillon, for, on the contrary, he had rightly measured the dangers spawned by the false conceptions of social life proposed by the movement.

The Suppression and Levelling of the Classes

Indeed, the Sillon proposes to raise up and re-educate the working class. But in this respect the principles of Catholic doctrine have been defined, and this history of Christian civilization bears witness to their beneficent fruitfulness. Our Predecessor of happy memory re-affirmed them in masterly documents, and all Catholics dealing with social questions have the duty to study them and to keep them in mind. He taught among other things, that "Christian democracy must preserve the diversity of classes which is assuredly the attribute of a soundly constituted State, and it must seek to give human society the form and character which God, its Author, has imparted to it." Our Predecessor denounced "a certain Democracy which goes so far in wickedness as to place sovereignty in the people and aims at the suppression of classes and their levelling down.

Yet this is what the perpetrators of the false doctrines seek: the suppression and levelling of the classes. St. Pius X recalls the principles that Leo XIII had denounced:

> At the same time, Leo XIII laid down for Catholics a program of action, the only program capable of putting society back onto its centuries old Christian basis. But what have the leaders of the Sillon done? Not only have they adopted a program and teaching different from that of Leo XIII... but they have openly rejected the program laid out by Leo XIII on the essential principles of society; they place authority in the people, or gradually suppress it and strive, as their ideal, to effect the levelling down of the classes. In opposition to Catholic doctrine, therefore, they are proceeding towards a condemned ideal.

Once again we touch upon the principle of equality. What Leo XIII often denounced in his encyclicals, as we have already seen, were the modern principles that are set on imposing equality, that is to say, levelling: equal possession of the goods of this world, of means, of riches, etc.

The popes have always reiterated that this equality is inexistent. There is equality of men before God: yes, we are all equal before God; but as for temporal equality, the equality of possessions and of natural faculties, this is not so. It does not exist. And if it does not exist, it is in the nature of men, which means that God wanted it that way. And if the good God wanted it so, it is for the sake of good and not evil. How can it be for the good?— Because men are made to live in society and to communicate to others the talents and the goods they possess. The one who is more intelligent must communicate the goods of his understanding to others; this is normal. This also concerns the generations: those who possess knowledge must communicate it to those who are ignorant, and educate the youth, etc. The rich practice charity by communicating some of their goods to the needy. It is by the intercommunication of the different goods each possesses that charity is manifested. All those who work are useful to society. What kind of cities would we be living in if there were no one to sweep the streets? The humblest services are useful to society. And everyone has a place, his place. To desire the absolute levelling of society is ridiculous:

> We know well that they flatter themselves with the idea of raising human dignity and the discredited condition of the working class. We know that they wish to render just and perfect the labor laws and the relations between employers and employees, thus causing a more complete justice and a greater measure of charity to prevail upon earth, and causing also a profound and fruitful transformation in society by which mankind would make an undreamt-of progress. Certainly, We do not blame these efforts; they would be excellent in every respect if the Sillonists did not forget that a person's progress consists in developing his natural abilities by fresh motivations to operate within the frame of, and in conformity with, the laws of human nature. But on the contrary, by ignoring the laws governing human nature and by breaking the bounds within which they operate, the human person is led, not towards progress, but towards death.

The frame in question is, precisely, the social framework. Not everyone can be a worker or employee; not everyone can be a company owner. Everyone has his place in society and the places can change according to the aptitudes, the intelligence, and the know-how of each one. Someone who was an employee becomes a low-level manager, and if he succeeds well, a high-ranking one. This is normal. A natural selection takes place in society when justice is observed. All this is willed by God:

> This nevertheless, is what they want to do with human society; they dream of a Future City built on different principles, and they dare to proclaim these more fruitful and more beneficial than the principles upon which the present Christian City rests.

Then the Pope writes this very forceful passage:

> No, Venerable Brethren, We must repeat with the utmost energy in these times of social and intellectual anarchy when everyone takes it upon himself to teach as a teacher and lawmaker—the City cannot be built otherwise than as God has built it;

society cannot be set up unless the Church lays the foundations and supervises the work; no, civilization is not something yet to be found, nor is the New City to be built on hazy notions; it has been in existence and still is: it is Christian civilization, it is the Catholic city.

It is for this reason that those who founded the "*Cité catholique*" chose this expression, formulated by Pius X:

> It has only to be set up and restored continually against the unremitting attacks of insane dreamers, rebels and miscreants. *Omnia instaurare in Christo.*

It is really simple. And yet it is all the more difficult to demystify the nefarious action of these false ideologues because they conceal their real agenda by calling for popular reforms. They say that they want social justice. They use the language the Church has always used [in expressing her social doctrine], but as their ideas are different, in their mouths the words have a different meaning. Their language is inspired by liberal ideas, which impart a revolutionary meaning to the words liberty, equality and fraternity.

Third Error: An Erroneous Notion of Human Dignity

In the third point, the Pope notes that "the Sillon has a praiseworthy concern for human dignity," but:

> ...it understands human dignity in the manner of some philosophers, of whom the Church does not at all feel proud. The first condition of that dignity is liberty, but viewed in the sense that, except in religious matters, each man is autonomous. This is the basic principle from which the Sillon draws further conclusions: today the people are in tutelage under an authority distinct from themselves; they must liberate themselves: political emancipation.

Thus human dignity equals liberty; liberty equals autonomy; autonomy equals political emancipation. Afterwards:

> They are also dependent upon employers who own the means of production, exploit, oppress and degrade the workers; they must shake off the yoke: economic emancipation.

Political emancipation, economic emancipation, shake off the yoke of those who manage in the economic domain; it is very clear. And finally:

> ...they are ruled by a caste called intelligentsia, which, by its very nature, enjoys undue preponderance in the direction of affairs. The people must break away from this domination: intellectual emancipation.

Along with these three sorts of liberation, political, economic and intellectual, the Pope has said that the Sillonists want to escape equally from ecclesiastic authority; thus it is also religious emancipation that is inscribed in their program. If the Sillonists do not dare to say openly and categorically that they desire religious emancipation, it is only because they do not dare go so far, for this would be open revolt against the Church, but their reasoning and their conduct lead them to it. The triple emancipations that they seek to obtain will inevitably lead them to religious emancipation. And this became apparent when they became the "Great Sillon." The "Great Sillon" is completely emancipated from religious submission.

Sillonist Democracy

> A socio-political set-up resting on these two pillars of Liberty and Equality, to which Fraternity will presently be added, is what they call Democracy. However, liberty and equality are, so to speak, no more than a negative side. The distinctive and positive aspect of Democracy is to be found in the largest possible participation of everyone in the government of public affairs. And this, in turn, comprises a three-fold aspect, viz. political, economical, and moral.

In the political order, if the Sillon does not abolish authority, it affirms nonetheless that authority resides in the people and must remain in the people. As fundamentally each citizen, as an elector, becomes a sort of head of State: each participates in the government:

Taken away from a specific group, management will be so well multiplied that each worker will himself become a kind of employer.

As for the moral element:

Since, as we have seen, authority is much reduced, another force is necessary to supplement it and to provide a permanent counterweight against individual selfishness. This new principle, this force, is the love of professional interest and of public interest, that is to say, the love of the very end of the profession and of society.

Sillon's Ideal Society: Liberty, Equality, Fraternity

In order to attain this goal, the Sillonists dream of turning the people into perfect citizens. If all the citizens were perfect people, they would only seek the public interest and not their own personal interest; and then there would be a society which would possess more authority, and everything would be perfect:

Snatched away from the pettiness of private interests, and raised up to the interests of the profession and, even higher, to those of the whole nation and higher still, to those of the human race (for the Sillon's field of vision is not bound by national borders, it encompasses all men even to the ends of the earth), the human heart, enlarged by the love of the commonwealth, would embrace all comrades of the same profession, all compatriots, all men. Such is the ideal of human greatness and nobility to be attained through the famous popular trilogy: liberty, equality, fraternity.

To sum up, such is the theory, one could say the dream of the Sillon; and that is what its teaching aims at, what it calls the democratic education of the people, that is, raising to its maximum the conscience and civic responsibility of every one, from which will result economic and political Democracy and the reign of justice, liberty, equality, fraternity.

This brief explanation, Venerable Brethren, will show you clearly how much reason We have to say that the Sillon opposes doctrine to doctrine, that it seeks to build its City on a theory contrary to Catholic truth, and that it falsifies the basic and essential notions which regulate social relations in human society.

The Pope does not fear to say that the three points that he just set forth are on the whole contrary to Catholic doctrine.

False Liberation Leads to Violence

What the Pope said then remains very pertinent. The problems that he discusses are far from being resolved. All worker-priests who are currently in the factories and work, they claim, in the midst of the workers, still speak the language of progressive priests who preach the liberation of the workers, their economic, social and moral liberation, etc. They use the resounding phrases, progress, liberty, and, at the same time of course, universal charity and mutual love—the same pathetic sentiments which moreover bore the few faithful who still go to church and hear the same thing every Sunday.

To discuss social problems, they take examples from the press. They talk about murders. Why are there murders? Of course, they condemn the assassins, but, they add, one cannot gauge the situation they were in and which pushed them to act. Ultimately they come to defend all the murderers. They justify their actions by saying, that they found such bad social circumstances, because society is bad and badly ordered; because people are unjust, etc. Are we supposed to conclude that these people were forced to kill! It is society that is called into question. As for the murderers, they are not guilty!

Even in Switzerland, a land once renowned for its tranquillity, peace and order, things have changed quite a bit. People used to say about Switzerland that it is the country where everyone is nice, they do not insult each other. They have peace. Presently, it is quite different. About six months ago, veritable insurrections took place in Zurich, Berne, Lausanne and Geneva. The instigators of the disturbances even tried to come to Sion.

At the beginning three hundred young people were demonstrating, but the last time they numbered six thousand at Zurich. They demolished everything. And in *Le Nouvelliste*, the newspaper of the Valais, a well-known journalist wrote: "We must not condemn them all; it is necessary to consider the profound motives that determine mob action, etc." And if the police are constrained to use arms, or if they put the rioters in prison, it is they who are held responsible for not having understood the profound motives that push the demonstrators to break everything. If Switzerland has come to this, then her days are numbered. Switzerland will be afflicted by the same difficulties and the same disequilibrium that afflict Italy, Spain and other countries. The police will no longer be able to do anything, because they are always in the wrong as soon as they oppose a demonstration. It is true that if societies have reached such a point, it did not come about over night. It is because they rejected the foundations of the moral and social education of peoples, and this was done according to the principles born of the Revolution, which have led to the destabilization of societies.

Refutation of the Sillonist System

In the first part of his letter to the French bishops on the Sillon, Pope Pius X explained first of all the movement's doctrine, in particular the point concerning authority, and the way in which the Sillonists consider and judge authority. Then he touched on the question of how, according to their principles, they envisage social doctrine; and lastly, how they understand human dignity. In relation to this, the Pope refers especially to the idea of emancipation that, moreover, animates the progressives of our day, who have inherited all the modernist and Sillonist doctrines, according to which the adult must emancipate himself at the political, economic, and intellectual levels, all of which are encompassed in the Pope's condemnation of this way of understanding human dignity:

> This brief explanation, Venerable Brethren, will show you clearly how much reason We have to say that the Sillon opposes doctrine to doctrine, that it seeks to build its City on a theory contrary to Catholic truth, and that it falsifies the basic and essential notions which regulate social relations in human society. The following considerations will make this opposition even more evident.

After having set forth the doctrine of the Sillon, the Pope reviews the principles in order to judge them and condemn them one after the other: firstly, authority; second, social doctrine; and thirdly, human dignity.

Authority Comes From God

The Sillon places public authority primarily in the people, from whom it then flows into the government in such a manner however, that it continues to reside in the people....

Here is where the error lies.

....But Leo XIII absolutely condemned this doctrine in his Encyclical *Diuturnum Illud* on political government in which he said: "Modern writers in great numbers, following in the footsteps of those who called themselves philosophers in the last century, declare that all power comes from the people; consequently those who exercise power in society do not exercise it from their own authority, but from an authority delegated to them by the people, and on the condition that it can be revoked by the will of the people from whom they hold it. Quite contrary is the sentiment of Catholics....

So the Catholic doctrine is the contrary of that:

...who hold that the right of governing derives from God as its natural and necessary principle. Admittedly, the Sillon holds that authority—which it first places in the people—descends from God, but in such a way: "as to return from below upwards, whilst...

Now note how the Sillonists admit it:

...in the organization of the Church power descends from above downwards." But besides its being abnormal for the delegation of power to ascend, since it is in its nature to descend, Leo XIII refuted in advance this attempt to reconcile Catholic Doctrine with the error of philosophism. For, he continues: "It is necessary to remark here that those who preside over the government of public affairs may indeed, in certain cases, be chosen by the will and judgment of the multitude without repugnance or opposition to Catholic doctrine. But whilst this choice marks out the ruler, it does not confer upon him the authority to govern it; it does not delegate the power, it designates the person who will be invested with it."

It is very important to emphasize this and make it understood. We have now become so used to seeing everything settled by elections. It is the people who command. The people keep the power and can take back authority from the officials by means of referendums. Ultimately, one comes to concede that authority truly resides in the people and remains there. And this is contrary to the doctrine of the Church. The Catholic says that while the people can designate who exercises authority, it does not confer authority: authority comes from God.

In the Church, clearly, the authorities in general are named by the superiors in the ecclesiastic hierarchy, except for the pope, who is elected by a conclave. This is also an election, but in this case, it is not the conclave that gives the authority to the pope; it comes from God. Once the person has been designated, the authority comes from God. This is one of the main errors of our times, the error of this unnatural reversal of reality:

> For the rest, if the people remain the holders of power, what becomes of authority?

If it is the people who holds power, then the authority does not exercise its own power; what can such an authority be?

> A shadow, a myth; there is no more law properly so-called, no more obedience. The Sillon acknowledges this: indeed, since it demands that threefold political, economic and intellectual emancipation in the name of human dignity, the Future City in the formation of which it is engaged will have no masters and no servants. All citizens will be free; all comrades, all kings. A command, a precept would be viewed as an attack upon their freedom; subordination to any form of superiority would be a diminishment of the human person, and obedience a disgrace.

And this is indeed what they seek to arrive at little by little, to leave total freedom to men and no longer impose anything upon them, save uniquely for the maintenance of public order. But as this cannot be achieved, a country ends up with a Socialist or Communist government, that allows no liberty whatsoever. On paper, the authority is vested in the people, but in reality it is in the hands of the intelligentsia. Look at Poland, where the authority is not in the hands of the people, far from it, and their trade union Solidarity notwithstanding; the people are aware of it! They obtain little freedoms and feeble concessions, but soon they shall lack bread to eat. This is where the false notion of authority leads.

The Soviet government is a socialist government. Under the regime of State Socialism, under the pretext of having received the delegation of the people, the rulers—the ruling class—maintain power and do not give it up. Nothing is more Totalitarian than Socialism.

Liberty and Authority

Is it in this manner, Venerable Brethren, that the traditional doctrine of the Church represents social relations, even in the most perfect society? Has not every community of people, dependent and unequal by nature, need of an authority to direct their activity towards the common good and to enforce its laws? And if perverse individuals are to be found in a community (and there always are), should not authority be all the stronger as the selfishness of the wicked is more threatening? Further, unless one greatly deceives oneself in the conception of liberty, can it be said with an atom of reason that authority and liberty are incompatible?

We saw this point made in the encyclical *Libertas* of Pope Leo XIII. When liberty, which exists for the good and not for evil, is well defined, as well as law, then there is no opposition, but rather a correlation between liberty and authority, which both converge towards the common good and consequently the good of families and persons. Can one teach that obedience is contrary to human dignity, and that the ideal would be to replace it by consent to authority? Is the religious state, founded upon obedience, contrary to the ideal of human nature? Were the saints, who were the most obedient of men, slaves? degenerates?

It is difficult to believe how such errors could spread so easily among Catholics, even among those who have kept the faith. St. Pius X refutes the error of the Sillon which affirms that the authority is in the people. He demonstrates that such a conception is not

Catholic, and that if they want to remain Catholic, the Sillonists must renounce it.

Teaching such doctrines, and applying them to its internal organization, the Sillon therefore sows erroneous and fatal notions on authority, liberty and obedience among your Catholic youth.

Justice and Equality

The Pope takes up the question of social doctrine:

> The same is true of justice and equality; the Sillon says that it is striving to establish an era of equality which, by that very fact, would be also an era of greater justice. Thus, to the Sillon, every inequality of condition is an injustice, or at least a diminution of justice.

Then necessarily, if the fact that inequality in society exists is an injustice, the consequences of that principle are grasped immediately, namely, that it is necessary to fight against inequality. But, says St. Pius X, it is a principle that "conflicts sharply with the nature of things."

The same point was made by Pius IX, Leo XIII and by all those who refute the false principle that is constantly to be found in the modern errors. Of course, and this is obvious, by our common nature we are all equal before God. But by the inequality of physical capacity, intellectual gifts, and external goods we are not all made to hold an identical place in society; the inequality of the parts results in their complementarity, and the harmony of the whole. This is what is called order. Thus this social equality that is falsely urged does not exist in reality. There is no equality:

> Here we have a principle that conflicts sharply with the nature of things, a principle conducive to jealously, to injustice and subversive to any social order.

The quest for total equality in society leads infallibly to the introduction of subversion in society. Undoubtedly St. Pius X is open to the idea of a more normal sharing of goods within society, but to want to level everything by putting everyone in the same place and in the same conditions is impossible. For, he adds, without authority there is no viable society possible. Moreover, according to the Sillon:

>...Democracy alone will bring about the reign of perfect justice!

For the Sillonists there is then only one form of government possible: democracy. Every other form of government is a government to fight against, because it is an unjust government, as it enshrines inequality. Therefore monarchy and oligarchy are out of the question:

> Is this not an insult to other forms of government which are thereby debased to the level of sterile makeshifts? Besides, the Sillonists once again clash on this point with the teaching of Pope Leo XIII...[in which he] alludes to the three well-known forms of government, thus implying that justice is compatible with any of them....he was teaching that in this respect Democracy does not enjoy a special privilege. The Sillonists who maintain the opposite view either turn a deaf ear to the teaching of the Church or form for themselves an idea of justice and equality which is not Catholic.

Fraternity and Pluralism

The Pope also demonstrates that, as regards social relations, not only is the equality promoted by the Sillonists false, but so is their notion of fraternity:

>...Catholic doctrine tells us that the primary duty of charity does not lie in the toleration of false ideas, however sincere they may be, nor in theoretical or practical indifference towards the errors and vices in which we see our brethren plunged, but in zeal for their intellectual and moral improvement as well as for their material well-being.

The Sillonists claimed to want to establish this false fraternity between all the religions, and between all ideologies. Their position constitutes an exaggerated tolerance of error. Error and truth would enjoy the same conditions and the same privileges in society. It is just unthinkable. This is what is advanced nowadays under the name of pluralism.

No Real Brotherhood Outside of Christian Charity

Catholic doctrine further tells us that love for our neighbor flows from our love for God, Who is Father to all, and goal of the human family; and in Jesus Christ whose members we are, to the point that in doing good to others, we are doing good to Jesus Christ Himself. Any other kind of love is sheer illusion, sterile and fleeting.

Indeed, we have the human experience of pagan and secular societies of ages past to show that concern for common interests or affinities of nature weigh very little against the passions and wild desires of the heart. No, Venerable Brethren, there is no genuine fraternity outside Christian charity.

These are expressions that may seem too strong, but they express the truth. "There is no genuine fraternity outside Christian charity." Because the fraternity that can exist in a certain form is in reality practically selfish. It is a humanitarian, philanthropic sentiment that ends by showing itself to be self-love. Apparently, this behavior can give the impression of fraternity, but it is not real.

It is only Our Lord who came to bring us by His grace the Holy Ghost, the source of true charity, the source of a veritable love, a completely disinterested love because it is directed towards God. By working for one's neighbor, one works for God. Ultimately, it is not for one's neighbor personally that one works, it is for the glory of God. For the neighbor's good is also the glory of God. The object of our love for our neighbor is God. It is always the same love. As St. Augustine and St. Thomas have said: "There is only one love, the love of God" in which the love of neighbor is integral.

To the degree that we do not love our neighbor in order to lead him to God, as St. Thomas says, *ut in Deo sit*,[2] and also as St. Thomas says elsewhere in a beautiful formulation, *propter it (sic) quod Dei est in ipso*, "For what there is of God in him,"[3] we do not really love him. One loves one's neighbor for what there is of God in him and not for what he puts of himself in himself, that is, his

---

[2] *Summa Theologica* II, II, 25, 1.
[3] *Ibid.*, ad 1.

sins, his whims, his personal ideas; no. We love him in the measure that he is with God, and that he recognizes that all his gifts natural and supernatural come from God and that all his activity is for God. And we must love him, moreover, to lead him to God. And this is true even with respect to material goods: everything must be oriented towards God. And this can only be found in the love of the Holy Ghost that inspires men towards this goal.

That is why the Pope permits himself to express these strong words: "There is no genuine fraternity outside Christian charity." It will be objected that we condemn every form of fraternity among the Protestants, the Buddhists and the Moslems. Is there no fraternity amongst them?

We reply: It is not Christian fraternity, and it is not the Holy Ghost that inspires it. It is a philanthropy, a purely human sentiment that is founded upon egoism. One loves one's neighbor because one needs him, because he loves us, but it will not be truly for God:

> No, Venerable Brethren, there is no genuine fraternity outside Christian charity. Through love of God and His Son Jesus Christ our Savior, Christian charity embraces all men, comforts all, and leads all to the same faith and same heavenly happiness.
>
> By separating fraternity from Christian charity thus understood, Democracy, far from being a progress, would mean a disastrous step backwards for civilization. If, as We desire with all Our heart, the highest possible peak of well-being for society and its members is to be attained through fraternity or, as it is also called, universal solidarity, all minds must be united in the knowledge of Truth, all wills united in morality, and all hearts in the love of God and His son Jesus Christ. But this union is attainable only by Catholic charity, and that is why Catholic charity alone can lead the people in the march of progress towards the ideal of civilization.

One God, One Faith

Pope St. Pius X had the faith. Now many bishops no longer do; they no longer believe in Our Lord Jesus Christ; they no longer know who Our Lord Jesus Christ is. From the beginning of his pontificate, St. Pius X stood square with his faith, and said, *Omnia instaurare in Christo* [to restore all things in Christ]. For him there is no other God than Our Lord Jesus Christ, God the Son, united to the Father and the Holy Ghost. It is by this affirmation that we conclude all our prayers.

From the moment of his accession to the throne of Peter, St. Pius X wanted to reaffirm that there is only Our Lord Jesus Christ, and that He holds the key to all our problems. It is Our Lord Jesus Christ who gave us the one true religion, hence the one way of salvation. As everything on earth must be ordered to the salvation of souls, Our Lord is the only way that can lead them there, as He said: "I am the way, the truth, and the life." There are no others. So St. Pius X does not want to abandon his convictions, and reaffirms that there is but one way to salvation, one path to happiness and true civilization, one way of truth: Our Lord Jesus Christ. And all those who would like to find a way beside Our Lord Jesus Christ, these the Pope tries to bring back into the true way, or else he condemns them.

Charity must above all be exercised for the salvation of souls, for the true good of men, including the body which is ordered to the soul. As Our Lord Jesus Christ is the only object of charity, He is also the source of true charity:

> ...Catholic charity alone can lead the people in the march of progress towards the ideal of civilization.

The facts of history prove it. It is the Church that brought true civilization to the pagan world.

The Greeks, of course, built beautiful monuments; a visit to the Acropolis of Athens and the temples still manifests the splendor. The Greeks had not lost their senses; men were not so corrupt that they were incapable of reasoning correctly and creating true works of art. And it is true that the Egyptians built their pyramids, etc. It cannot be denied. But next to that, what were the morals at these different epochs of human civilization? It was slavery; human life was held as worthless. In almost all the religions there were human sacrifices. When we read the Old Testament, we see that as soon as the Jews strayed from God in order to adopt the religion of the neighboring peoples, human sacrifices began to be offered. The psalms themselves reflect the reality: the Jews killed their children, their sons and their daughters, immolating them to Baal and to the pagan gods. Undoubtedly these pagan peoples achieved great works of art. They knew how to work gold and weave fine fabrics. At the time of Solomon, art reached a pinnacle, not only among the Jews, but also among the pagans. Whether they have been reconstructed or whether archeology has discovered them, the palaces of Nabuchodonosor, the pharaohs of Egypt or the queen of Sheba have all outstripped in splendor whatever has been built subsequently. But these extraordinary monuments were founded upon tyranny. Because the elite who governed the people drew everything to themselves. They constrained the entire nation to work for the satisfaction of their ambition, pride and personal glory. Thus there existed civilizations which were materially and artistically extraordinary, but morally abominable.

It is really only the Church which, with the one true religion founded by Our Lord Jesus Christ, brought forth a veritable civilization. True charity, the love of neighbor, the dignity of marriage, the dignity of women and children, the suppression of slavery, all are the work of the Church. It is the Church, faithful to the teachings of Our Lord Jesus Christ, that allowed the blossoming of a society whose foundation and crown was the true religion. The magnificent cathedrals were constructed, the abbeys, convents and monasteries built. Where else can one find similar testimonials? There are Buddhist monasteries, yes; but if one goes to see what happens there and discovers the reality, one quickly sees that it is but a mask, a facade behind which there reigns a certain immorality. The adepts of these false religions are given to such exaggeration that they end by destroying themselves. It is thus that some hold that, in order to give to the soul its spiritual principle, its liberty, the act of destroying oneself by fire constitutes an act of virtue. Things which are absolutely contrary to the natural law of God can be found in all the false religions.

But unfortunately, if at the time when he lived, St. Pius X was able to express himself so forcefully, he would not have been able to do so now in the same manner without arousing a vigorous opposition. Almost a century has passed. Contaminated by false doctrines, people would now no longer accept it; many among them deem that there is not just the Catholic religion. The consequences follow necessarily.

False Definition of Human Dignity

Unfortunately, a good part of public opinion is now imbued with false ideas concerning social doctrine.

The Pope then, in his third point, denounces a false definition of human dignity. And one is forced to conclude that he was not well heeded, because this definition corresponds exactly to the notion of human dignity that can be discerned in the texts of Vatican II. It is the same thing!

> According to [the Sillon], Man will be a man truly worthy of the name only when he has acquired a strong, enlightened and independent consciousness (There's the conscience.), able to do without a master (And there's human dignity.), obeying only himself, and able to assume the most demanding responsibilities without faltering. Such are the big words by which human pride is exalted....

A consciousness strong, enlightened and independent, able to do without a master, obeying only self: this is exactly the meaning adopted by the Council. "Now men are becoming increasingly conscious of their dignity, man has become an adult." These words are, moreover, the very title of the *Declaration on Religious Liberty*: *Dignitatis Humanae*, the famous human dignity:

> Contemporary man is becoming increasingly conscious of the dignity of the human person.[4]

As if all those who have gone before us lacked the consciousness of human dignity, of the true human dignity which is to be sons of God, to submit to Him, to obey His law and to be attached to the truth and charity.

The second phrase of this declaration is equally significant:

> More and more people are demanding that men should exercise fully their own judgment and a responsible freedom in their actions...

---

[4] *Vatican Council II*, p.799.

Here it is exactly: strong, enlightened and independent, obeying only himself. It is incredible that the like should be found in an official document. Man must act by the light of his conscience and no one must apply any pressure. We are indeed forced to observe that those who are in error, the modernists and the progressives are, alas, ever more numerous.

In the same text, coercion is often mentioned: there must be no coercion. And it is not, of course, a matter of physical coercion, but moral coercion, the coercion of the magisterium. Every kind of coercion must be suppressed. That is to say that everyone must be autonomous, and must not depend upon a superior: no authority. It is incredible!

> ...[M]en...should not be subject to the pressure of coercion but be inspired by a sense of duty.[5]

Everyone will determine his duty and form his own conscience. This is exactly the expression of false human dignity, by which man would only be man by obeying his own independent conscience free of the objective authority of truth. St. Pius X made very clear to what such a conception of human dignity can lead:

> Such are the big words by which human pride is exalted, like the dream carrying man away without light, without guidance, and without help into the realm of illusion in which he will be destroyed by his errors and passions whilst awaiting the glorious day of his full consciousness.

By repeating "no constraint," all teaching comes to be rejected. The truth must not be taught. Everyone must find his own truth. The text of *Dignitatis Humanae*, unbelievably, develops the point:

> It is in accordance with their dignity that all men, because they are persons, that is, beings endowed with reason and free will and therefore bearing personal responsibility, are both impelled by their nature and bound by a moral obligation to seek the truth....[6]

Thus no one would be held to obey the truth he is taught, that is, the truth of Our Lord Jesus Christ, who imposed Himself upon

---

[5] *Ibid.*
[6] *Vatican Council II*, p.801.

us as our Master when He said: "He that believeth and is baptized shall be saved: but he that believeth not shall be condemned" (Mk. 16:16). Our Lord did indeed present Himself as Master. He did not simply say to men, seek the truth and let every man follow his conscience. Our Lord was clear: behold the truth, and you must obey it. They have the audacity now to pretend that their theory, by which everyone is free to follow his conscience, was taught by Sacred Scripture, and that it was Our Lord who taught it.

A few days ago I met Cardinal Oddi and I told him: "It is a blasphemy! To affirm such an anti-truth is blasphemous!" This is indeed what St. Pius X said about the erroneous conceptions of the Sillon. The Sillon transformed the Gospel too, and by so doing it blasphemed. To assert that Our Lord told everyone to follow his conscience is to do like the Sillon. It is odious to dare commit such an offense. Nonetheless, it continues. The conciliar Declaration goes on:

> ...men...help one another in the search for truth. Moreover, it is by personal assent that men must adhere to the truth they have discovered.[7]

But it really is a duty that is imposed upon us by our masters, our priests, by the authority, by those who know the truth and who teach it to us. We need to be taught. If everyone must seek his truth one can no longer teach the catechism to children. For, according to this argument, it would be to constrain them. It would be constraining the children to teach them something and to oblige them to follow the truth. Rather they must seek it themselves and adhere to it according to their own conscience and by the act of their own will. And they tell us: "You have no right to impose any constraint." It is unthinkable as well as unbelievable.

> But men cannot satisfy this obligation in a way that is in keeping with their own nature...

As if all constraint frustrated nature, as if the good God had wanted there to be no constraint!

---

[7] *Ibid.*

...unless they enjoy both psychological freedom and immunity from external coercion.[8]

It is clear that physical coercion is not in question, even though St. Augustine himself wrote:

> Yes, at the beginning, I also believed that one could not constrain men to believe in the truth. But now that I have seen, and observed that thanks to the orders given by the emperor to pursue the error of the Donatists, thanks to the force that was used to impede their meetings and close their temples, to threaten them with exile and the loss of their goods, the Catholics who had fallen into the error had a chance to reflect and have now returned to the truth and say, "Blessed coercion that helped us to recover the truth. Now we recognize that we were in error, but now we have found the true path thanks to the emperor, who sent soldiers to combat error"; now I understand that force can very well be used to reduce the enemies of the faith and prevent the diffusion of error and, indirectly, cause men to return to the truth.[9]

It is St. Augustine himself who said this. Of course, it is only a question of using constraint in certain cases. But what is and remains a duty is to pursue error and vice, to prevent error from spreading and to drive it out. For Catholics, for all those who believe and have the Faith, a duty exists to defend the Faith against the error that seeks to destroy it.

"Immunity from external coercion," says the Council. It speaks, not of physical constraint, but of moral constraint. Now, when Our Lord said, "If you refuse belief, you will be condemned," wasn't that psychological constraint? The threatened condemnation is hell. Is it not a rather rude constraint to say, either this or hell? It is indeed a moral constraint that causes the one to whom it is addressed to tremble: It is the fire of hell for all eternity if you do not believe. Would Our Lord then not have the right to do it? According to the principles of the *Declaration on Religious Liberty*,

---

[8] *Ibid.*, p.801.
[9] Cf. St. Augustine, Letter 93. St. Thomas explains that one can legitimately exercise coercion on those who apostatized from the Catholic faith, "in order to oblige them to perform what they promised" by receiving baptism, that is, to keep the faith (cf. *Summa Theologica*, II, II, q. 10, a. 8).

one is free to follow his conscience: no constraint. Hence parents do not have the right to discipline their children. Consequently, they do not have the right to baptize their children. "Perhaps he would not wish to be baptized," and so on. From the false notion of human dignity spring forth, evidently, unbelievable consequences.

St. Pius X thus concludes his reflections on the errors of the Sillon:

> Unless human nature can be changed, which is not within the power of the Sillonists, will that day ever come? Did the Saints who brought human dignity to its highest point, possess that kind of dignity? And what of the lowly of this earth who are unable to raise so high but are content to plough their furrow modestly at the level where Providence placed them? They who are diligently discharging their duties with Christian humility, obedience and patience, are they not also worthy of being called men? We close here our observations on the errors of the Sillon.

The Sillon's Action

Having studied and stigmatized the errors of doctrine, the Pope opens a second chapter on the action of the Sillon:

> We do not claim to have exhausted the subject, for We should yet draw your attention to other points that are equally false and dangerous, for example on the manner to interpret the concept of the coercive power of the Church. But We must now examine the influence of these errors upon the practical conduct and upon the social action of the Sillon.

Since the Sillon does not limit its activity to the realm of abstraction, as St. Pius X says; but acts to influence society, it is necessary to examine how it acts. The Pope describes this action in three points: Firstly, the manner of forming its members, their education; second, its lack of discipline, and finally the relations of the Sillon with the Church.

If what we ourselves are witnessing were not so heartbreaking and disastrous, one might be tempted to smile, for what the Pope describes exactly corresponds to what is happening now; it is precisely what the modernists and the progressives want.

No More Master

> The governing elite has emerged from the rank and file by selection, that is, by imposing itself through its moral authority and its virtues. People join it freely, and freely they may leave it. Studies are carried out without a master, at the very most, with an adviser. The study groups are really intellectual pools in which each member is at once both master and student.

St. Pius X, who always kept a sense of humor, chose well the expression "intellectual pools."

According to such a plan, what follows? Why not create the same sort of "pools" in the seminaries, where, to be taught, the seminarians would put in common all their ideas, and so on!

The Dignity of the Priesthood Debased

The Pope continues this examination of "intellectual pools" by describing how they function:

> The most complete fellowship prevails amongst its members, and draws their souls into close communion; hence the common soul of the Sillon. It has been called a "friendship." Even the priest on entering, lowers the eminent dignity of his priesthood, and by a strange reversal of roles, becomes a student, placing himself on a level with his young friends, and is no more than a comrade.

This is still a reality among a good number of modernists and progressives. And exactly the same thing happened in the J.O.C.[10] circles, as I observed when I was in Dakar. When the group met, the chaplain was a comrade! He was one among the members of the little group of youth and, in principle, he had no say. It was the group as a whole that was responsible for the meetings, and they said, that when the priest comes, he must only listen and give advice from time to time. The spirit of the Sillon, denounced by Pope Pius X in 1910, had passed into the J.O.C. movement founded in 1925 by Fr. Cardijn.[11]

---

[10] Young Catholic Workers [tr. note].
[11] Prelate of His Holiness in 1950, he was to be made a cardinal by Paul VI in 1965.

So, even after having been condemned, the spirit of the Sillon remains, and this perseverance in the propagation of these baneful ideas has resulted in the spread of terrible errors. In vain have the popes spoken and condemned, addressing the bishops in order to mobilize and second their efforts, as indeed it was their pastoral duty to do; it has been as if they had never spoken nor condemned anything. And even if there were bishops who proved themselves to be true disciples of St. Pius X, supporting his action and following his directives, a good number of them refused to hear, and continued to act as if the Pope had never made known his judgment by condemning these ideas.

Unfortunately, the spirit of the Sillon entered the seminaries and infected numerous seminarians who became priests, and some of them even bishops and cardinals. When the Council was convened, one found bishops there quite imbued with the spirit of the Sillon: a false notion of human dignity, comradeship.

Opposition to Authority

After studying their formation, the Pope comes to the second point, namely describing what results this brings in practice:

> In these democratic practices and in the theories of the Ideal City from which they flow, you will recognize, Venerable Brethren, the hidden cause of the lack of discipline with which you have so often had to reproach the Sillon. It is not surprising that you do not find among the leaders and their comrades trained on these lines, whether seminarians or priests, the respect, the docility and the obedience which are due to your authority and to yourselves; nor is it surprising that you should be conscious of an underlying opposition on their part....

When such a spirit enters a body, a seminary, for example, the consequences are terrible, because it does not reveal itself, it is not perceptible, because the opposition to authority is very subtle.

Then the Pope expresses some considerations that are quite applicable to what is being said now about those of us who desire to keep tradition:

> ...and that to your sorrow, you should see them withdraw altogether from works which are not those of the Sillon or, if com-

pelled under obedience, that they should comply with distaste. You are the past; they are the pioneers of the civilization of the future. You represent the hierarchy, social inequalities, authority and obedience, worn out institutions to which their hearts, captured by another ideal, can no longer submit. Occurrences so sad as to bring tears to Our eyes bear witness to this frame of mind. And we cannot, with all Our patience, overcome a just feeling of indignation. Now then! Distrust of the Church, their Mother, is being instilled into the minds of Catholic youth; they are being taught that after nineteen centuries She has not yet been able to build up in this world a society on true foundations; She has not understood the social notions of authority, liberty, equality, fraternity and human dignity; they are told that the great Bishops and Kings, who have made France what it is and governed so gloriously, have not been able to give their people true justice and true happiness because they did not possess the Sillonist Ideal!

This is the language that is being proffered at present and which we heard during the course of the Council. The Church has not succeeded in converting the world, she has failed in her apostolic role. Then it is necessary to change, to adapt the Church to the modern world. The Church did not know how to adapt herself to the peoples, and it is for this reason that there have been so few fruits. During the Council, this spirit was to be found lodged in not a few episcopal heads.

In the encyclical the Pope speaks of the seminarians and priests. But these seminarians and priests became bishops, and there were many who, during the Council, proved themselves to have been won over by this nefarious spirit. They did not want to see or to accept the situation of the Church, that difficulties in the apostolate existed and still exist and needed to be remedied.

Even at that epoch, for instance, vocations were drying up; the priests had less and less influence over the families and the children. A kind of discouragement overtook them as they saw that their apostolate did not bear fruit as they had wished, and that, despite their efforts, families disappeared from the parish. The young people would go to clubs or sports associations and the like, and so their parishes emptied.

Seek the Causes

What should they have done? They should have reflected. From what do these things proceed? What are the causes? For the cause is known: It comes from the persecution by the Protestants that the Church has been suffering for four centuries. It is also the result of secularism which has been introduced into all State schools. And as secularism little by little consolidated its foothold, it was atheism that spread. Necessarily, in such conditions, atheism could not help but gain an increasing number of adherents.

Then the lay State put pressure on people, telling them in effect not to go to church if they wished to keep their position or advance in their careers in the administration or the army. One must not be Catholic, one must not go to church. Confronted by these pressures which were applied in every domain, in the lay institutions, and in the secular or even the Communist communes, what can be done? This is the question that the bishops should have asked. This should have been their essential preoccupation.

But instead of seeing the evil where it was and still is to be found, namely, in the vast conspiracy of secularism against the Church and against Our Lord Jesus Christ, the bishops preferred to say, that it was the Church that had been mistaken, and did not know what to do. They averred that if the Church had known how to get along with everyone who is against her, and who fight against us, this would not have happened.

This is a complete error.

Then, at the Council, they wanted to formalize a marriage between the Catholic ideas of the Church and the modern ideas which, as we have seen, have been condemned by all the popes prior to Vatican II. Such a marriage is absolutely impracticable, impossible.

Secularism and Desecration: A Total Disaster

The result is complete, radical catastrophe. How can one think that it is possible to reach an arrangement with those whose end has always been and still is the destruction of the Catholic religion and the Church. They bring to bear the weight of their moral authority, of the priesthood, for the destruction of the Church.

And the disaster is worse still. It is they who have succeeded in secularizing the Church. They began by casting aside the cassock, thus, by secularizing, they have become laymen.
Then they removed everything that was sacred in the churches. The Blessed Sacrament was withdrawn from the tabernacles and exiled to a niche in the wall—or, even worse, many times one does not know where it is. The altars, the beautiful altars representing sacred mysteries, were thrown out and replaced by a table. Nothing was left. The stations of the cross were taken down. The holy objects carted to the flea markets. They secularized everything, believing that by acting in this way they would attract all the people with increasingly secular ideas into the churches. It was madness. The priests associated with the enemies of Our Lord. They no longer believe in Our Lord.

The priests thought that by dressing in lay fashion the laymen would be much more amiable towards them—and that they would be everyone's friend—and that they would bring them to church. Not only did they not draw anyone, they practically chased away half of the Catholics from the churches. As for them, what are they now? They are no longer men of the Church. It is over. People no longer recognize them as being men of the Church. It is a frightful result.

Our own position was constant. We told them that they were taking a wrong turn, that the solution was to return to the tradition of the Church, and do once more what the Church had always done. We warned them that those who fight against the Church are enemies, and that we should not compromise with them; that we should not resemble them. On the contrary, more than ever, we must be true representatives of Our Lord Jesus Christ, and emphasize the mystery, the supernatural, and grace. We affirmed that this should be manifest in the churches, that the churches should be somewhat an antechamber of paradise. Consequently, when we see statues of the saints, they should be models for us. Our churches should make us think of heaven and all the virtues that the Church has brought forth.

But they tell us, You are the past and we are the future. We are marching with progress, and we shall prevail! But they will come to nothing, because they nonetheless represent authority and obedience, even if according to their own theses, there is no more authority nor obedience, no more social inequalities, yet these differences have, in reality, been willed by God and cannot be eliminated. For that does not depend on us. They are willed by Him for the practice of charity.

No longer accepting the Church as it had been before, they changed everything: the Bible, the catechism, the Mass. They have changed everything.

The Lead Came from the Top

The churchmen themselves accused the Church. All the bad examples leading to change came from above: the bishops wrote letters to this effect. All the commissions, liturgical and other, had but one goal: change!

When Pope John XXIII read his letter at the beginning of the Council, in which, in essence, in the name of the Church he beat his breast and said *"Mea culpa, mea culpa,"* to the Protestants, it was profoundly scandalous. That the Pope should practically accuse his predecessors of having acted badly towards the Protestants, and then add that had they proceeded differently perhaps the Protestants would never have separated from the Church, was utterly scandalous.

On the contrary, if the popes had been firmer and more severe towards the Protestants as soon as they manifested themselves, perhaps the princes would have fought against Protestantism from its inception. It would have died in the egg. But, because out of the goodness of their hearts they were willing to discuss interminably, while they talked the heresy spread. And once the princes themselves began to convert to Protestantism, it became a political matter. All hope was ended and the massacres began, as well as the looting and destruction of churches. Then the wars of religion opened fire; and they were horrible. If one might formulate a reflection, it would be to remark that the popes were too good towards the Protestants, and not to say that they should have tried to be more understanding!

The Church's Past Discredited

This is somewhat the spirit of John Paul II. I do not know what he will say at Geneva, but I am afraid that he is going to make more declarations similar to the ones he made in Germany, begging pardon of the Protestants for what the Catholics may have done to them. Some deem that these are words spoken only out of courtesy. No. It is extremely grave, because it discredits the Church's entire past, as well as all the popes who preceded him, and who, according to him, did not know how to do what needed to be done. The Church did not know how to exercise her ministry as she ought to have done. A very grave responsibility is incurred for holding forth such language.

And this ties in perfectly with what Pope St. Pius X was saying about what the Sillon taught its members, namely:

> ...after nineteen centuries She has not yet been able to build up in this world a society on true foundations; She has not understood the social notions of authority, liberty, equality, fraternity, etc.

Presently, the progressives no longer use such language concerning politics, but, much more serious, concerning the apostolate:

> The Church has not known how to bring solutions to the social question; the Church has not known how to solve the problems of the apostolate....

The Pope concludes his remarks on the lack of discipline by saying:

> The breath of the Revolution has passed this way.

The Breath of the Revolution

Without a doubt it can be said that the breath of the Revolution passed by Vatican II. It is absolutely certain. And for those who were there, as I myself was, it was really palpable. I would go so far as to say that one physically felt the revolutionary breath blow against the past, against all that the Church had done, and against tradition. These were really atrocious times: the self-destruction and self-criticism of the Church. This was especially felt during the interventions. Each time that the Church was ridiculed—or a traditional cardinal, be it Cardinal Ottaviani or another, or the Roman Curia—all the young bishops applauded. Essentially, they demonstrated against papal authority. They did not express this clearly, of course, but in their interventions against the Roman Curia, Roman authoritarianism, certain cardinals, or whatever, these bishops indirectly attacked the Pope. For, ultimately, who is in charge of the Roman Curia, and who commands, or who established it if not the Pope?

In the back of the basilica there were hundreds of young bishops who would applaud. As for me, I was among the ranks of the old archbishops, having been such for some time. At that time I was ranked sixty-fourth among the archbishops. There were the cardinals, then the archbishops, and then the multitude of bishops.

Among the young bishops there were rousing ovations each time something was said against the Church. It was truly frightful, truly the revolution had entered the Church. Revolutionary minds wanted to overthrow everything, to topple the edifice, so to speak. And this is indeed what they succeeded in doing. It was appalling then; and indeed it is manifest now that they broke everything..

Already Pope St. Pius X said:

> The breath of the Revolution has passed this way, and We can conclude that, whilst the social doctrines of the Sillon are erroneous, its spirit is dangerous and its education disastrous.

After considering the formation of the Sillon's members, the Pope takes up the topic of their action, in particular their insubordination vis-à-vis the bishops. What is the relation of the Sillon to the Church?

> But then, what are we to think of its action in the Church? What are we to think of a movement so punctilious in its brand of Catholicism that, unless you embrace its cause you would almost be regarded as an internal enemy of the Church, and you would understand nothing of the Gospel and of Jesus Christ!

If we place these allegations in the current situation, we observe that the bishops and all the progressives tell us exactly the same thing, that we understand nothing about the Gospel of Our

Lord. According to them, it is we who do not understand the Gospel of Our Lord.

St. Pius X's Judgment of the Sillon

> We deem it necessary to insist on that point because it is precisely its Catholic ardor which has secured for the Sillon until quite recently, valuable encouragements and the support of distinguished persons. Well now, judging the words and deeds, we feel compelled to say that in this action as well as in its doctrine, the Sillon does not give satisfaction to the Church.

The Pope does not declare formally that the Sillon is heretical, but that "it does not give satisfaction to the Church," and further on he adds that it is no longer Catholic. But it would have been something else to actually qualify it as heretical. And, on this point, I would like to caution those who have a tendency to decry as a heretic anyone who says the least thing that may not be completely in accordance with the Faith. Beware; do not go faster than the popes themselves. St. Pius X only says that "the spirit of the Sillon does not give satisfaction to the Church." In the same way, when he says that Modernism is the synthesis of all the heresies, he does not add that all those favorable to Modernism are heretics. He only says, that it is the synthesis of all the heresies in its doctrine.

If they professed this doctrine pertinaciously and openly, then it could be said that they are heretics. But how many are there who profess a Modernist or Sillonist doctrine, and yet who are not totally in accord with these ideas? It is necessary to be careful and to be nuanced in our appreciations, as the popes were, as St. Pius X was.

Catholicism Not Linked to Any Form of Government

The Pope formulates two criticisms about the Sillon in its relation to the Church: Firstly, it subjects its religion to a political party, and secondly, it tries to unite all the religions. Firstly, it subjects its religion to a political party:

> ...Its brand of Catholicism accepts only the democratic form of government which it considers the most favorable to the

Church, and so to speak, identifies it with her. The Sillon therefore, subjects its religion to a political party. We do not have to demonstrate here that the advent of universal Democracy is of no concern to the action of the Church in the world; we have already recalled that the Church has always left to the nations the care of giving themselves the form of government which they think most suited to their needs. What We wish to affirm once again, after Our Predecessor, is that it is an error and a danger to bind down Catholicism by principle to a particular form of government. This error and this danger are all the greater when religion is associated with a kind of democracy whose doctrines are false.

He specifies a democracy based upon false principles, because it cannot be maintained that all democracies are based on a false principle. As the Pope says: If, for example, the people merely designate the holders of authority, but without giving it to them, the Church does not condemn such a system. Such is the case of Switzerland, for example, which has long been democratic, where the people designate the subjects of authority.

What is false, and what the Sillonists maintained, was that the authority remains in the people, and that it is conferred by the people and not by God. Moreover, the absolute egalitarianism and exaggerated liberty the Sillonists professed are false principles which they wanted the Church to espouse, as well as to be linked to this kind of democracy.

Against such false conceptions of democracy which the Sillonists dreamed of establishing and which violated the Church's principles, Pope St. Pius X rose up.

The Sillon Stood Back While the Church Was Despoiled

And after expressing this principled opposition, he clearly states the reasons for his assessment:

> For the sake of a particular political form, [the Sillon] compromises the Church, it sows division among Catholics, snatches away young people and even priests and seminarians from purely Catholic action, and is wasting away as a dead loss part of the living forces of the nation.

While they should have defended the Church and come to her aid when she was attacked in France from all sides, they stood back with their arms crossed. It must be remembered that this was the period during his pontificate when Pope Pius X had witnessed the separation of Church and State in France, and the persecution of the Church that was unleashed by Emile Combes resulting in the forced seizure of all the church buildings, the despoliation of the Church's property, etc. It would have been necessary for the Sillon, for example, to come to the aid of the Church in order to defend her against the State's open attack. But they did no such thing, as the Pope describes:

> At the sight of the violences thus done to the Church, we are often grieved to see the Sillonists folding their arms except when it is to their advantage to defend her; we see them dictate or maintain a program which nowhere and in no degree can be called Catholic. Yet this does not prevent the same men, when fully engaged in political strife and spurred by a provocation, from publicly proclaiming their faith. What are we to say except that there are two different men in the Sillonist; the individual who is Catholic, and the Sillonist, the man of action, who is neutral.

This is proof again of the trait that characterizes Liberalism: duplicity, two modes of being, as we have seen on several occasions. Cardinal Billot defined Liberalism as such: the liberal Catholic always finds himself in a state of incoherence. He is a walking contradiction. Even the very expression "liberal Catholic" suffices to manifest the contradiction, for if one is a Catholic, one cannot be a liberal in the sense of Liberalism as condemned by the popes. The two things are fundamentally contradictory, the expression "liberal Catholic" is an oxymoron, and Pope Paul VI was the living demonstration.

Paul VI: Liberal and Symbol of Contradiction

Pope Paul VI embodied contradiction. He was fundamentally liberal, and this is somewhat the case of the reigning Pope. These are people who were formed with false doctrines, and who have not wanted to heed the teachings of their predecessors. Thus formed, they are imbued with ideas of universalism, human dignity, accord with the Church's enemies, and all the modern current of false notions.

Nonetheless, they engage themselves in this new path, then suddenly notice that all is not well. Pope Paul VI said that they had hoped that the Council would produce good fruits, but then they had been obliged to acknowledge that it had not. When they have felt this, fear moves them to make a few more traditional speeches. This is the case of Pope John Paul II when he is addressing seminarians, religious or nuns; his remarks could well be placed in the mouths of a more distant predecessor, like Pope Pius XII, etc. But in other circumstances he makes speeches which, like his encyclicals, utilize nebulous language, and improbable expressions that are incomprehensible. One does not find the clear doctrine of the Church such as it is found in the documents of the popes we have studied, which were always expressed in limpid style. It was always the same doctrine, simple and luminous.

False Ecumenism

Now the opposite is true; a total confusion of ideas and equivocal expressions are met with. The false ecumenism practiced by John Paul II towards the Church's enemies is frightening. His mind is ecumenical, and he is lost. Never would Pope Pius XII have made declarations similar to his. Not even John XXIII would have uttered them. Undoubtedly John XXIII let himself be led astray by weakness of soul and by those who pushed him to make certain risky or surprising statements which did not echo the traditional language of the Church. But in his own mind he still possessed the traditional doctrine. Whereas, coming from Pope Paul VI and Pope John Paul II these kinds of declarations are very grave, because they are imbued with Liberalism. Pope John Paul II may have had a good course of study at Rome during the time he was there, but how much of it did he assimilate? He frequented the liberals so much that he wound up by adopting their mentality. Thus he makes utterly incredible statements when dealing with the enemies of the Church. There are two men in him: the Ecumenist and the Catholic.

As Pope Paul VI told me: "You say that I am half Protestant, half Catholic." Unfortunately, this was true. Within myself I thought it without saying anything. But he himself made the gesture of dividing his face in two: two faces. That is pretty strong, for a pope. And I believe that this duality within tortured him. Paul VI was an anguished man, a man torn interiorly because of this fundamental contradiction in himself. When he made this remark to me, he really felt that he had a dual behavior and that there was some truth in the assertion when he was accused of being half Catholic, half Protestant. In this terrible situation there was something frightening, especially for a pope.

Pope John Paul II does not have the same anguished air, nor does he have the same temperament or character as Paul VI, but I fear—I am not a prophet, but I think that if he does not restore the Mass and return to tradition, grave events will occur. It is not possible otherwise, for almighty God cannot tolerate this situation.

In a few days Poland may be invaded. If Poland were invaded again, this would be an extremely grave event which would have incalculable consequences for this poor country, as the Czechs let us know when, after the "Prague spring," they were savagely crushed by the Russians. They sent us photocopied letters saying that if we did not help them, soon the stone covering the well into which they had been plunged would be sealed, and they would remain entombed for how long?

For Poland, the same thing may come to pass. They are, as it were, in a well. The Czechs hoped that Europe would come to their aid; the Poles are trying to push away the stone that weighs on them, but the Russians are surely going to intervene, and who then will fly to their rescue? I do not especially know, but I presume that they are going to let the Russians have their way, as they did in Afghanistan. The Russians have been allowed to get away with everything they have undertaken in Europe, even by force, as long as there has been no immediate danger to us. "Better red than dead," is the current motto.

We are now reaping the fruit of the false ideas that invaded the seminaries at the time of the Sillon, and which reached the Council in our own time.

The Union of Religions

Another of the ideas proposed by the Sillon and which was unfurled at the Council was the union of the religions:

> There was a time when the Sillon as such was truly Catholic. It recognized but one moral force—Catholicism; and the Sillonists were wont to proclaim that Democracy would have to be Catholic or would not exist at all. A time came when they changed their minds. They left to each one his religion or his philosophy. They ceased to call themselves Catholics and for the formula "Democracy will be Catholic," they substituted "Democracy will not be anti-Catholic," any more than it will be anti-Jewish or anti-Buddhist. This was the time of "the Greater Sillon." For the construction of the Future City they appealed to the workers of all religions and all sects. These were asked but one thing: to share the same social ideal, to respect all creeds, and to bring with them a certain supply of moral force. Admittedly they declared that "The leaders of the Sillon place their religious faith above everything. But can they deny others the right to draw their moral energy from whence they can? In return, they expect others to respect their right to draw their own moral energy from the Catholic Faith. Accordingly, they ask all those who want to change today's society in the direction of Democracy, not to oppose each other on account of the philosophical or religious convictions which may separate them, but to march hand in hand, not renouncing their convictions, but trying to provide on the ground of practical realities, the proof of the excellence of their personal convictions. Perhaps a union will be effected on this ground of emulation between souls holding different religious or philosophical convictions." And they added at the same time (but how could this be accomplished?) that "the Little Catholic Sillon will be the soul of the Greater Cosmopolitan Sillon."

This is the very same spirit that holds sway today under the name of ecumenism. It is called ecumenism, but this word is equivocal and signifies some kind of union of all the religions. All must collaborate to build the world. This is indeed what *Gaudium et Spes* suggests, especially in the last chapter, which sounds the same note. In the conclusion (no. 91) which follows the chapter devoted to "The Construction of the International Community," we read:

> Drawn from the treasures of the teaching of the Church, the proposals of this Council are intended for all men, whether they believe in God or whether they do not explicitly acknowledge him (—All the religions, then, even the atheist ones); they are intended to help them to a keener awareness of their own destiny, to make the world conform better to the surpassing dignity of man, to strive for a more deeply rooted sense of universal brotherhood...[12]

Upon what deeper foundation they fail to specify. They should have said: based on Our Lord Jesus Christ; this is the foundation of universal union:

> ...and to meet the pressing appeals of our times with a generous and common effort of love.

How vague all this is. What can be the foundations upon which to build a universal community of those who believe and those who do not believe? How frightening it is that the Council puts forth the very theses maintained by the Sillon.

The last part of the Conclusion, entitled "A World to Be Built Up and Brought to Fulfillment" (no. 93), is even more shocking, if that were possible:

> Mindful of the words of the Lord: "By this all men will know that you are my disciples, if you have love for one another" (Jn. 13:35), Christians can yearn for nothing more ardently than to serve the men of this age with an ever growing generosity and success. Holding loyally to the Gospel, enriched by its resources, and joining forces with all who love and practice justice, they have shouldered a weighty task here on earth and they must render an account of it to him who will judge all men on the last day. Not everyone who says "Lord, Lord," will enter the kingdom of heaven, but those who do the will of the Father, and who manfully put their hands to the work.[13]

---

[12] *Vatican Council II: The Conciliar and Post Conciliar Documents*, p.999.
[13] *Ibid.*, p.1001.

What does that mean? It is not clear what one must work towards, nor in what direction to tend, nor why:

> It is the Father's will that we should recognize Christ our brother in the persons of all men....[14]

If they are sinners, how can one recognize Christ in every man? Rather one desires to restore them in Christ so that they believe in God:

> ...and love them with an effective love, in word and deed....

The style adopted is unbelievable. One should love one's neighbor in the measure that he is attached to Our Lord, and so we should attempt to bring them to believe in Our Lord!

> ...and love them with an effective love, in word and in deed, thus bearing witness to the truth; and it is his will that we should share with others the mystery of his heavenly love. In this way men all over the world will awaken to a lively hope (the gift of the Holy Spirit) that they will one day be admitted to the haven of surpassing peace and happiness in their homeland radiant with the glory of the Lord.

And how is this to be done? Without conversion, without Baptism, and without the preaching of the Gospel?

> ...We are all called to be brothers. And since we are destined to one and the same divine vocation, we can and we must cooperate, without violence and without hidden motives, in the building up of the world in true peace.

What can this mean? how can those who believe and those who do not believe build up the world and establish true peace? What world is being referred to? and what world do they want to build up? It is scarcely credible that this could be written in an official document issued by Vatican Council II, a Catholic Council, and promulgated by a pope! This is not Catholic teaching. But it corresponds exactly to the language employed by the Sillonists.

In the course of his letter, Pope Pius X judges the action of the Sillon:

---

[14] *Ibid.*

These declarations and this new organization of the Sillonist action call for very serious remarks. Here we have, founded by Catholics, an inter-denominational association that is to work for the reform of civilization, an undertaking which is above all, religious in character....

Without the True Religion, No Real Civilization

St. Pius X replies in anticipation to the Second Vatican Council's summons to build up the world and civilization by declaring that it is "an undertaking which is above all, religious in character":

> ...for there is no true civilization without a moral civilization, and no true moral civilization without the true religion: it is a proven truth, an historical fact.

Fortunately, popes like St. Pius X made themselves heard before Vatican Council II, for by giving us the truth, they have enabled us to better understand the current situation. Pope St. Pius X is very clear in his affirmations. He does not employ this modern style that is incomprehensible and ambiguous. One never knows exactly what they mean, but is this not intentional?

St. Pius X defines civilization as principally a matter of religion, and he explains why: "For there is no true civilization without a moral civilization." A people's morals are an essential element of civilization; there is no true moral civilization without the true religion. It is simple; it is a clear undeniable fact: "It is a proven truth, an historical fact." All those who pretend to seek a civilization apart from the Church, the truth, Our Lord Jesus Christ, have completely veered off course. As the Pope says, it is an historical fact. To be convinced of this truth it suffices to reread history.

And the new Sillonists are wrong to pretend that:

> ...they are merely working on "the ground of practical realities" where differences of belief do not matter. Their leader is so conscious of the influence which the convictions of the mind have upon the result of the action, that he invites them, whatever religion they may belong to, "to provide on the ground of practical realities, the proof of the excellence of their personal convictions."

Again, this is what we are witnessing now, and which we frequently have occasion to observe. For example, nowadays one speaks frequently of "the three great monotheist religions." According to the logic, these three monotheistic religions should unite to create a better world. Not only is this completely utopian, but such language uttered by Catholics, bishops, and even the Vatican, constitutes a veritable insult to Our Lord Jesus Christ. To thus put the Moslems, Jews and Christians on a par is untenable. Beside the fact that such remarks are in some way blasphemous, the attitude maintained by the Vatican is completely illusory.

The errors propagated by the Vatican, however, do not call into question the promises of Our Lord on the infallibility of the pope and His assistance to the Holy See. Over the centuries there have indeed been some errors made by the popes in carrying out their duties, but they never violated the Church's universal doctrine on faith and morals.

Impossible to Be Both Jew and Catholic

All these utopians who betray the duties of their office did not escape the slap they were given when a cardinal went to a meeting with the Moslems under pretext of creating a kind of Catholic-Islamic union. He was quite correctly despised and treated in an odious manner by the Moslems. It was a good lesson he well deserved to receive. For the utopians refuse to believe history; they do not believe what the popes have taught; and they do not believe the truth of Our Lord. If they imagine they can reach an understanding with the Moslems, they are badly deceiving themselves. The Moslems hate the Catholics.

The same goes for the Jews, as the Rabbi Kaplan said recently to the new archbishop of Paris, who affirmed that he is both Catholic and Jew: "It is impossible to be a Jew and a Christian at the same time." That would be like "a round square." Of course he is right. The Jews are the inheritors of those who crucified Our Lord, and they boast of the fact, because for them Our Lord was not the Messias; they are still waiting for him. Being the inheritors of those who crucified Our Lord, they are essentially against the Church. It is impossible to be simultaneously a Christian, that is, a disciple of Jesus Christ, and a Jew. Now, if they are Jews like the

Blessed Virgin, Sts. Peter and Paul and all those who converted and became disciples of Our Lord, and yet remained Jews because they were by nature Jewish, this goes without saying. Had the archbishop of Paris meant that, there would have been nothing to remark. Even the chief rabbi could only have said that he was powerless to prevent a Jew from converting to Catholicism. But for this man, being Catholic and moreover archbishop of Paris and cardinal of the Holy Church, to say, "I am a Jew and in union with the Jewish community, this persecuted minority," is untenable.

It Is the Jews Who Have Persecuted the Catholics

And when he speaks of the "persecuted minority," the cardinal shows that he does not know his history very well, because it is the Jews, after all, who persecuted the Christians. The Christians did not persecute the Jews. Just the contrary is true.

If it were necessary to set them apart in what were called ghettos, as existed at Rome, Venice, throughout Italy and in all the great Catholic cities, it was to protect them. But they enjoyed great liberties and even privileges. They carried out their trade and business in all tranquillity and freedom. And in these ghettos—which signifies a place where Jews lived apart—they were officially protected by the Church.

As for them, as soon as they could, they worked against Catholics. They have always worked against the Church. They have never been willing to accept submission to the laws of a Christian State. They have always remained outside, and this in every domain. It is thus that they have been able to get control of all the financial institutions, all the while refusing to recognize the laws of the countries in which they lived. It is fantastic.

There is no people or race or foreigner who lives in a country who insists that he dwells there but refuses to submit himself to the country's laws. The Jews refuse to submit to the laws of a country because they are Jews! "I am a Jew, I cannot submit to the laws of a Christian State." This is the reason why it has happened that they have been persecuted, for practicing usury, for remaining segregated, and for not working for the common good.

Hence it is obvious that it is impossible to act in concert with these people. A Moslem adage puts it: "Kiss the hand you cannot cut off." Yes, only force can intervene. When force is present, they kiss the hand; but when it is they who wield the force, they chop off the hand. It has always been so.

Recently the newspapers reported that the Egyptian Moslem communities have decreed that any Moslem who converts to Catholicism will be put to death. The representatives of these Moslem communities wanted to see this clause inserted into their constitution, or at least have this decretal ratified by official acts. The newspapers reported it because it is an official decision: any Moslem converting to Catholicism would suffer the death penalty.

It is forgotten, but this is the reality of Islam. For the Moslems, only Islam exists and everyone must be subject to it, either by becoming Moslem, or by being the slave of Islam; it is one or the other. It is thus that they set about reducing to slavery all those who refused to submit. Remember the religious orders of the Trinitarians and of Our Lady of Ransom, which were founded to deliver captive Christians who were being held in bondage by the Moslems. For centuries the Moslems would raid all the coasts of France, Spain and the Mediterranean, seizing Christians, whom they made slaves. This is still in their mind. If they could do it tomorrow, they would resume these ignoble practices. One must not imagine that their frame of mind has changed in the least.

Respect for Error Prevents Conversion

The Pope, then, deems it impossible to work with those people, and reaffirms that the only true civilization is Catholic, founded upon Our Lord Jesus Christ; and by the very fact he condemns every manifestation of union with the other religions:

> This being said, what must be thought of the promiscuity in which young Catholics will be caught up with heterodox and unbelieving folk in a work of this nature? Is it not a thousand-fold more dangerous for them than a neutral association? What are we to think of this appeal to all the heterodox, and to all the unbelievers, to prove the excellence of their convictions in the social sphere in a sort of apologetic contest? Has not this contest lasted for nineteen centuries in conditions less dangerous for the faith of Catholics? And was it not all to the credit of the Catholic Church? What are we to think of this respect for all errors, and of

this strange invitation made by a Catholic to all the dissidents to strengthen their convictions through study so that they may have more and more abundant sources of fresh forces?

And this is the very language employed now by bishops. If one asks a bishop of France if it is necessary to try and convert the Moslems, be it in France or elsewhere, or the animists and the Buddhists, the reply is an exasperated no, no, one must not try and convert them. On the contrary, one must uphold them in their religion, help them to appreciate the beauties of their religion. This response is unbelievable, yet typical.

The Rev. Fr. Maurice Avril, at Salérans, has been persecuted by the bishops, and has endured all sorts of harassment because after the Algerian war he looked after the *harkis*, the Algerians faithful to France, who had been able to escape and take refuge in France. The *harkis* had fought in the war to defend French Algeria and to wrest it from the revolutionary stranglehold.

Tens of thousands of them were massacred at the time when De Gaulle abandoned Algeria into the hands of the F.L.N. [National Liberation Front]. The latter, of course, had no sympathy for the harkis who had fought with the French troops to deliver French Algeria from terrorism and the revolution. Those who had been unable to flee by boat to France were tortured, massacred, buried alive, burned alive. Those responsible for this betrayal carry a horrible crime on their consciences. People who had devoted themselves to France, ready to die to defend French Algeria, as certain had done when they came to France in 1939-40, and then again during the Liberation when they arrived in Italy, in Corsica and Provence, and again against the Communists in Indochina: they were abandoned into the hands of a cruel enemy who tortured them in the cruelest ways. It was an atrocious event. Many of their children have remained in France; they only sent back the adults. Fr. Avril, who was a priest in French Algeria, was able to gather together about one hundred of these orphans. He educated them and brought them up; he took good care of them. The children of the *harkis* found themselves in the care of a priest who educated them and who gently tried to convert them by persuasion, and without forcing them, of course. Seeing the devotion of this priest and of the persons who helped him, many at last understood the beauties of the Catholic religion, and most of them asked to convert.

This was not to the liking of several bishops, who wrote letters of admonition to Fr. Avril: Leave them in their Moslem religion; they must not be converted.

They Put Their Flags in Their Pocket

What have such bishops become? Do they still believe in Our Lord? Do they believe in the one true religion founded by Our Lord?

St. Pius X had well foreseen where the erroneous doctrines of the Sillon would lead:

> What are we to think of an association in which all religions and even Free-Thought may express themselves openly and in complete freedom? For the Sillonists who, in public lectures and elsewhere, proudly proclaim their personal faith, certainly do not intend to silence others, nor do they intend to prevent a Protestant from asserting his Protestantism, and the skeptic from affirming his skepticism. Finally, what are we to think of a Catholic who, on entering his study group, leaves his Catholicism outside the door so as not to alarm his comrades who, "dreaming of disinterested social action, are not inclined to make it serve the triumph of interests, coteries and even convictions whatever they may be"?

So, he does not even work for his religion! Frightful! It is very interesting to compare all that this holy pontiff says to the text of Vatican II on religious liberty. Never would St. Pius X have consented to promulgate a text like the one on religious freedom. Compare what he himself affirmed with this assertion of the conciliar declaration:

> Also included in the right to religious freedom is the right of religious groups...not to be prevented from freely demonstrating the special value of their teaching for the organization of society... and the inspiration of all human activity.

This is exactly the opposite of what Pope St. Pius X said: "...There is no true moral civilization without the true religion: it is a proven truth, an historical fact." Then the Pope concludes:

Alas! Yes, the *équivoque* has been broken: the social action of the Sillon is no longer Catholic. The Sillonist, as such, does not work for a coterie, and "the Church," he says, "cannot in any sense benefit from the sympathies that his action may stimulate." A strange situation indeed! They fear lest the Church should profit for a selfish and interested end by the social action of the Sillon, as if everything that benefited the Church did not benefit the whole human race! A curious reversal of notions! The Church might benefit from social action! As if the greatest economists had not recognized and proved that it is social action alone which, if serious and fruitful, must benefit by the Church!

The same mindset reigns today: no privileges for the Church. And when they speak of "privileges" for the Church, it is a misnomer, for they are not privileges, but rights. They speak as if it were not the Church who is entirely at the service of peoples, and nations; as if it were not the Church who quickens them, who gives everything necessary for civilization, for the fostering of justice and civic peace.

Verbal Confusion and Social Chimera

But stranger still, alarming and saddening at the same time, are the audacity and frivolity of men who call themselves Catholics and dream of re-shaping society under such conditions, and of establishing on earth, over and beyond the pale of the Catholic Church, "the reign of love and justice" with workers coming from everywhere, of all religions and of no religion, with or without beliefs, so long as they forego what might divide them—their religious and philosophical convictions, and so long as they share what unites them—a "generous idealism and moral forces drawn from whence they can."

When we consider the forces, knowledge and supernatural virtues which were necessary to establish the Christian City, and the sufferings of millions of martyrs, and the light given by the Fathers and Doctors of the Church, and of the self-sacrifice of all the heroes of charity, and a powerful hierarchy ordained in heaven, and the streams of Divine Grace—the whole having been built up, bound together, and impregnated by the life and spirit of Jesus Christ, the Wisdom of God, the Word made man—when we think, I say, of all this, it is frightening to behold new apostles eagerly attempting to do better by a common interchange of vague idealism and civic virtues. What are they going to produce? What is to come out of the collaboration? A mere verbal and chimerical construction in which we see, glowing in a jumble, and in seductive confusion, the words of Liberty, Justice, Fraternity, Love, Equality and human exaltation, all resting upon an ill-understood human dignity. It will be a tumultuous agitation, sterile for the end proposed, but which will benefit the less Utopian exploiters of the people. Yes, we can truly say that the Sillon, its eyes fixed on a chimera, brings Socialism in its train.

Pope Pius X crushes this chimera. Subsequent facts have shown that he was right. Were he to come back into the world, seeing the current state of affairs, he would conclude that his objurgations had not been heeded, for we find ourselves enmeshed in Socialism. All of Europe has been entangled by Socialism, and often this came about with the concurrence of Catholics. Behold our pitiful state, until such time as outright Communism takes hold, again with the concurrence of Catholics.

The Pope then outlines how it was possible for the Sillonists to arrive at such excesses of thought and deed.

Towards a One-World Religion

> We fear that worse is to come: the end result of this developing promiscuousness, the beneficiary of this cosmopolitan social action, can only be a Democracy which will be neither Catholic, nor Protestant, nor Jewish. It will be a religion (for Sillonism, so the leaders have said, is a religion) more universal than the Catholic Church, uniting all men to become brothers and comrades at last in the "Kingdom of God." "We do not work for the Church, we work for mankind."

It must be noted that, since Paul VI, the documents issuing from Rome frequently employ a language entirely similar to that of the Sillon, and which Pope St. Pius X denounced.

"I am an expert on humanity," Paul VI said. First of all, what does that mean exactly? It seems that now the very idea of the

Church is set aside; it is no longer defended. One no longer works for the Church, or for the reign of Our Lord, which is the same thing. The Church is the mystical body of Our Lord; if one works for the Church, one is working for the extension of the mystical body of Christ Our Lord: He must reign. This is the role of all the popes, the bishops, priests and all Christians. We should be apostles in order to increase the mystical body of Our Lord which here below is the Church Militant, then the Church Suffering in purgatory, and the Church Triumphant in heaven.

Now they claim that the Church seems like a special interest group where they work for their own interests, for Catholics only, for a particular association. In opposition the liberals claim that they must work for humanity. They reason as if working to build up the mystical body of Christ, by converting men and making them members of Our Lord Jesus Christ, were not working for humanity.

This is very serious, because the modernists have a completely different perspective; they reproach us, when we speak of the Church, for placing outside her all those who do not belong to her, and of treating them as strangers, as if they were not our brothers. Yet, precisely, the modernists fail to awaken in the Protestants and all those who are not Catholics the idea that they should come or return to the Catholic Church in order to become truly brothers in Our Lord Jesus Christ. What will be the result? A sort of humanitarianism and philanthropy which will ultimately serve the society of Masonic nations, which is in the process of preparing something that Pope Pius X foresaw very clearly:

> ...a religion (for Sillonism, so the leaders have said, is a religion) more universal than the Catholic Church, uniting all men to become brothers and comrades at last in the 'Kingdom of God.'

One could even say, in the reign of the Great Architect! For this is the objective of the Freemasons, and with them, the Jews: the establishment of this universal religion that will exert its empire over all men. The Pope, moreover, refers to it:

> And now, overwhelmed with the deepest sadness, We ask Ourselves, Venerable Brethren, what has become of the Catholi-

cism of the Sillon? Alas! This organization which formerly afforded such promising expectations, this limpid and impetuous stream, has been harnessed in its course by the modern enemies of the Church, and is now no more than a miserable affluent of the great movement of apostasy being organized in every country for the establishment of a One-World Church which shall have neither dogmas, nor hierarchy; neither discipline for the mind, nor curb for the passions, and which, under the pretext of freedom and human dignity, would bring back to the world (if such a Church could overcome) the reign of legalized cunning and force, and the oppression of the weak, and of those who toil and suffer.

Baneful Doctrines

This is the state to which we have come. The Catholics who wanted to do something other than what the Church had always done let themselves be co-opted by the Socialists and the Freemasons. The Pope clearly says so:

> We know only too well the dark workshops in which are elaborated these mischievous doctrines which ought not to seduce clear-thinking minds. The leaders of the Sillon have not been able to guard against these doctrines. The exaltation of their sentiments, the undiscriminating good-will of their hearts, their philosophical mysticism, mixed with a measure of illuminism, have carried them away towards another Gospel which they thought was the true Gospel of our Savior. To such an extent that they speak of Our Lord Jesus Christ with a familiarity supremely disrespectful, and that—their ideal being akin to the Revolution—they fear not to draw between the Gospel and the Revolution blasphemous comparisons for which the excuse cannot be made that they are due to some confused and over-hasty composition.

St. Pius X puts his finger on the wound; the dark workshops are simply the Masonic sects. He practically says that it is the Masonic sects that profit from the current of Sillonism in order to reach their goal, which is the destruction of Catholic civilization. Indeed, this is what all the popes, and especially Leo XIII, pointed out quite explicitly. The goal of Freemasonry is the destruction of all the Christian institutions; that is, to make everything that is Christian or proceeds from Christ disappear. This is the goal of the Freemasons, and they use the liberal and falsely Catholic movements, the Sillonists and the Modernists, in order to succeed, because these are useful in the struggle that they have engaged in to destroy the Church. It is thus that they used the Second Vatican Council. Thanks to its "pastoral," non-doctrinal character, they were able to exert an influence throughout its course with the purpose of destroying the Church.

Before judging, Pope Pius X makes a last remark on the reconciliation of the Gospel and the revolution which the Sillon pretends to accomplish:

> We wish to draw your attention, Venerable Brethren, to this distortion of the Gospel and to the sacred character of Our Lord Jesus Christ, God and Man, prevailing within the Sillon and elsewhere.

There are absolutely abominable things in the theories developed by the Sillon. The Sillon maintains that democracy is equality, and that the prophet of equality is in some way Our Lord Jesus Christ. The Sillon goes even further, affirming that not only is Our Lord the symbol of equality, but that the Blessed Trinity is too, because the Three Persons are equal! The Sillonists state that Our Lord was sent by the Blessed Trinity in order to make men equal, and that, by being associated with Our Lord and becoming his brothers, they become the equals of the Persons of the Blessed Trinity!!! These are abominable assertions. Certainly, it is true that the good God wants us to participate in the Holy Trinity, but to claim that we are the equals of Our Lord and the Persons of the Blessed Trinity is blasphemous.

The Mystery of the Blessed Trinity

The Persons of the Blessed Trinity, while equal in all things, are nevertheless distinct. And this is a very great mystery. It is possible to emphasize the equality of the Divine Persons as well as their distinction, for they are indeed distinct, otherwise there would not be three Persons in the Trinity.

In the Blessed Trinity there are the Father, the Son and the Holy Ghost. As the Son said: He has received everything from the

Father. And He has received from the Father everything such that there is nothing in Him that is not equal to the Father. Evidently, this is the great mystery: this passing of everything that is in the Father into the Son into the Holy Ghost, and from the Holy Ghost returning to the Father, and this from all eternity: this is God, one God.

This is what the theologians call *circumincession*, this constant flux of the Father, the Son, and the Holy Ghost, such that the Persons are equal while at the same time they receive everything, that the Son receives everything from the Father, and with the Father He gives everything to the Holy Ghost, and the Holy Ghost gives all in the bosom of the Father and the Son. It is undoubtedly a great mystery.

But it is truly a blasphemy for the Sillon to express such opinions on equality, as if there were not in reality distinction between the Persons of the Blessed Trinity. One can say that the image of the Blessed Trinity is found in creation, because there are spiritual and physical paternities. It is truly the image of the Trinity, which is the fundamental distinction of the Persons, which is found as well in the fundamental distinction in society: parents and children, and which is of a radical inequality.

Now, this is the same reasoning of the adherents of liberation theology. They say that they base themselves on the Gospel to affirm that Our Lord Jesus Christ is the first revolutionary. It is monstrous to propagate such infamies.

Instruct, Convert, and Save Souls

> True, Jesus has loved us with an immense, infinite love, and He came on earth to suffer and die so that, gathered around Him in justice and love, motivated by the same sentiments of mutual charity, all men might live in peace and happiness. But for the realization of this temporal and eternal happiness, He has laid down with supreme authority the condition that we must belong to His flock, that we must accept His doctrine, that we must practice virtue, and that we must accept the teaching and guidance of Peter and his successors. Further, whilst Jesus was kind to sinners and to those who went astray, He did not respect their false ideas, however sincere they might have appeared. He loved

them all, but He instructed them in order to convert them and save them. Whilst He called to Himself in order to comfort them, those who toiled and suffered, it was not to preach to them the jealousy of a chimerical equality. Whilst He lifted up the lowly, it was not to instill in them the sentiment of a dignity independent from, and rebellious against, the duty of obedience. Whilst His heart overflowed with gentleness of the souls of good-will, He could also arm Himself with holy indignation against the profaners of the House of God, against the wretched men who scandalized the little ones, against the authorities who crush the people with the weight of heavy burdens without putting out a hand to lift them. He was as strong as He was gentle. He reproved, threatened, chastised; knowing and teaching us that fear is the beginning of wisdom, and that it is sometimes proper for a man to cut off an offending limb to save his body. Finally, He did not announce for future society the reign of an ideal happiness from which suffering would be banished; but, by His lessons and by His example, He traced the path of the happiness which is possible on earth and of perfect happiness in heaven: the royal way of the Cross. These are teachings that it would be wrong to apply only to one's personal life in order to win eternal salvation; these are eminently social teachings, and they show in Our Lord Jesus Christ something quite different from an inconsistent and impotent humanitarianism.

Today it is the same: they pretend to base religious liberty on the Gospel! As I had the chance to say to Cardinal Oddi, this is blasphemous. One reads in the *Declaration on Religious Liberty*, in the section on how Christ and his apostles acted:

> God calls men to serve him in spirit and in truth. Consequently they are bound to him in conscience but not coerced. God has regard for the dignity of the human person which he himself created; the human person is to be guided by his own judgment....[15]

If God does not physically coerce man to serve Him, nonetheless he constrains him morally. According to this passage, man would be free to adhere to God or not!

---

[15] *Vatican Council II*, p.807.

Texts Not Inspired by the Holy Ghost

And one reads a little farther on:

> At the same time [the apostles] showed respect for the weak even though they were in error, and in this way made it clear how "each of us shall give account of himself to God" (Rom. 14:12) and for that reason is bound to obey his conscience.[16]

But what did the apostles say when they began to preach? "You have crucified the Lord; what must you do now? You must do penance," be baptized, and keep the commandments. That they would have added, "Now you are free, each must follow his own conscience," is unthinkable.

If those who heard the apostles had said, "Listening to my own conscience, I find that I cannot obey," then the apostles would have threatened them with hell fire and the chastisements of God. They would not have said, "You are perfectly free to believe or not believe; you must follow your own conscience. Oh yes, you do equally well by following your own conscience and in not obeying when you listen to us." And yet, this is essentially what is said in the *Declaration on Religious Liberty*.

It is not possible that this document was inspired by the Holy Ghost. Fortunately, they wanted this to be a pastoral council, not a dogmatic one. This is the first time in history that the Church was met in a pastoral Council; the other councils had always been dogmatic. A pastoral council is nothing but a long homily, that is only worth what it is worth, as they themselves said.

The Authority of the Vatican II Decrees

So, then, what must be retained from this Council? How must it be understood. When the Secretariat was queried on the question, the answer was that nothing could be specified, and that it was necessary to compare the documents of the Council to those that are binding in matters of faith, and then grade them according to the varying degrees of theological certitude.

Hence the conciliar texts are not necessarily infallible. Consequently there is no moral obligation to give firm adherence to these

---

[16] *Ibid.*, p.809.

writings, except in so far as they echo texts which have already been defined by the Church. One can, then, very well discuss texts of Vatican II without being thereby against the Church or opposed to the faith of the Church.

When I was a member of the Central Preparatory Commission of the Council, I had proposed that each commission present two documents, a theologically scientific text for the use of theologians and the more learned members of the faithful, and which eventually could have been designated as infallible; and another text written in a more pastoral language accessible to all persons whether Catholic or non-Catholic or infidel.

The dogmatic texts elaborated with such care and of such utility for presenting the truth to priests, and especially professors and theologians, would have remained as the rule of faith. The pastoral texts, more easily translatable into the vernacular, would have been presented in more accessible language, good for presenting the truth to all men, even those educated in letters and science, yet not theologians. Of a pastoral nature, these texts would have been conceived and drafted in the form of an invitation to the faithful, a more apologetic appeal because non-dogmatic.

This suggestion was well enough received by the Central Commission; nearly half the members showed that they were favorable. At the beginning of the Council I again made the suggestion, and was seconded by several Cardinals, among whom were Cardinals Ruffini and Roy, who said that they were in agreement with the proposal. After I concluded my intervention, Cardinal Roy came and showed me the text of an intervention he wanted to make in the same line. "I agree with you completely. It would be much better. At least then there would be certain clear and definitive texts, and others that would allow greater scope for clarifying certain questions. Whereas, otherwise we are going to remain in a kind of fog, and nothing really will be defined. It will not be known what must be adhered to, and what not."

Holy Ghost Not Obliged to Intervene

But the progressives were furious. They were frightened when they heard Cardinal Ruffini, one of the presidents of the Council, express his sympathy for the idea: "I agree with Archbishop

Lefebvre that we should proceed in the manner he has suggested." Seeing that this idea was beginning to advance and make headway, they went over to the counterattack, and the next day it was affirmed once again that the Council was not a dogmatic council, and that it would remain strictly pastoral. There was no question of defining anything, but simply of setting forth the truth in a pastoral manner.

Thus it became simple to conclude that, if there were to be no definitions, it was not worth anything; it was simply a big homily. Ultimately, it was not unfortunate that the progressives clearly reaffirmed the pastoral character of the Council. At least everyone was clear about what to think of it.

The Holy Ghost is not obliged to intervene to prevent committing errors. Whereas had the Council been dogmatic, the Holy Ghost would have been obliged to intervene. He would not have allowed the Church to err. And so one can accept as granted that the Holy Ghost did not intervene during this pastoral council. The modernists prevailed as pastors, and one is now forced to recognize the disastrous results of the Council.

Pope Pius X concludes his letter on the Sillon with an urgent appeal to the bishops:

> As for you, Venerable Brethren, carry on diligently with the work of the Savior of men by emulating His gentleness and His strength. Minister to every misery; let no sorrow escape your pastoral solicitude; let no lament find you indifferent. But, on the other hand, preach fearlessly their duties to the powerful and to the lowly; it is your function to form the conscience of the people and of the public authorities. The social question will be much nearer a solution when all those concerned, less demanding as regards their respective rights, shall fulfill their duties more exactingly.

At least he did not say that it was left to consciences to judge, but rather that consciences had to be formed.

Finally, the Pope requested that they pray; and he launched one last appeal to the members of the Sillon to cast off their errors and listen to his instruction.

Chapter XII

THE ENCYCLICAL *DIVINI REDEMPTORIS* OF POPE PIUS XI ON COMMUNISM
(MARCH 19, 1937)[1]

Elected on February 6, 1933, Pope Pius XI died February 10, 1939. The very important encyclical we are going to study, *Divini Redemptoris* dated the feast of St. Joseph, March 19, 1937, is thus one of the very last that he wrote. There is a curious coincidence: Pope St. Pius X died just before the outbreak of World War I, and Pope Pius XI died on the eve of World War II.

The letter is comprised of a prologue followed by five major parts.

The Pope begins by alluding to the combat that has existed since original sin:

> The promise of a Redeemer brightens the first page of the history of mankind, and the confident hope aroused by this promise softened the keen regret for a paradise which had been lost. It was this hope that accompanied the human race on its weary journey, until in the fullness of time the expected Savior came to begin a new universal civilization....

Christian Civilization

The allusion to a new universal civilization is very important, for this is what the progressives and modernists want: a new age. The Communists employ the same expressions. They all accord to call out for a new era, evidently desiring to destroy the era that began with Our Lord:

---

[1] *Divini Redemptoris, Encyclical Letter of Pius XI on Atheistic Communism.* Available from Angelus Press. Archbishop Lefebvre makes a point of letting the students know that he was citing the French version translated by Jean Madiran.

...The Savior came to begin a new universal civilization, the Christian civilization, far superior even to that which up to this time had been laboriously achieved by certain more privileged nations.

We have seen how the Modernists, like the Sillonists, for all intents and purposes rejected the idea of Christian civilization and denied its benefits. Now they accuse the Europeans of identifying Christian civilization with European civilization, while saying that the non-European peoples have always said that this was false. They accuse us of wanting to impose European civilization on other cultures.

The popes, however, have always said that their accusation was false, because a European civilization has never existed. No, it is a question of Catholic civilization. The ancient pagan civilization which existed before the Christian era, before the coming of Our Lord, was comparable to that of other peoples still pagan, who do not yet acknowledge Our Lord. Europe was in the same state.

If Europe became civilized it was under the influence of Our Lord Jesus Christ; it was by the effect of His doctrine, under the influence of the Holy Ghost, the sacraments and the holy sacrifice of the Mass. Europe was transformed by what Our Lord gave. Certain elements adopted by the Church were secondary, yet to condemn this civilization because of these elements is unthinkable. But the Modernists insist that this civilization should not be communicated and transmitted to non-European peoples.

It is clear that some adaptation is necessary, simply in consideration of the challenge posed by the multiplicity of languages. Criticisms were raised over the use of Latin in preference to the local languages. This was especially the case when discussing the peoples of the Far East: China, Japan. Problems arose and there were difficulties. The Holy See could have judged whether it was entirely useful to allow the use of Chinese as a liturgical language. But these are problems of a secondary nature.

The very principles of Christian civilization, however, remain ever the same: the principles of the family, of civil society, of the human person, of the spiritual nature of the soul, and all the philosophical principles taught by the Church. All of these are valid for all peoples; that cannot be changed. Men are everywhere the same.

The popes have always objected to the idea that European civilization must not be transmitted to others, as if European civilization were not simply Christian civilization!

> ...the Christian civilization [was] far superior even to that which up to this time had been laboriously achieved by certain more privileged nations.

The pope alludes to the Greeks, Egyptians, etc. No one can deny that it was Our Lord who brought us this civilization.

The Fight Began With Original Sin

> Nevertheless, the struggle between good and evil remained in the world as a sad legacy of the original fall. Nor has the ancient tempter ever ceased to deceive mankind with false promises.

Today no one wants to hear about original sin; the Pope, nonetheless, begins with a reminder that the struggle began with original sin:

> It is on this account that one convulsion following upon another has marked the passage of the centuries, down to the revolution of our own days. This modern revolution, it may be said, has actually broken out or threatens everywhere, and it exceeds in amplitude and violence anything yet experienced in the preceding persecutions launched against the Church. Entire peoples find themselves in danger of falling back into a barbarism worse than that which oppressed the greater part of the world at the coming of the Redeemer.

Their Goal: Annihilate Christian Civilization

Such are the Pope's predictions. It was not too long ago, and I think that if he were alive today, he would repeat the same thing. A little farther on, the Pope says that the consequences of these errors, this revolution, were foreseeable, and he concludes his prologue with this sentence:

> This all too imminent danger, Venerable Brethren, as you have already surmised, is bolshevistic and atheistic Communism, which aims at upsetting the social order and at undermining the very foundations of Christian civilization.

For the Pope, then, there is one civilization whose destruction Communism has set itself as goal: Christian civilization. That is why Pope Pius XI will say in the penultimate section of the en-cyclical that Communism is intrinsically perverse. The progressives of our day hold that Communism is reprehensible for its atheism, but that the solutions it offers for social life and the commonweal are valid. The Pope is wholly against this estimation. Communism is not only atheist, which it is, but it "aims at upsetting the social order and at undermining the very foundations of Christian civilization." The Pope will show how it does this.

We come to the first part in which the Pope gives the reasons and the ends of the present encyclical:

> In the face of such a threat the Catholic Church could not and does not remain silent. This Apostolic See, above all, has not refrained from raising its voice, for it knows that its proper and special mission is to defend truth, justice and all those eternal values which Communism ignores or attacks. Ever since the days when groups of "intellectuals" were formed in an arrogant attempt to free civilization from the bonds of morality and religion, Our Predecessors overtly and explicitly drew the attention of the world to the consequences of the dechristianization of human society. With reference to Communism, Our venerable Predecessor, Pius IX, of holy memory, as early as 1846 pronounced a solemn condemnation, which he confirmed in the words of the Syllabus....

It is interesting to see that Pope Pius XI invokes that terrible *Syllabus* that makes the progressives' hair stand on end. Yet it was even earlier, in 1846, when Pope Pius IX in his encyclical letter *Qui Pluribus* condemned Communism. He wrote:

> The sacred celibacy of clerics has also been the victim of conspiracy. Indeed, some churchmen have wretchedly forgotten their own rank and let themselves be converted by the charms and snares of pleasure. This is the aim too of the prevalent but wrong method of teaching, especially in the philosophical disciplines, a method which deceives and corrupts incautious youth in a wretched manner and gives it as drink the poison of the serpent in the goblet of Babylon. To this goal also tends the unspeakable

doctrine of *Communism*, as it is called, a doctrine most opposed to the very natural law.

Pope Pius XI repeats in almost the same terms what Pope Pius IX had written, and even cites his appreciation of Communism:

> ...that infamous doctrine of so-called Communism which is absolutely contrary to the natural law itself, and if once adopted would utterly destroy the rights, property and possessions of all men, and even society itself.

A Monstrous Doctrine

The text is not exactly the same as what is cited in the encyclical, but it has the same meaning. Pope Pius XI quotes this passage from the encyclical of Pius IX and states that the latter condemned Communism too. It suffices to refer to the fourth chapter of the *Syllabus* to find all the references where Communism is condemned. These references to the *Syllabus* and to the encyclical *Qui Pluribus*, published 9 November 1846 by Pius IX are very interesting, and it is very useful to consult them.

Pope Pius XI cites four other documents, five all together, of Pope Pius IX condemning Communism. If today it is still possible to read the *Syllabus*, it is much more difficult to find the other writings of Pius IX. Those of Pope Leo XIII and subsequent pontiffs can still be found, but it is impossible to find those of Pius IX, short of sifting through the used bookdealers' stalls.

The encyclicals of Pius IX are really extraordinary and admirable because they are still quite topical. It would be good to see them reprinted and circulated so that people could see what was already being said at the time of Pius IX. His writings constitute a kind of extraordinary premonition.

Pope Pius XI quotes the encyclical *Quod Apostolici Muneris* against the errors of the modern world, published by Pope Leo XIII on December 18, 1878:

> Later on, another of Our Predecessors, the immortal Leo XIII, in his Encyclical *Quod Apostolici Muneris* defined Communism as "the fatal plague which insinuates itself into the very marrow of human society only to bring about its ruin." With clear intuition he pointed out that the atheistic movements exist-

ing among the masses of the Machine Age had their origin in that school of philosophy which for centuries had sought to divorce science from the life of the Faith and of the Church.

You understand as a matter of course, Venerable Brothers, that We are alluding to that sect of men who, under the motley and all but barbarous terms and titles of Socialists, Communists, and Nihilists, are spread abroad throughout the world and, bound intimately together in baneful alliance, no longer look for strong support in secret meetings held in darksome places, but standing forth openly and boldly in the light of day, strive to carry out the purpose long resolved upon, of uprooting the foundations of civilized society at large.

...They leave nothing scatheless or uninjured of that which human and divine laws alike have wisely ordained to ensure the preservation and honor of life.[2]

This, then, is what Pope Leo XIII wrote. In the next paragraph, Pius XI recalls his own discourses and the condemnations that he has levied against Communism:

During Our Pontificate We too have frequently and with urgent insistence denounced the current trend to atheism which is alarmingly on the increase. In 1924 when Our relief-mission returned from the Soviet Union.

There was a terrible famine in Russia in 1924, and so the Holy See had sent an aid mission, which had been accepted with much difficulty. Its members had to conceal the fact that they were religious. They practically had to disguise themselves as laymen to be able to work there and distribute the supplies and provisions sent by the Holy See to relieve the famine:

...We condemned Communism in a special Allocution which We addressed to the whole world. In Our Encyclicals *Miserentissimus Redemptor, Quadragesimo Anno, Caritate Christi, Acerba Animi, Dilectissima Nobis*, We raised a solemn protest against the persecutions unleashed in Russia, in Mexico and now in Spain.

---

[2] *The Great Encyclical Letters of Pope Leo XIII* (Rockford, Illinois: TAN Books & Publishers, 1995), p.22.

The civil war that was to erupt in Spain in 1936 had not yet broken out—the last document cited appeared in 1933—but Communism was already beginning to spread in that country.

In Mexico, the Pope had been sorely deceived. He had trusted the government and asked the *Cristeros* to lay down their arms. They obeyed the Holy See, and as soon as they had disarmed, the others took up theirs and the *Cristeros* were all massacred and atrocities were committed. The Pope had been fooled and deceived.

The Popes' Clairvoyance

The Pope repeats what he had said shortly before, as the Spanish Civil War was reaching its conclusion, and he writes:

> In fact, the most persistent enemies of the Church, who from Moscow are directing the struggle against Christian civilization, themselves bear witness, by their unceasing attacks in word and act, that even to this hour the Papacy has continued faithfully to protect the sanctuary of the Christian religion, and that it has called public attention to the perils of Communism more frequently and more effectively than any other public authority on earth.

The Russians recognize that it is the Pope, the Sovereign Pontiff, who opposes Communism more strenuously and more persuasively than any other public power on earth. Unfortunately, that changed completely with Vatican Council II. It was almost treason, because if for more than a hundred years the popes had judged it well and good to condemn Communism, how could Rome suddenly fall silent about Communism and refuse to condemn it?

This was not the case of Pius XI, and he did not fear or hesitate to do so.

In defense of the modern stance, it is alleged that if the pope condemns Communism, the Catholics will be persecuted even more in the countries under the Communist yoke. This is not true.

Abandonment Worse Than Persecution

The Communists are afraid of those who attack them publicly. Those who were behind the iron curtain would have felt themselves to be supported by the Holy See and understood by all the Catholics who do not live under a Communist regime. It would have given them real courage. Whereas in the absence of this clear stance, they felt anguished, and wondered if they were still supported, and if their combat were still approved by Rome.

This is the case of the Lithuanians, who often wonder if the combat they are engaged in today is approved by the Holy See, because they notice that in a number of States, the bishops who are being named, like Bishop Lekai in Hungary or Bishop Tomasek in Czechoslovakia, silence and shunt aside the priests who fight against Communism.

They experience something like what is happening to us in the Church, and yet which is not behind the iron curtain. They would like to silence us, they would like to suppress us. Over there, it is the same thing. In the countries situated behind the iron curtain, it is actually the cardinals and those who are in episcopal curias who forbid people to fight or oppose the Communist government. So they no longer know what they should do. They wonder if the Church is still against atheistic Communism or not. For them it is an anguish even more terrible than persecution. When you are persecuted, you defend the Church, you defend the faith. But to not know whether one's reason for fighting, for which one may endure prison and torture, is approved or not by the Church is worse. Not to know whether their own leaders or our superiors are with them or against them causes a greater moral suffering than the physical pain that they endure in the prisons.

It is somewhat the same thing for us. To be chased and disliked by the episcopal authorities is a cause of great suffering. But for Rome to shunt us aside and despise us is worse! because we wonder if the Church approves of our combat against the modern errors, the same combat of the popes for two centuries. Should the fight against errors cease? Should the fight for truth be abandoned? Unthinkable. And this suffering is increased when we consider what the Church has become since Vatican II. It is extremely painful for many Catholics. How many laymen and priests suffer a real martyrdom from this situation. They no longer know what to think, whereas before everything was clear. With those popes, it was the whole Church that fought.

One no longer knows what to think. They no longer want to fight Communism openly; and yet the Pope has lived under a Communist regime! Since his accession to the pontificate, has he ever said or read or written anything where he openly took a stand against Communism? Perhaps he has alluded to it on one occasion or other, but there is no real combat against this revolution which, as Pope Pius XI wrote, is "the most horrible that has ever been endured."

Aggravation of the Peril

Before writing his encyclical, Pope Pius XI had already addressed the topic frequently:

> To Our great satisfaction, Venerable Brethren, you have, by means of individual and even joint pastoral Letters, accurately transmitted and explained to the Faithful these admonitions.

He congratulates the bishops for having disseminated his declarations. The Pope continues:

> Yet despite Our frequent and paternal warnings the peril only grows greater from day to day because of the pressure exerted by clever agitators.

In all the papal documents, we find the observation that, despite their warnings, the evil spreads. It would seem that to try us, despite all that the popes have done to combat the evil, God permits us to be unable to uproot the errors and halt the flood of false ideas that, for the last two or three centuries, has been dragging the world to its destruction:

> Therefore We believe it to be Our duty to raise Our voice once more, in a still more solemn missive, in accord with the desire of the whole Catholic world, which makes the appearance of such a document but natural. We trust that the echo of Our voice will reach every mind free from prejudice and every heart sincerely desirous of the good of mankind. We wish this the more because Our words are now receiving sorry confirmation from

the spectacle of the bitter fruits of subversive ideas, which We foresaw and foretold, and which are in fact multiplying fearfully in the countries already stricken, or threatening every other country of the world.

It can be said that the Pope was right. If he were to return, he could say that he had foreseen it. Since Pius XI, how many nations that were not yet enslaved have fallen under the yoke of the Communists? There were almost none in Africa. Russia and China were under Communist domination, but in the Far East, Vietnam, had not yet fallen to Communist regimes. In Africa now almost half the continent has fallen into Communist hands. To complete the survey it would be necessary to include the Americas, Mexico, Central America, Cuba, as well as to consider the penetration of communist influence in the so-called free countries. The Communists have made enormous progress in Italy, France and Spain, where they have made a come back. It is quite worrisome.

The Imposture Decried

Hence We wish to expose once more in a brief synthesis the principles of atheistic Communism as they are manifested chiefly in bolshevism. We wish also to indicate its method of action and to contrast with its false principles the clear doctrine of the Church, in order to inculcate anew and with greater insistence the means by which Christian civilization, the true *civitas humana*, can be saved from the satanic scourge, and not merely saved, but better developed for the well-being of human society.

In the second part, Pius XI describes the theory and practice of the communists.

Counterfeit Redemption of the Poor

The Communism of today, more emphatically than similar movements in the past, conceals in itself a false messianic idea.

This is how the Pope understands Communism. Communism presents itself to the world as the redemption of the lowly, coming to bring salvation to the poor, the wretched, the hungry. It is a counter-redemption, so to speak, as the devil is wont to do; he imitates, to a certain degree, the Christian religion, as it was Our Lord who truly came to bring redemption to souls and Christian civilization, the most beautiful of civilizations. So to destroy this Christian civilization, it is necessary to present to the world a kind of counterfeit redemption. They have concocted this strategy: present themselves to the world as those who bring redemption to the lowly:

> A pseudo-ideal of justice, of equality and fraternity in labor impregnates all its doctrine and activity with a deceptive mysticism....

And indeed, the Communists present themselves as animated by a real mystique, as having a new religion and a new gospel. This is the means they use to ensnare the humble, by calling themselves the liberators of the poor and the workers:

> ....which communicates a zealous and contagious enthusiasm to the multitudes entrapped by delusive promises. This is especially true in an age like ours, when unusual misery has resulted from the unequal distribution of the goods of this world.

The Capitalist Economy: Fruit of the Revolution

With the capitalist economic system, which is the fruit of the French Revolution, the same people distilled the poison of this so-called freedom, because behind it—as the Pope says—were the secret societies. It was they who broke with every social structure that existed to protect the workers: the corporations, the guilds. All was broken at the time of the Revolution. The worker then found himself standing alone face to face with his employers; and at the same time unrestricted freedom was granted: "liberal" economy, freedom of trade, freedom of industry, etc. Clearly, those who possessed money profited from the situation to accumulate immense fortunes at the expense of the workers, who found themselves defenseless. They were no longer united by any bond; all the guilds had been broken up and disbanded.

Nonetheless, during the 19th century, it must be recognized that thanks to the efforts of the Catholic Church, the efforts of Pope Leo XIII and French Catholics like La Tour du Pin, and in other countries, for example Germany, they tried to restore to the workers some kind of organization in order to defend them against those who exploited their work and their weakness.

All these sufferings and injustices are the fruit of the modern errors, and not those of the Christian civilization inaugurated by the Church. Rather they are the fruits of the errors that had been propagated initially by Protestantism, and then by the Revolution: the liberal spirit, that gave total freedom to trade and industry, whereas before there had been rules. No one could set up an industry just anywhere, crush others, destroy the small businessmen, form trusts, as is done now. These are all practically the result of the liberal economy. It is not the work of the Church.

Even priests often accuse the Church, saying that the current miseries are the result of Christian civilization. This is absolutely false. It is the work of the Revolution! The revolutionaries broke the social framework that existed previously, which protected the worker and united together patron and worker in associations, the corporations, which often took on a religious aspect: they had a patron saint and even religious feasts. These were organizations established for the sake of the work, the trade, the profession; all was done in a Christian spirit. The whole edifice was torn down! The defenseless workers found themselves face to face with lawless immoral men, who profited from the situation to abuse the workers. It has to be acknowledged: there were enormous abuses, and shameful forms of exploitation of the workers.

Unfortunately, it was at that moment that Communism presented itself as the liberator. They arrived on the scene at the very moment when they could find an enormous well-disposed audience amongst the populace, especially among the workers. The Pope continues:

> This is especially true in an age like ours, when unusual misery has resulted from the unequal distribution of the goods of this world. This pseudo-ideal is even boastfully advanced as if it were responsible for a certain economic progress. As a matter of fact, when such progress is at all real, its true causes are quite different, as for instance the intensification of industrialism in countries which were formerly almost without it, the exploitation of immense natural resources, and the use of the most brutal

methods to insure the achievement of gigantic projects with a minimum of expense.

Evoking the exploitation the Communists were able to make of a situation that begat social injustices, Pius XI then indicates the source whence Communism draws its ideas.

Dialectical Materialism, the "Class Struggle"

> The doctrine of modern Communism, which is often concealed under the most seductive trappings, is in substance based on the principles of dialectical and historical materialism previously advocated by Marx, of which the theoreticians of bolshevism claim to possess the only genuine interpretation.

The Pope does not expound their doctrine at length; he exposes it in a few lines:

> According to this doctrine there is in the word only one reality, matter, the blind forces of which evolve into plant, animal and man.

The theory is close to the evolutionist system: everything is contained in matter!

> Even human society is nothing but a phenomenon and form of matter, evolving in the same way. By a law of inexorable necessity and through a perpetual conflict of forces, matter moves towards the final synthesis of a classless society.

A society completely leveled, completely equal. Behold, according to communist principles, what should be a fatal, relentless, inevitable evolution, brought about by the application of a principle inherent in matter which tends to this evolution against which no one can do anything. But there is a way to precipitate it, and bring it about more rapidly. "In such a doctrine, as is evident," the Pope says:

> ...there is no room for the idea of God; there is no difference between matter and spirit, between soul and body; there is neither survival of the soul after death nor any hope in a future life. Insisting on the dialectical aspect of their materialism, the communists claim that the conflict which carries the world towards its final synthesis can be accelerated by man.

The means by which they accelerate this movement is dialectic:

> Hence they endeavor to sharpen the antagonisms which arise between the various classes of society. Thus the class-struggle with its consequent violent hate and destruction takes on the aspect of a crusade for the progress of humanity.

It could be added that the expression "class-struggle" should not be taken uniquely to mean the struggle of workers against bosses, but can express in general every facet of social demolition. Of course, it is a wonderful opportunity for goading the workers and provoking clashes between employees and employers. According to the Communists, only a perpetual state of struggle and combat permit society to progress economically.

It is not only the class struggle that they seek to exacerbate, but also the struggle of citizens against the authorities and the government. They seek to profit from any occasion to provoke the citizens to rise up against authority. Demonstrations are multiplied; they instigate occasions if need be. This also constitutes the class struggle. Everywhere, within every society, the Communists try to set one group against another. They preach the emancipation of children from parental authority, and even in religious societies they try to set the so-called lower clergy against the higher clergy. Wherever they can, they insinuate or incite this kind of dialectic, this internecine conflict, for this is one of their principles: one must fight constantly. The Pope continues:

> Thus the class-struggle with its consequent violent hate and destruction takes on the aspect of a crusade for the progress of humanity. On the other hand, all other forces whatever, as long as they resist such systematic violence, must be annihilated as hostile to the human race.

Depersonalization

Then comes the privation of freedom:

> Communism, moreover, strips man of his liberty, robs human personality of all its dignity, and removes all the moral restraints that check the eruptions of blind impulse.

Nowadays, one would speak of depersonalization, because this has been accentuated since the time that Pope Pius XI wrote his encyclical; one can judge even better the veracity of his judgment when he wrote that it "strips man of his liberty, robs human personality of all its dignity, and removes all the moral restraints." One no longer has the right to govern his own morals. They seek to remove all will, personality and independence from the human person, because for them:

> ...human personality...is a mere cog-wheel in the communist system. In man's relations with other individuals, besides, communists hold the principle of absolute equality, rejecting all hierarchy and divinely-constituted authority, including the authority of parents. What men call authority and subordination is derived from the community as its first and only font. Nor is the individual granted any property rights over material goods or the means of production, for inasmuch as these are the source of further wealth, their possession would give one man power over another. Precisely on this score, all forms of private property must be eradicated, for they are at the origin of all economic enslavement.

This depersonalization has become the classic communist system. They put all their enemies—those against whom they have a grudge—in concentration camps; undoubtedly, this still continues. Needing manual labor, they use these unfortunates in the mines and the forests that they exploit in unendurable regions like Siberia, in unimaginable conditions. Courageous writers have recounted these things in books where they reveal the horrors of the gulags and deportation camps, absolutely horrible, unheard of things. And deportations to fill the requirements for manual labor continue.

They no longer dare to send certain of their enemies into the camps, those whose names are too well-known worldwide and whose arrest would create too much of a stir in the free world, yet they endure something like prison anyway. They are injected with chemicals that depersonalize them: they no longer enjoy the freedom of their faculties, they become like robots. The Communists were already using this kind of procedure at the time of Cardinal Mindszenty, as the former Primate of Hungary wrote in a letter:

Henceforth do not trust everything that I say or may sign, because I am going into this prison, and in the prison they put us into such states that one is capable of signing or saying anything.

How far can this destruction of man go? It is abominable. The depersonalization extends to every domain, such that they leave no free rein to any private initiative: nothing! They expropriate all private property. One can no longer own any private property, or own the instruments of one's work, nor one's house nor one's fields. Everything belongs to the State. One is lodged. One is fed. One must think like the party. This conditioning is frightful. They treat man like a veritable beast, a beast of burden good for working, producing and consuming—if it is possible to speak of consuming! They keep the products of work to make cannons and equip their armies with weapons of mass destruction, they let the people almost die of starvation, as is the case in Poland. Hence, no more private property.

Destruction of Marriage and Family Life

Then comes the discussion of marriage: the communist system results in the destruction of family life. Undoubtedly, they have taken a step backwards, because they weighed the disadvantages of what they had undertaken at first. But they do not want marriage, and advocate free unions and concubinage. The children are brought up in governmental organizations and completely taken away from their parents. Pope Pius XI writes:

> Refusing to human life any sacred or spiritual character, such a doctrine logically makes of marriage and the family a purely artificial and civil institution, the outcome of a specific economic system. There exists no matrimonial bond of a juridico-moral nature that is not subject to the whim of the individual or of the collectivity. Naturally, therefore, the notion of an indissoluble marriage-tie is scouted (*sic*). Communism is particularly characterized by the rejection of any link that binds woman to the family and the home, and here emancipation is proclaimed as a basic principle. She is withdrawn from the family and the care of her children, to be thrust instead into public life and collective production under the same conditions as man. The care of home and children then devolves upon the collectivity.

They pushed this to the utmost limit, which created quite a few difficulties. So, quietly, they let husband and wife live together and take back their children's upbringing, somewhat. They realized that the situation they had created was so abnormal and that it encumbered them with so many tasks—picking up the children, housing them to keep them from knowing their parents—that finally they backed away from their initial decision. Who would imagine putting into practice such unnatural things. The same thing was done in China in an odious manner...:

> Finally, the right of education is denied to parents, for it is conceived as the exclusive prerogative of the community, in whose name and by whose mandate alone parents may exercise this right.

Constant Surveillance

At school it is still this way: they alone can teach. It is very difficult to give religious education to children. I do not know how things are in Poland, but in countries like Czechoslovakia and Hungary, they keep track of all the children who go to catechism. They make trouble for the parents, take away their employment, reduce their salaries, harass them in countless ways. Everything is done to make the parents decide to withdraw their children from catechism. Nonetheless, they let a few catechism classes remain, where the number of children attending is very low, because the parents have been persecuted so much that they finally succumb to the pressure. They allow them uniquely to give the appearance of religious liberty, for propaganda to the West, to make them believe that in the Communist countries there is religious freedom and that religious education is given.

Communications from truly Catholic priests, not the "Peace priests," inform us of the difficulties they encounter in getting the children to catechism, and even the problems they have in exercising their ministry. There are always agents of the party present to listen to the sermons. In all the religious ceremonies, an agent of the party is present to note if any adverse comments on the government are made. It would be reported right away to the party bosses. The priests are summoned, interrogated, reprimanded, and even threatened.

A Machiavellian Persecution

If they go out to visit the sick, bring the sacraments, permission must always be requested. They are authorized, but they are followed. They know where they are going, and why. It is difficult for us to form an idea of such a Machiavellian persecution.

Here is an example that illustrates the conditioning that is practiced by the Communists. It did not happen in a Communist country, or at least it had not been for long. I remember having received, at Dakar, the Archbishop of Konakry, Bishop de Milleville, who moreover has since been expelled by the Communists. At that time he was still Archbishop of Konakry, and the Communists had been in power for about a year. He had received permission to come to Dakar; he came, he stayed with me. When I asked him questions, we two were alone together and I asked him how he was, he hesitated to answer. A few days later he told me, "You know, it is incredible, but you are watched so much over there, you have such a strong feeling that someone is listening to your conversation, and that someone else will know what you have said, that soon you no longer dare to say anything. Coming here, when you were asking me questions, I felt that I was still under surveillance. I had the feeling that I was in a setting where I was not free."

Unceasing Fear

This fear, this anguish that comes over you and finally never leaves is terrible. Children no longer dare to speak to their parents, parents are careful not to say anything against the party in front of their children, because afterwards the children may be interrogated. Inadvertently, the children may say that papa or mama said this or that, and this will immediately be reported to the party. Interrogations and prosecution follow. They are no longer really free to think, they endure a continual constraint. It is inconceivable that men should be foiled in every personal endeavor, and even in mind. It is monstrous. The Pope writes:

What would be the condition of a human society based on such materialistic tenets? It would be a collectivity with no other hierarchy than that of the economic system. It would have only one mission: the production of material things by means of collective labor, so that the goods of this world might be enjoyed....

Contrary to what the Communists claim, we must still wait! For the people who live under the communist yoke are far from obtaining the enjoyment of terrestrial goods. Having undertaken the destruction of the family, society disposes of an unlimited right. It possesses all the rights, and can compel men to work.

Banish God From the Earth

In a word, the communists claim to inaugurate a new era and a new civilization which is the result of blind evolutionary forces culminating in a "humanity without God."

Such is the goal of their society. Next comes a society without classes. In waiting to reach this goal, it is the State that holds all the power and is responsible for bringing about the ideal of the classless society:

Such, Venerable Brethren, is the new gospel which bolshevistic and atheistic Communism offers the world as the glad tidings of deliverance and salvation! It is a system full of errors and sophisms. It is in opposition both to reason and to divine Revelation. It subverts the social order, because it means the destruction of its foundations; because it ignores the true origin and purpose of the state; because it denies the rights, dignity and liberty of human personality.

A Counterfeit of the Truth

A few paragraphs follow concerning the dissemination of this doctrine. How could it have happened?

How is it possible that such a system, long since rejected scientifically and now proved erroneous by experience, how is it, We ask, that such a system could spread so rapidly in all parts of the world?

Pope Pius XI asks the question, and then provides several explanations. First of all, they deceive the people by their promises; one of the means, then, is deception:

> The explanation lies in the fact that too few have been able to grasp the nature of Communism. The majority instead succumb to its deception, skillfully concealed by the most extravagant promises. By pretending to desire only the betterment of the condition of the working-classes, by urging the removal of the very real abuses chargeable to the liberalistic economic order, and by demanding a more equitable distribution of this world's goods (objectives entirely and undoubtedly legitimate), the communist takes advantage of the present world-wide economic crisis to draw into the sphere of his influence even those sections of the populace which on principle reject all forms of materialism and terrorism.

Of course, they profited from the consequences of the introduction of economic liberalism in the world, which had certainly reduced the workers to a miserable condition. They exploited that state of affairs to gain an audience and adherents:

> If we would explain the blind acceptance of Communism by so many thousands of workmen, we must remember that the way had been already prepared for it by the religious and moral destitution in which wage-earners had been left by liberal economics.

To the misdeeds of liberal economics the laicism of the governments was joined. The consequences were such that the people had more or less lost the faith: religious practice and religious convictions disappeared. So Communism was able to spread more easily in these minds, where it excited little reaction. In nature, an organism that is already sick and weakened succumbs more easily to another illness than does a healthy organism whose powers of resistance are normal. In our countries the populations were already secularized, and so when attacked had fewer religious reflexes by which to repel the invading organism.

Fraud of Propaganda

There is another explanation for the rapid diffusion of the communistic ideas now seeping into every nation, great and small, advanced and backward, so that no corner of the earth is free from them. This explanation is to be found in a propaganda so truly diabolical that the world has perhaps never witnessed its like before. It is directed from one common center. It is shrewdly adapted to the varying conditions of diverse peoples. It has at its disposal great financial resources, gigantic organizations, international congresses, and countless trained workers. It makes use of pamphlets and reviews, of cinema, theater and radio, of schools and even universities. Little by little it penetrates into all classes of the people and even reaches the better-minded groups of the community, with the result that few are aware of the poison which increasingly pervades their minds and hearts.

The Spike: Astounding Silence of So-Called "Free" Press

Another powerful factor in the diffusion of Communism is "... the conspiracy of silence on the part of a large section of the non-Catholic press of the world." These are not Catholic newspapers, of course, but they certainly could and even should have objectively reported on what happens in the Communist countries: the massacres, the concentration camps, the coercions. But no, a complete silence was observed. As Pope Pius XI writes:

> We say a conspiracy, because it is impossible otherwise to explain how a press usually so eager to exploit even the little daily incidents of life has been able to remain silent for so long about the horrors perpetrated in Russia, in Mexico and even in a great part of Spain; and that it should have relatively so little to say concerning a world organization as vast as Russian Communism. This silence is due in part to short-sighted political policy, and is favored by various occult forces which for a long time have been working for the overthrow of the Christian Social Order.

The silence of the press is yet another of the means that has helped the Communists to expand. For if they had headlined even a little of what has happened in Russia—the massacres perpetrated, the tens of millions of people who were exterminated, as well as the persecutions in Spain and Mexico—it might have helped prevent the communist subjugation of entire peoples.

In the third part, Pope Pius XI restates Christian doctrine on man, his dignity and his rights, on the family, on the relations between man and civil society, on the corporatist order, and the entire social order.

The fourth part proposes the means of defending Christian civilization: spiritual renewal, the practice of the beatitude of poverty, Christian charity, the practice of justice, not only commutative (between men) but also "social justice" (towards the commonweal), and distributive justice (of society towards every member of the social body to allow him to accomplish his social function). The Pope recalls the recent deceits of Communism: slogans of world peace, the infiltration of Catholic associations, humanitarian and charitable collaboration.

He condemns this Communism "more criminal than anything criminal that has ever existed" in precise and definitive terms, addressing the bishops:

> See to it, Venerable Brethren, that the Faithful do not allow themselves to be deceived! Communism is intrinsically wrong, and no one who would save Christian civilization may collaborate with it in any undertaking whatsoever. Those who permit themselves to be deceived into lending their aid towards the triumph of Communism in their own country, will be the first to fall victims of their error. And the greater the antiquity and grandeur of the Christian civilization in the regions where Communism successfully penetrates, so much more devastating will be the hatred displayed by the Godless.

Then, denouncing "an evil of the spiritual order," the Pope writes:

> It is from a radical corruption of ideas that (...) the lamentable, impious monstrosities of Communism proceed.

Pope Pius XI, in a fifth part, gives particular tasks to certain states of life: to priests, to the activists of Catholic Action, to all the sons of the Church, and to the governors of the Christian States:

> At the same time the State must allow the Church full liberty to fulfill her divine and spiritual mission, and this in itself will be an effectual contribution to the rescue of nations from the dread torment of the present hour.

Pope Pius XI does not hesitate to warn, not only the faithful, but the whole world against the perversity of Communism and the "fatal poison" that it distills.

Yet it was as if he had never spoken, for nothing changed, on the contrary, because the outcome of the second world war was that the Soviet Union extended its domination over all the countries of Eastern Europe, and at Vatican II the subject became taboo. No one wanted to speak about Communism and still less reiterate the condemnation that had been levied by solemn acts of the magisterium.

Accompanied by Bishop Sigaud, Archbishop of Diamantina, I myself carried to Bishop Felici, Secretary of the Council, a document bearing the signatures of 450 Fathers, out of the total of 2,350 bishops present, to demand that the Council officially condemn Communism. Not only was that not done, but the request was never even mentioned! When I asked Bishop Felici in order to learn the reasons why, he answered that this document signed by 450 bishops had been forgotten in a drawer!